SRA Reading Mastery

Signature Edition

Literature Guide
Grade 4

Siegfried Engelmann
Jean Osborn
Steve Osborn
Leslie Zoref

McGraw Hill SRA

Columbus, OH

Contents

SRAonline.com

Copyright © 2008 by SRA/McGraw-Hill.

All rights reserved. No part of this publication may be reproduced or distributed in any form or by any means, or stored in a database or retrieval system, without the prior written consent of The McGraw-Hill Companies, Inc., including, but not limited to, network storage or transmission, or broadcast for distance learning.

Permission is granted to reproduce the printed material contained on pages with a permission-to-reproduce copyright line on the condition that such material be reproduced only for classroom use; be provided to students, teachers, or families without charge; and be used solely in conjunction with Reading Mastery Signature Edition.

Printed in the United States of America.

Send all inquiries to this address:
SRA/McGraw-Hill
4400 Easton Commons
Columbus, OH 43219

ISBN: 978-0-07-612628-6
MHID: 0-07-612628-5

3 4 5 6 7 8 9 10 MAZ 13 12 11 10 09 08

INTRODUCTION

The stories in the *Reading Mastery Signature Edition*, Grade 4, *Literature Anthology* complement the content and themes of *Reading Mastery Signature Edition,* Grade 4, *Textbooks A* and *B.* The *Literature Anthology* provides twelve stories for your students to read and enjoy. The *Literature Anthology* also provides a set of *Before Reading Activities* and a set of *Extending Comprehension Activities* for each story. These activities will help your students understand, discuss, and write about the meanings of these stories.

Scheduling the Literature Anthology Stories

The *Literature Anthology* stories are arranged in the order the students are to read them. The appropriate *Literature Anthology* story and its related activities can be presented any time after each tenth lesson in *Reading Mastery,* starting after lesson 10. A list of the stories, their authors, and the earliest *Reading Mastery* lesson after which each story is to be presented appears below. A short summary of each story follows this schedule.

Follows Lesson	Literature Lesson	Title	Author
10	1	*Hans in Luck*	The Brothers Grimm
20	2	*The Bracelet*	Yoshiko Uchida
30	3	*The Jacket*	Steven Otfinoski
40	4	*Ginger's Challenge*	Josephine Noyes Felts
50	5	*Brown Wolf*	Jack London
60	6	*Like Jake and Me*	Mavis Jukes
70	7	*Thank You, M'am*	Langston Hughes
80	8	*The Circuit*	Francisco Jiménez
90	9	*Salmon Count*	Clifford E. Trafzer
100	10	*The No-Guitar Blues*	Gary Soto
110	11	*Raymond's Run*	Toni Cade Bambara
120	12	*Without a Shirt*	Paul Jennings

The stories and activities of the *Literature Anthology* are a supplement to the *Reading Mastery Signature Edition, Grade 4* program and are to be scheduled in addition to the regular lessons.

Hans in Luck is a variation on a theme common in many cultures: I want what I don't have. Hans has worked for seven years as a servant and is now a free man. He is paid with a lump of gold that he thinks is too heavy to carry. But Hans is in luck—he trades his gold for a horse. And so the story goes as Hans trades one thing for another until he has nothing.

The Bracelet is a fictionalized account of a Japanese American girl whose family is forced to move to an internment camp during World War II. Before Ruri moves, her best friend gives her a bracelet as a keepsake. Ruri loses the bracelet when she gets to the camp and is heartbroken. Ruri's mother uses this event as an opportunity to teach her daughter how to remember people by keeping them alive in her heart.

The Jacket is a story about self-confidence. Walter receives a jacket that turns him into one of the most self-assured, popular students in his school. After he loses his jacket, Walter discovers the jacket wasn't magical after all—the successes were his own.

Ginger's Challenge is a horse story with a familiar theme: a girl loves a horse that is too unruly to ride. Ginger is faced with a grave dilemma while babysitting the children of the family who owns Dark Boy. The barn catches fire, and Ginger must notify the fire department without the benefit of a phone or a car. She decides to leave the children behind and ride Dark Boy to town by taking the quickest—but not the easiest—route. Her heroic efforts are justly rewarded.

Brown Wolf is the classic Jack London tale of a dog's undying loyalty to its owner. A dog appears in California and is adopted by a couple who name him Wolf. For the first year, Wolf runs away repeatedly, traveling north and covering tremendous distances. Wolf is not friendly to strangers until he meets up with Skiff Miller, who is visiting from the Yukon. Skiff claims Wolf is his dog, and he sets out to prove it. All three people decide to let the dog choose who his owner or owners will be.

Like Jake and Me is a humorous, touching story about the relationship between Alex and his stepfather, Jake. Alex thinks Jake doesn't like him because they are so different. Jake is a cowboy; Alex likes ballet. The two seem to have little in common until an encounter with a spider changes how Jake and Alex feel about each other.

Thank You, M'am is the story of a teenage boy named Roger who has no idea what he's in for when he mugs Mrs. Luella Bates Washington Jones. She believes Roger is worth saving, so she drags him home with her. While she feeds and lectures him, Roger begins to understand that Mrs. Jones really cares about what happens to him.

The Circuit is about the nomadic and difficult lives of migrant workers as they move from one job to another. In this story, a young boy thinks he is finally going to settle in one place for a year and go to school. Unfortunately, things don't work out that way.

Salmon Count is about the efforts of the Nez Perce tribe to regain their salmon fishing rights. In the story, the elders of the tribe remind the younger members that while the tribe has the right to fish any time and any place, it also has the responsibility to respect nature by not being greedy with its resources.

The No-Guitar Blues is the story of Fausto, an adolescent boy who aspires to be a guitar player. His family is poor and it's up to Fausto to figure out how to earn the money he needs to buy a guitar. A chance encounter with a lost dog belonging to affluent owners offers Fausto a solution. Fausto embellishes his story to the owners, hoping to increase the reward amount. Their graciousness and generosity leave Fausto feeling guilty. He makes restitution for his deceitfulness, with satisfying results.

Raymond's Run is about a girl nicknamed Squeaky, who is in charge of her brother, Raymond. Squeaky is highly competitive, and verbally and physically tough. She never hesitates to come to Raymond's defense. Squeaky is a serious runner. While competing in a race she has always won, Squeaky notices Raymond has developed his own unique style of running. Her competitiveness yields to feelings of compassion for Raymond's show of strength.

Without a Shirt is a ghost story. Brian is a student who involuntarily adds the phrase "without a shirt" at the end of everything he says. When he, his mom, and their dog Shovel have to move to the caretaker's house at a cemetery, Shovel starts bringing home bones. These bones arrange themselves into a leg. Brian figures out that the bones belong to his great-great-grandfather and gives them a proper burial, promising not to bury them "without a shirt." From then on, Brian stops saying "without a shirt."

Before Reading Activities and Extending Comprehension Activities

Each story is accompanied by a set of *Before Reading Activities* and a set of *Extending Comprehension Activities*. *Before Reading Activities* include *New Vocabulary Words* and *Definitions*. In addition, the *Story Background* section provides students with relevant information about each story. Finally, just before reading the story, the students read a set of *Focus Questions* that help them track the development of the ideas and themes of the story.

After reading a story, the students are offered three different types of *Extending Comprehension Activities.* These activities—*Story Questions, Discussion Topics,* and *Writing Ideas*—are often found in the broader language arts curriculum. You may choose to have the students do one, two, or all three of the activities, depending on the time and the strengths and needs of your students.

Presenting the Before Reading Activities

The *New Vocabulary Words* and *Definitions* activities are similar to the word practice and vocabulary routines of *Reading Mastery Signature Edition,* Grade 4.

New Vocabulary Words—So that the students will hear the correct pronunciation of words that may be new to them, you first model the pronunciation of potentially difficult words selected from the story.

Definitions—So that students have the opportunity to hear how vocabulary words are used in the context of each story, students read definitional sentences that contain the words. Then the entire group practices using these words. To present these important exercises, you call on a student to read a definition. Then you present the questions and sentence-construction tasks for that definition to the entire group.

Story Background—The *Story Background* passages provide students with some historical or literary information about the story or its author that will enhance their understanding of the story. To ensure that the students benefit from these passages, ask individual students to read two or three sentences aloud. At the end of each section, ask the group the questions that appear in this guide.

Focus Questions—The *Focus Questions* help students focus on the important concepts and themes of the story. Call on individual students to read these questions aloud and remind the group to think about these questions as they read the story.

Reading the Story

You may have the students read the story independently, or you may divide them into pairs or small groups to read the story orally. As a general rule, if student response is not strong in the vocabulary and comprehension activities of the *Reading Mastery Signature Edition,* Grade 4 lessons, you should have those students work in pairs or in small groups to read the stories aloud. You may circulate among these pairs or groups of students as they take turns reading the story.

Presenting the Extending Comprehension Activities

The *Extending Comprehension Activities* are optional. For each story, you decide which of these activities you want your students to do. For some stories, you may want to have your students respond to all three of the activities; for other stories, you may choose to have them do only one or two of the activities. Your choices depend on the needs of your students and the time you have available for your students to read, understand, and reflect on the messages of these stories.

Story Questions—The *Story Questions* help the students reflect on specific information from the story as well as on its general themes. Often, the *Story Questions* are closely aligned with the *Focus Questions*. Your options for this activity include calling on different students to read and answer the questions orally, or more typically, having students work independently to write their answers to these questions. (An answer key is included in this guide.)

Discussion Topics—The *Discussion Topics* are intended to foster student discussions that are based on conflicts and dilemmas in the stories. These discussions can take place in small groups or with the entire class. Discussion groups can address one or more of the suggested topics, or different groups can take on different topics. You may wish to enhance these topics by adding a related writing assignment.

Writing Ideas—The *Writing Ideas* span a variety of writing skills, from composing friendly letters to taking the perspective of one of the story's characters. Your options include having your students choose which of the writing ideas they want to respond to, or assigning specific *Writing Ideas* to individual students or to the entire group.

The box below lists the activities for each *Literature Anthology* lesson:

New Vocabulary Words

Definitions

Story Background

Focus Questions

Extending Comprehension
    Story Questions
    Discussion Topics
    Writing Ideas

Introducing the First Literature Anthology Story

You may want to use the following introduction to provide a preview of the *Literature Anthology* activities for your students.

1. Everybody, take out your Literature Anthology. ✔
    • This book contains stories that you'll read after every tenth lesson or so in your reading program.
2. Everybody, look at the Table of Contents. ✔
    • The Table of Contents shows all the stories in the book.
    • What's the title of the first story? (Signal.) *"Hans in Luck."*
    • What page does it begin on? (Signal.) *One.*

3. Everybody, turn to page one. ✔
    • Read the first heading. (Signal.) *New Vocabulary Words*.
    • Look at the headings under New Vocabulary Words. Read the heading. (Signal.) *Definitions.*
    • You'll talk about the meanings of some of the words that the author uses in the story.

4. What's the next heading? (Signal.) *Story Background.*
    • When you read the Story Background passage, you'll learn some important information that will help you understand the story.

5. What's the next heading? (Signal.) *Focus Questions.*
    • Those questions will help you look for some of the most important parts of the story.

6. What's the next heading? (Signal.) *"Hans in Luck."*
   • You'll read the story either on your own or with others.

7. What's the next heading? (Signal.) *Extending Comprehension.*

8. You'll see three more headings. Read the first one. (Signal.) *Story Questions.*
   • After you read the story, you may answer these questions about the story.

9. What's the next heading? (Signal.) *Discussion Topics.*
   • You'll have a chance to discuss these topics from the story with other students.

10. What's the last heading? (Signal.) *Writing Ideas.*
    • You will choose one of these writing ideas to write about the story.

Additional Materials

At the back of this guide, you will find a bibliography of correlated trade literature that

   • lists every *Reading Mastery Signature Edition* selection.
   • notes the lessons in which the selection is presented.
   • recommends trade books that relate to the selection.
   • denotes the genre of each trade book.

Following the bibliography is an *Additional Reading* program that includes activities for several popular children's novels.

Story 1

Hans in Luck

New Vocabulary Words

Everybody, take out your *Literature Anthology*. Turn to page 1. ✔
What is the title of this story? (Signal.) *"Hans in Luck."*
Who are the authors? (Signal.) *The Brothers Grimm.*

1. First we'll read some words from the story, and then we'll talk about what they mean.
2. Word 1 is **exchange.** What word? (Signal.) *Exchange.*
   - (Repeat for every numbered word.)
3. It's your turn to read all the words.
4. Word 1. What word? (Signal.) *Exchange.*
   - (Repeat for every numbered word.)

1. exchange	4. butcher	7. trudge
2. peasant	5. slaughter	8. vex
3. fend	6. remedy	9. bargain
		10. grindstone

Definitions

(For each definition, call on a student to read the definition aloud; then, present the tasks for that definition to the group.)

1. *When you **exchange** something, you trade one thing for another thing.*
   - Everybody, what's another way of saying **Tricia traded her hair ribbon for a comb?** (Signal.) *Tricia exchanged her hair ribbon for a comb.*
2. *A **peasant** is a person who lives and works on a farm.*
   - Everybody, what do you call a person who lives and works on a farm? (Signal.) *A peasant.*
3. *When you **fend** for yourself, you take care of yourself.*
   - Here's another way of saying **The dog had to take care of himself: The dog had to fend for himself.**
   - Everybody, what's another way of saying **The dog had to take care of himself?** (Signal.) *The dog had to fend for himself.*
4. *A **butcher** is a person who kills animals and cuts meat.*
   - Everybody, what do you call a person who kills animals and cuts meat? (Signal.) *A butcher.*

5. When people **slaughter** animals, they kill the animals.
   - Everybody, what's another way of saying **The butcher killed the goat?** (Signal.) *The butcher slaughtered the goat.*
6. A **remedy** is a solution to a problem.
   - Everybody, what's another way of saying **Josef drank orange juice as a solution for his cold?** (Signal.) *Josef drank orange juice as a remedy for his cold.*
7. A person who is **trudging** is walking in a tired way.
   - Here's another way of saying **The dog walked home in a tired way: The dog trudged home.**
   - Everybody what's another way of saying **The dog walked home in a tired way?** (Signal.) *The dog trudged home.*
8. If a person is **vexed** with you, he or she is annoyed with you.
   - Everybody, what's another way of saying **Her mother was annoyed when Teresa spilled the soup?** (Signal.) *Her mother was vexed when Teresa spilled the soup.*
9. A **bargain** is a good deal.
   - When you make a bargain, you make a good deal.
   - What's another way of saying **Those blue jeans are a good deal?** (Signal.) *Those blue jeans are a bargain.*
10. A **grindstone** is a flat stone used to polish and sharpen blades.
    - Everybody, what is a flat stone used to polish and sharpen blades? (Signal.) *A grindstone.*

Story Background

1. (Call on individual students to read two or three sentences.)
2. (After students complete a section, ask the questions for that section.)

> "Hans in Luck" is a type of story called a folktale. Many folktales are old stories that people told aloud. Parents would tell these stories to their children, and when the children became parents themselves, they would tell same the stories to their own children. Some stories were passed on in this way for hundreds of years without ever being written down.
>
> In the early 1800s, two brothers from Germany named Jacob and Wilhelm Grimm began listening to folktales and writing them down. The folktales they collected were from Germany and other countries in Europe. Many of these folktales were hundreds of years old.

- How did people pass on the folktales without writing them down? (Idea: *Parents told them to their children.*)
- About how long ago did the Brothers Grimm begin collecting folktales? (Idea: *About two hundred years ago.*)
- Where did those folktales come from? (Ideas: *Germany; other countries in Europe.*)

> In the folktale you will read, Hans works as a servant for a master. Like many young people of that time, Hans had worked for his master for seven years. During that period, Hans had earned no money, but at the end of the seven years, his master pays Hans all his earnings in one payment. That payment is a lump of gold. The story tells what happens to Hans as he makes the long walk back to his mother's home with the lump of gold.

- Why did Hans receive a lump of gold? (Idea: *As payment for seven years of work.*)
- How long did Hans work before he got paid. (Signal.) *Seven years.*
- Why did Hans have to walk home? (Idea: *People didn't have cars, buses, or trains.*)
- What do you think might happen to Hans as he walks home? (Ideas: *People will try to steal the gold; he might get tired; he might lose the gold.*)

Focus Questions

1. (Call on individual students to read the Focus Questions aloud.)
2. (Remind students to think about these questions as they read the story.)
   - *What is the value of the exchanges that Hans makes, beginning with the lump of gold?*
   - *Why are the people Hans meets so interested in making exchanges with him?*
   - *How did Hans feel at the end of the story?*
   - *Why do you think the story is titled "Hans in Luck"?*

Hans in Luck
by the Brothers Grimm

Illustrated by Allen Davis

Hans had served his master seven years, and at the end of the seventh year he said, "Master, my time is up. I want to go home and see my mother, so give me my wages."

"You have served me truly and faithfully," said the master, and he gave Hans a lump of gold as big as his head. Hans pulled his handkerchief out of his pocket and tied up the lump of gold. Then he hoisted the gold on his shoulder and set off on his way home.

As Hans was trudging along, a man came riding by on a spirited horse, looking very lively. "Oh," cried Hans aloud, "how splendid riding must be! You sit at ease and don't stumble over stones." The horseman heard Hans say this, and called out to him, "Well, what are you doing on foot?"

"I can't help myself," said Hans. "I have this great lump to carry. To be sure, it is gold, but then I can't hold my head straight because of it, and it hurts my shoulder."

"I'll tell you what," said the horseman, "we will trade. I will give you my horse, and you shall give me your lump of gold."

"Yes," said Hans. "But I warn you, you will find it heavy." And the horseman got down, took the gold, and, helping Hans up, he gave the reins into his hand.

"When you want to go fast," said he, "you must click your tongue and cry "'Gee-up!'"

And Hans, as he sat upon his horse, was glad at heart and rode off with merry cheer. After a while he thought he should like to go quicker, so he began to click with his tongue and to cry "Gee-up!" The horse began to trot, and Hans was thrown before he knew what was happening. There he lay in the ditch by the side of the road. The horse was caught by a peasant who was passing that way and driving a cow before him.

Hans pulled himself together and got upon his feet, feeling very vexed. "Riding is a poor business," said he, especially on a mount like this, who starts off and throws you before you know where you are going. Never shall I try that game again. Now, your cow is something worth having. One can jog comfortably after her and have her milk, butter, and cheese every day, as part of the bargain. What would I not give to have such a cow!"

"Well now," said the peasant, "since it will be doing you such a favor, I don't mind exchanging my cow for your horse."

Hans agreed most joyfully, and the peasant, swinging himself into the saddle, was soon out of sight. Hans went along driving his cow quietly before him, and thinking all the while of the fine bargain he had made.

"With only a piece of bread I shall have everything I can possibly want, for I shall always be able to add butter and cheese to it. And if I am thirsty I have nothing to do but to milk my cow. What more is there for a heart to wish?"

And when he came to an inn he made a stop. He ate up all the food he had brought with him, and bought half a glass of milk with his last two pennies. Then he went on again, driving his cow toward the village where his mother lived.

It was now near the middle of the day, and the sun grew hotter and hotter. Hans began to feel very hot, and so thirsty that his tongue stuck to the roof of his mouth.

"Never mind," said Hans, "I can find a remedy. I will milk my cow at once." And tying her to a tree, and taking off his leather cap to serve for a pail, he began to milk, but not a drop came. And as he set to work rather awkwardly, the impatient beast gave him such a kick on the head with her hind foot that Hans fell to the ground. For some time he could not think where he was. Luckily a butcher came by wheeling along a young pig in a wheelbarrow.

"This is terrible," cried the butcher, helping poor Hans on his legs again. Then Hans related to him all that had happened. The butcher handed him a jug of water, saying, "Here, take a drink, and you'll feel fine again. Of course the cow would give no milk, because she is old and only fit to pull burdens, or to be slaughtered."

"Well, to be sure," said Hans, scratching his head. "Who would have thought it? Of course it is a very handy way of getting meat when a man has a beast of his own to kill. But for my part I do not care much about beef, it is rather tasteless. Now, if I had but a young pig, that is much better meat, and then the sausages!"

"Look here, Hans," said the butcher, "just for love of you I will exchange. I will give you my pig instead of your cow."

"Heaven reward such kindness," cried Hans. Handing over the cow, he received in exchange the pig. The butcher lifted the pig out of the wheelbarrow and Hans led it away by a rope.

So on went Hans, thinking how everything turned out according to his wishes. After a while he met a peasant, who was carrying a fine white goose under his arm. They bid each other good-day, and Hans began to tell about his luck, and how he had made so many good exchanges. And the peasant told how he was taking the goose to a feast.

"Just feel how heavy it is," said the peasant, taking it up by the wings. "It has been fattening for the last eight weeks. When it is roasted, won't the fat run down."

"Yes, indeed," said Hans, weighing it in his hand, "very fine to be sure. But my pig is also desirable."

The peasant glanced cautiously on all sides of the animal and shook his head. "I am afraid," said he, "that there is something not quite right about your pig. In the village I have just left, a pig had actually been stolen from the sheriff's yard. I fear you have it in your hand. They have sent after the thief, and it would be a bad situation if the pig was found with you. At the least, they would throw you into a dark hole."

Poor Hans grew pale with fright. "For heaven's sake," said he, "help me out of this scrape. I am a stranger in these parts. Take my pig and give me your goose."

"It will be running some risk," answered the man, "but I will do it so you won't experience grief." And so, taking the rope in his hand, he drove the pig quickly along a by-path, and lucky Hans went on his way home with the goose under his arm.

"The more I think of it," said he to himself, "the better the bargain seems. First I get the roast goose and then the fat. That will last a whole year for bread and dripping. And lastly, I can stuff my pillow with the beautiful white feathers. How comfortably I shall sleep upon my pillow, and how pleased my mother will be."

And when he reached the last village, he saw a knife grinder. As the knife grinder's wheel went whirring round, he sang:

> My scissors I grind, and my wheel I turn,
> And all good fellows my trade should learn,
> For all that I meet with just serves my turn.

Hans stood and looked at him. At last Hans said, "You seem very well off, and merry with your grinding."

"Yes," answered the knife-grinder, "my handiwork pays very well. I call a man a good grinder who finds money every time he puts his hand in his pocket. But where did you buy that fine goose?"

"I did not buy it. I exchanged it for my pig," said Hans.

"And the pig?"

"That I exchanged for a cow."

"And the cow?"

"That I exchanged for a horse."

"And the horse?"

"I gave for the horse a lump of gold as big as my head."

"And the gold?"

"Oh, that was my wage for seven years' service."

"You seem to have fended very well for yourself," said the knife-grinder. "Now, if you could have money in your pocket every time you put your hand in, your fortune would be made."

"How shall I manage that?" said Hans.

"You must be a knife-grinder like me," said the man. "All you want is a grindstone, and the rest comes of itself. I have one here. To be sure, it is a little damaged, but I don't mind letting you have it in exchange for your goose. What do you say?"

"How can you ask?" answered Hans. "I shall be the luckiest fellow in the world. If I find money whenever I put my hand in my pocket, there is nothing more left to want."

And so he handed over the goose to the knife-grinder and received a grindstone in exchange.

"Now," said the knife-grinder, taking up a heavy common stone that lay near him, "here is another sort of stone that you can hammer out your old nails upon. Take it with you, and carry it carefully."

Hans lifted up the stone and carried it off with a contented mind. "I must have been born under a lucky star," cried he, while his eyes sparkled with joy. "I have only to wish for a thing and it is mine."

After a while he began to feel rather tired, because he had been on his legs since daybreak. He also began to feel rather hungry, for he had eaten up all he had. At last he could scarcely go on at all. He had to stop every few moments, for the stones weighed him down. He wished that he did not have to drag them along.

And so on he went at a snail's pace until he came to a well. He thought he would rest there and take a drink of the fresh water. He placed the stones carefully by his side at the edge of the well. As he stooped to drink, he happened to give the stones a little push, and they both fell into the water with a splash.

Hans watched the stones disappear and jumped for joy. He thanked his stars that he had been so lucky as to get rid of the stones that had weighed upon him for so long.

"I really think," cried he, "I am the luckiest man under the sun." So on he went, free of care, until he reached his mother's house.

Extending Comprehension

(The following Extending Comprehension activities can be presented after students finish reading the story. The activities also appear in the *Literature Anthology*.)

1. (Students can answer the Story Questions either orally or in writing. If the questions are presented orally, use the script below.)
2. (Students can select one or more Discussion Topics. Discussions can take place in small groups or with the entire class.)
3. (Students can use the Writing Ideas to respond to the story in writing.)

Story Questions

1. Make a list of the exchanges Hans made, beginning with "He exchanged the lump of gold for a horse."
   - (List: *He exchanged the lump of gold for a horse, the horse for a cow, the cow for a pig, the pig for a goose, the goose for a grindstone, and the grindstone for freedom from cares.*)
2. Tell why the people Hans met were so interested in making exchanges with him.
   - (Ideas: *Because they wanted what he had; because they got good bargains; because it was easy to talk him into an exchange.*)
3. Why did Hans think exchanging the gold for the horse was a good idea?
   - (Ideas: *Because the gold was heavy; because he could ride the horse.*)
4. Why did Hans feel lucky at the end of the story?
   - (Ideas: *Because he was free of care; because he made so many bargains on his journey; because he had gotten rid of the heavy stones; because he was almost home.*)

5. Why do you think the story is titled "Hans in Luck"?
  - (Ideas: *Because Hans thought he was lucky; because the author is making fun of Hans.*)
6. What do you think Hans's mother said about his exchanges when he got home?
  - (Ideas: *I'm so glad to see you; where is your payment for seven years' work? Accept all other reasonable responses.*)

Discussion Topics

1. This story can be interpreted in different ways. In one interpretation, Hans is unlucky because he keeps giving up valuable things until he ends up with nothing. In another interpretation, Hans is lucky because he gets rid of all the things that were a burden to him. Discuss these two interpretations with your classmates. During your discussion, try to answer the following questions:
  - Which interpretation do you agree with? Why?
  - Do you have another interpretation of the story? If so, what is it?

2. This story tells about people who make exchanges to get the things they want. With your classmates, discuss how you might get some things you want. During your discussion, try to answer the following questions:
  - What types of things would you like to get?
  - What kind of exchanges could you make to get those things?

3. People who are **gullible** believe everything they hear. It is easy to trick **gullible** people. With your classmates, decide if **gullible** is a word that you should use to describe Hans. During your discussion, try to answer the following questions:
  - Do the exchanges Hans makes make him appear *gullible?* Explain your answers.
  - Do Hans's statements make him sound *gullible?* Give some examples.

Writing Ideas

1. Write out the conversation that Hans and his mother might have when Hans arrives home. Have Hans explain what happened on his journey. Tell what his mother says as she listens to his story.
2. Pretend that you could have any one of the things Hans had, including the lump of gold, the horse, the cow, the pig, the goose, the grindstone, or freedom from care. Which would you choose? Explain what you would do with your choice. Tell why you chose that thing.

Story 2

The Bracelet

New Vocabulary Words

Everybody, take out your Literature Anthology. Turn to page 17. ✔
What is the title of this story? (Signal.) *"The Bracelet."*
Who is the author? (Signal.) *Yoshiko Uchida.*
   1. First we'll read some words from the story, and then we'll talk about what they mean.
   2. Word 1 is **evacuated**. What word? (Signal.) *Evacuated.*
      • (Repeat for every numbered word.)
   3. It's your turn to read all the words.
   4. Word 1. What word? (Signal.) *Evacuated.*
      • (Repeat for every numbered word.)

1. evacuated	4. loyal	7. bayonets
2. concentration camp	5. register	8. barracks
3. interned	6. abandoned	9. cots

Definitions

   (For each definition, call on a student to read the definition aloud; then, present the tasks that go with that definition to the group.)
   1. *When families are **evacuated** by the government, they are forced to leave their homes and are taken to a different place to live.*
      • During a war, it is not unusual for groups of people to be **evacuated** by their government.
   2. *A **concentration camp** is like a prison where large groups of innocent people are forced to stay.*
      • Everybody, what do we call a place where large groups of innocent people are forced to stay? (Signal). *A concentration camp.*
   3. *When you are **interned**, you are taken to a place against your will and are not allowed to leave.*
      • Everybody, here's another way of saying **He was taken to a concentration camp against his will and was not allowed to leave: He was interned in a concentration camp.**

- Everybody, what's another way of saying **The families were taken to a concentration camp against their will and were not allowed to leave?** (Signal.) *The families were interned in the concentration camp.*

4. When you are **loyal** to your country, you support and defend the ideas your country stands for.
   - Everybody, here's another way of saying **The soldier supported and defended England: The soldier was loyal to England.**
   - Everybody, what's another way of saying **The woman supported and defended the United States?** (Signal.) *The woman was loyal to the United States.*

5. When you **register** somewhere, you give your name and important information about yourself.
   - Where are some places you would **register?** (Ideas: *School; hotels; camp; online.*)

6. When you feel **abandoned**, you feel completely alone and sad because someone you love has left you and is not coming back.
   - Everybody, here's another way of saying **Martin felt completely alone and sad after his friend moved away: Martin felt abandoned after his friend moved away.**
   - Everybody, what's another way of saying **The child felt completely alone and sad after the soldiers took her parents away?** (Signal.) *The child felt abandoned after the soldiers took her parents away.*

7. **Bayonets** are weapons that look like short swords. **Bayonets** are attached to the ends of guns.

8. **Barracks** are a group of large buildings where many people—usually soldiers—sleep.
   - Everybody, here's another way of saying **Large buildings where soldiers sleep are found in the desert: Barracks are found in the desert.**
   - Everybody, what's another way of saying **When we turned the corner, we saw large buildings where soldiers slept?** (Signal.) *When we turned the corner, we saw barracks.*

9. **Cots** are thin, portable beds. Soldiers sleep on **cots** in their barracks.
   - Everybody, what's another way of saying **We sleep on thin, portable beds when we go camping?** (Signal.) *We sleep on cots when we go camping.*

Story Background

1. (Call on individual students to read two or three sentences.)
2. (After students complete a section, ask the questions for that section.)

"The Bracelet" is an example of historical fiction. It is based on the experiences of Japanese Americans living on the West Coast of the United States during World War II. On December 7, 1941, the country of Japan bombed Pearl Harbor, Hawaii without any warning. Pearl Harbor was a very important base for the United States Navy, and many ships and lives were destroyed. The next day, the United States declared war against Japan.

- Which group of people is this story about? (Idea: *Japanese Americans.*)
- Where did these people live? (Idea: *On the West Coast of the United States.*)
- Everybody, which country bombed Pearl Harbor? (Signal.) *Japan.*
- What did the United States do after the bombs were dropped on Pearl Harbor? (Idea: *They declared war against Japan.*)

Because of the war, the United States government questioned the loyalty of Japanese Americans who were living in America. The United States government thought Japanese Americans might help Japan attack the United States, so the government forced over 100,000 Japanese Americans to move to relocation camps. The author of the story you will read calls these places concentration camps.

- Everybody, was the United States government sure that the Japanese Americans would remain loyal? (Signal.) *No.*
- Everybody, which country did the United States government think the Japanese Americans might try to help? (Signal.) *Japan.*
- What did the United States government do? (Idea: *Moved the Japanese Americans to relocation camps.*)

The United States government considered important Japanese American community and business leaders to be especially dangerous; it called them enemy aliens. (Aliens are people who are not from the country in which they are living.) The leaders who were identified as enemy aliens were the first Japanese Americans the government interned, but they were sent to prisoner-of-war (POW) camps instead of relocation camps. When the war ended, the Japanese Americans were permitted to leave all these camps. Sadly, most of them no longer had homes or businesses to return to. Many years later, the United States government paid money to all living Japanese Americans who had been interned. The money was a small way for the government to apologize to its loyal citizens.

- Why did the United States government consider the Japanese American community and business leaders to be dangerous? (Ideas: *Because they had a lot of influence over the other Japanese Americans; because they had connections with Japan.*)
- Who are aliens? (Idea: *People who are from a different country than the one they are living in.*)
- Where were the leaders who were thought of as enemy aliens sent? (Idea: *To prisoner-of-war camps.*)
- Why do you think the enemy aliens were sent to prisoner-of-war camps instead of to relocation camps? (Ideas: *Because the United States government thought they were more dangerous; because they had the most influence over the other Japanese Americans.*)
- When were the Japanese Americans released from their camps? (Idea: *When the war ended.*)
- Everybody, were most of the Japanese Americans' homes and businesses still available to them at the end of the war? (Signal.) *No.*
- What did the United States government do to show their Japanese American citizens that it was sorry for interning them? (Idea: *Paid them some money.*)

Focus Questions

1. (Call on individual students to read the Focus Questions aloud.)
2. (Remind students to think about those questions as they read the story.)
   - Why is Laurie's present so important to Ruri?
   - How is Ruri's life at the concentration camp different from her life in Berkeley?
   - What lesson does Ruri learn from her mother?

The Bracelet
by Yoshiko Uchida
Illustrated by Karen Jerome

"Mama, is it time to go?"

I hadn't planned to cry, but the tears came suddenly, and I wiped them away with the back of my hand. I didn't want my older sister to see me crying.

"It's almost time, Ruri," my mother said gently. Her face was filled with a kind of sadness I had never seen before.

I looked around at my empty room. The clothes that Mama always told me to hang up in the closet, the junk piled on my dresser, the old rag doll I could never bear to part with; they were all gone. There was nothing left in my room, and there was nothing left in the rest of the house. The rugs and furniture were gone, the pictures and drapes were down, and the closets and cupboards were empty. The house was like a gift box after the nice thing inside was gone; just a lot of nothingness.

It was almost time to leave our home, but we weren't moving to a nicer house or to a new town. It was April 21, 1942. The United States and Japan were at war, and every Japanese person on the West Coast was being evacuated by the government to a concentration camp. Mama, my sister Keiko and I were being sent from our home, and out of Berkeley, and eventually, out of California.

The doorbell rang, and I ran to answer it before my sister could. I thought maybe by some miracle, a messenger from the government might be standing there, tall and proper and buttoned into a uniform, come to tell us it was all a terrible mistake; that we wouldn't have to leave after all. Or maybe the messenger would have a telegram from Papa, who was interned in a prisoner-of-war camp in Montana because he had worked for a Japanese business firm.

The FBI had come to pick up Papa and hundreds of other Japanese community leaders on the very day that Japanese planes had bombed Pearl Harbor. The government thought they were dangerous enemy aliens. If it weren't so sad, it would have been funny. Papa could no more be dangerous than the mayor of our city, and he was every bit as loyal to the United States. He had lived here since 1917.

When I opened the door, it wasn't a messenger from anywhere. It was my best friend, Laurie Madison, from next door. She was holding a package wrapped up like a birthday present, but she wasn't wearing her party dress, and her face drooped like a wilted tulip.

"Hi," she said. "I came to say good-bye."

She thrust the present at me and told me it was something to take to camp. "It's a bracelet," she said, before I could open the package. "Put it on so you won't have to pack it." She knew I didn't have one inch of space left in my suitcase. We had been instructed to take only what we could carry into camp, and Mama had told us that we could each take only two suitcases.

"Then how are we ever going to pack the dishes and blankets and sheets they've told us to bring with us?" Keiko worried.

"I don't really know," Mama said, and she simply began packing those big impossible things into an enormous duffel bag—along with umbrellas, boots, a kettle, hot plate, and flashlight.

"Who's going to carry that huge sack?" I asked.

But Mama didn't worry about things like that. "Someone will help us," she said. "Don't worry." So I didn't.

Laurie wanted me to open her package and put on the bracelet before she left. It was a thin gold chain with a heart dangling on it. She helped me put it on, and I told her I'd never take it off, ever.

"Well, good-bye then," Laurie said awkwardly. "Come home soon."

"I will," I said, although I didn't know if I would ever get back to Berkeley again.

I watched Laurie go down the block, her long blond pigtails bouncing as she walked. I wondered who would be sitting in my desk at Lincoln Junior High now that I was gone. Laurie kept turning and waving, even walking backwards for a while, until she got to the corner. I didn't want to watch anymore, and I slammed the door shut.

The next time the doorbell rang, it was Mrs. Simpson, our other neighbor. She was going to drive us to the Congregational church, which was the Civil Control Station where all the Japanese of Berkeley were supposed to report.

It was time to go. "Come on, Ruri. Get your things," my sister called to me.

It was a warm day, but I put on a sweater and my coat so I wouldn't have to carry them, and I picked up my two suitcases. Each one had a tag with my name and our family number on it. Every Japanese family had to register and get a number. We were Family Number 13453.

Mama was taking one last look around our house. She was going from room to room, as though she were trying to take a mental picture of the house she had lived in for fifteen years, so she would never forget it.

I saw her take a long last look at the garden that Papa loved. The irises beside the fish pond were just beginning to bloom. If Papa had been home, he would have cut the first iris blossom and brought it inside to Mama. "This one is for you," he would have said. And Mama would have smiled and said, "Thank you, Papa San," and put it in her favorite cutglass vase.

But the garden looked shabby and forsaken now that Papa was gone and Mama was too busy to take care of it. It looked the way I felt, sort of empty and lonely and abandoned.

When Mrs. Simpson took us to the Civil Control Station, I felt even worse. I was scared, and for a minute I thought I was going to lose my breakfast right in front of everybody. There must have been over a thousand Japanese people gathered at the church. Some were old and some were young. Some were talking and laughing, and some were crying. I guess everybody else was scared too. No one knew exactly what was going to happen to us. We just knew we were being taken to the Tanforan Racetracks, which the army had turned into a camp for the Japanese. There were fourteen other camps like ours along the West Coast.

What scared me most were the soldiers standing at the doorway of the church hall. They were carrying guns with mounted bayonets. I wondered if they thought we would try to run away, and whether they'd shoot us or come after us with their bayonets if we did.

A long line of buses waited to take us to camp. There were trucks, too, for our baggage. And Mama was right; some men were there to help us load our duffel bag. When it was time to board the buses, I sat with Keiko and Mama sat behind us. The bus went down Grove Street and passed the small Japanese food store where Mama used to order her bean-curd cakes and pickled radish. The windows were all boarded up, but there was a sign still hanging on the door that read, "We are loyal Americans."

The crazy thing about the whole evacuation was that we were all loyal Americans. Most of us were citizens because we had been born here. But our parents, who had come from Japan, couldn't become citizens because there was a law that prevented any Asian from becoming a citizen. Now everybody with a Japanese face was being shipped off to concentration camps.

"It's stupid," Keiko muttered as we saw the racetrack looming up beside the highway: "If there were any Japanese spies around, they'd have gone back to Japan long ago."

"I'll say," I agreed. My sister was in high school and she ought to know, I thought.

When the bus turned into Tanforan, there were more armed guards at the gate, and I saw barbed wire strung around the entire grounds. I felt as though I were going into a prison, but I hadn't done anything wrong.

We streamed off the buses and poured into a huge room, where doctors looked down our throats and peeled back our eyelids to see if we had any diseases. Then we were given our housing assignments. The man in charge gave Mama a slip of paper. We were in Barrack 16, Apartment 40.

"Mama!" I said. "We're going to live in an apartment!" The only apartment I had ever seen was the one my piano teacher lived in. It was in an enormous building in San Francisco with an elevator and thick carpeted hallways. I thought how wonderful it would be to have our own elevator. A house was all right, but an apartment seemed elegant and special.

We walked down the racetrack looking for Barrack 16. Mr. Noma, a friend of Papa's, helped us carry our bags. I was so busy looking around, I slipped and almost fell on the muddy track. Army barracks had been built everywhere, all around the racetrack and even in the center oval.

Mr. Noma pointed beyond the track toward the horse stables. "I think your barrack is out there."

He was right. We came to a long stable that had once housed the horses of Tanforan, and we climbed up the wide ramp. Each stall had a number painted on it, and when we got to 40, Mr. Noma pushed open the door.

"Well, here it is," he said, "Apartment 40."

The stall was narrow and empty and dark. There were two small windows on each side of the door. Three folded army cots were on the dust-covered floor and one light bulb dangled from the ceiling. That was all. This was our apartment, and it still smelled of horses.

Mama looked at my sister and then at me. "It won't be so bad when we fix it up," she began. "I'll ask Mrs. Simpson to send me some material for curtains. I could make some cushions, too, and . . . well. . . ." She stopped. She couldn't think of anything more to say.

Mr. Noma said he'd go get some mattresses for us. "I'd better hurry before they're all gone." He rushed off. I think he wanted to leave so that he wouldn't have to see Mama cry. But he needn't have run off, because Mama didn't cry. She just went out to borrow a broom and began sweeping out the dust and dirt. "Will you girls set up the cots?" she asked.

It was only after we had put up the last cot that I noticed my bracelet was gone. "I've lost Laurie's bracelet!" I screamed. "My bracelet's gone!"

We looked all over the stall and even down the ramp. I wanted to run back down the track and go over every inch of the ground we'd walked on, but it was getting dark and Mama wouldn't let me.

I thought of what I'd promised Laurie. I wasn't ever going to take the bracelet off, not even when I went to take a shower. And now I had lost it on my very first day in camp. I wanted to cry.

I kept looking for it all the time we were in Tanforan. I didn't stop looking until the day we were sent to another camp, called Topaz, in the middle of a desert in Utah. And then I gave up.

But Mama told me never mind. She said I didn't need a bracelet to remember Laurie, just as I didn't need anything to remember Papa or our home in Berkeley or all the people and things we loved and had left behind.

"Those are things we can carry in our hearts and take with us no matter where we are sent," she said.

And I guess she was right. I've never forgotten Laurie, even now.

Extending Comprehension

(The following Extending Comprehension activities can be presented after students finish reading the story. The activities also appear in the *Literature Anthology*.)

1. (Students can answer the Story Questions either orally or in writing. If the questions are presented orally, use the script below.)

2. (Students can select one or more Discussion Topics. Discussions can take place in small groups or with the entire class.)

3. (Students can use the Writing Ideas to respond to the story in writing.)

Story Questions

1. How did Ruri feel about leaving her home? Give an example from the story that supports your answer.
   - (Ideas: *Upset—she cried; angry—she slammed the door; sad—she wondered who'd sit at her old desk.*)

2. Name at least two reasons why you think Laurie's present was so important to Ruri.
   - (Ideas: *Because it would remind her of Laurie; because it would keep her connected to her life in Berkeley; because her best friend gave it to her; because Laurie didn't want Ruri to forget about her.*)

3. Describe at least three different things Ruri observed when she reached her new home, Apartment 40.
   - (Ideas: *It was a horse stall; it was narrow, empty and dark; it had two small windows; the floor was dusty; one light bulb hung from the ceiling; it smelled like horses; there were three folded cots.*)

4. How did Ruri's mother react when she was faced with difficult situations?
   - (Ideas: *She tried to think of ways to make the situation better; she kept a positive attitude; she tried to find something good in the situation.*)

5. Why do you think the author never had Ruri find her bracelet?
   - (Idea: *Because the missing bracelet forced Ruri to realize she didn't need things to remind her how she felt about people and other things she loved.*)

Discussion Topics

1. What did Ruri's mother mean when she said, "Those are things we carry in our hearts and take with us no matter where we are sent"? During your discussion, try to answer the following questions:
   - What valuable lesson did Ruri learn when she lost the bracelet Laurie had given her?
   - Can you give an example from your own life of "things you carry in your heart"?
2. Do you think the United States government did the right thing when it interned the Japanese Americans during the war? During your discussion, try to answer the following questions:
   - What are some reasons for internment of the Japanese Americans?
   - What are some reasons against internment of the Japanese Americans?

Writing Ideas

1. Pretend you are Ruri. Write a letter to Laurie describing your experiences at Barrack 16, Apartment 40. Tell where you live and how you feel. Be sure to include all the parts of a friendly letter.
2. What do you think was the worst part of Ruri's internment? Explain your answer.

Story 3

The Jacket

New Vocabulary Words

Everybody, take out your *Literature Anthology*. Turn to page 32. ✔
What is the title of this story? (Signal.) *"The Jacket."*
Who is the author? (Signal.) *Steven Otfinoski.*

1. First we'll read some words from the story and then we'll talk about what they mean.
2. Word 1 is **customary.** What word? (Signal.) *Customary.*
   • (Repeat for every numbered word.)
3. It's your turn to read all the words.
4. Word 1. What word? (Signal.) *Customary.*
   • (Repeat for every numbered word.)

1. customary	6. candidate	11. expectant
2. bewildered	7. election	12. ovation
3. aroused	8. podium	13. landslide
4. flustered	9. improvise	14. frankly
5. fret	10. philosophical	15. potential

Definitions

(For each definition, call on a student to read the definition aloud; then, present the tasks that go with that definition to the group.)

1. **Customary** *is another way of saying* **usual.**
   • Everybody, what's another way of saying **I took my usual seat at the back table?** (Signal.) *I took my customary seat at the back table.*
2. **Bewildered** *is another way of saying* **confused.**
   • Everybody, what's another way of saying **I looked up at the teacher, confused?** (Signal). *I looked up at the teacher, bewildered.*
3. **Aroused** *is another way of saying* **awakened.**
   • Everybody, what's another way of saying **That picture awakened my curiosity?** (Signal.) *That picture aroused my curiosity.*
4. **Flustered** *is another way of saying* **nervous.**
   • Everybody, what's another way of saying **I felt nervous?** (Signal.) *I felt flustered.*

5. When you **fret,** you worry.
   - Everybody, what's another way of saying **I always worry the night before a test?** (Signal.) *I always fret the night before a test.*
6. A **candidate** is a person who is running for office.
   - Everybody, what do we call a person who is running for office? (Signal.) *A candidate.*
7. During an **election,** people vote for the candidates who are running for office.
8. A **podium** is a piece of furniture that a speaker stands behind.
   - Everybody, what do we call the piece of furniture that a speaker stands behind? (Signal.) *A podium.*
9. When you **improvise,** you do not prepare ahead of time to do something, you just do it.
   - Everybody, here's another way of saying **He didn't prepare his speech ahead of time: He improvised his speech.**
   - Everybody, what's another way of saying **She didn't prepare her presentation ahead of time?** (Signal.) *She improvised her presentation.*
10. If you feel **philosophical** about something that happened, you accept what happened, even though you may not be happy about it.
    - John was **philosophical** about losing the election because he accepted the fact that he didn't get enough votes.
11. When you are expecting something to happen, you may have an **expectant** expression on your face.
    - The **expectant** audience eagerly waited for the president's speech. Everybody, what kind of audience eagerly waited for the president's speech? (Signal.) *An expectant audience.*
12. An **ovation** is loud applause that lasts a long time. When the audience stands and applauds, it is called a standing **ovation.**
    - Everybody, here's another way of saying **The singer was given loud applause that lasted a long time: The singer was given an ovation.**
    - Everybody, what's another way of saying **The actor was given loud applause that lasted a long time?** (Signal.) *The actor was given an ovation.*
13. When you win an election by a **landslide,** you win by a lot of votes.
    - Everybody, what is winning an election by a lot of votes called? (Signal.) *A landslide.*
14. **Frankly** is another way of saying **honestly.**
    - Everybody, what's another way of saying **Honestly, I think your first idea was better?** (Signal.) *Frankly, I think your first idea was better.*
15. When you realize your **potential,** you become what is possible for you to be.

Story Background

1. (Call on individual students to read this passage.)
2. (After students complete a passage, ask the questions for that passage.)

> "The Jacket" is a modern fable about self-confidence and the power we each have inside of us. Walter is a "nerdy" student until he gets a magical jacket. When the jacket disappears, Walter is very worried. By the end of the story, you will find out what Walter learns about himself.

- What kind of story is "The Jacket"? (Ideas: *A modern fable; a story about self-confidence; a story about the power we have within us.*)
- What did Walter wear that he thought changed his life? (Idea: *A magical jacket.*)

Focus Questions

1. (Call on individual students to read the Focus Questions aloud.)
2. (Remind students to refer to these questions as they read the story.)
   - *How does wearing the jacket make Walter feel?*
   - *How are things different for Walter after he starts wearing the jacket?*
   - *Do you think the jacket is a magical jacket?*

The Jacket
by Steven Otfinoski
Illustrated by Anthony Accardo

My name is Walter, I'm in the sixth grade, and until a few weeks ago, I was the number one nerd at school. Then I put on the jacket and everything changed. But I think I'd better start at the beginning. Otherwise, I'm sure you won't believe what happened to me. I can hardly believe it myself.

It all started one Friday during lunch period. I was standing in line in the school cafeteria when "Gorilla" Gordon walked up to me. His real name is Gus, but everyone calls him Gorilla because he looks and acts like one. Of course, most kids only call him that behind his back. You live longer that way.

"Hi, punk," Gorilla said. "How about moving aside and letting me ahead of you? I'm really hungry today."

"Sure, Gus," I smiled. "Go right ahead."

To add insult to injury, Gorilla stomped on my foot as he walked past. It hurt, but I didn't say a word. Besides being a nerd, I was a coward, too.

After getting my lunch, I sat down at a table next to the new kid in school. His name is Bob and he's a pretty nice guy. At least he didn't get up and leave when I sat down next to him like the other kids do.

"Why do you take that stuff from that big ape?" Bob asked me. He had seen what happened in line.

"Simple," I replied. "If I didn't, he'd cream me."

"He's not so tough," said Bob. "If you only stood up to him, I bet he'd crumble in a minute."

I wasn't enjoying this conversation at all and wished I'd taken my customary seat at an empty table. "That's easy for you say," I told Bob. "You're bigger. Guys like Gorilla don't pick on you."

"Size doesn't have anything to do with it," replied Bob. "It's all in how you see yourself. I think I know someone who can help you."

Bob reached into his pocket, pulled out a small white business card, and handed it to me. I read the fine black print.

CALDUCCI'S CLOTHING SHOP
19 River Road
"Clothes that give confidence"

I looked up at Bob, bewildered. "I don't need any new clothes," I told him.

Bob just grinned. "Yes, you do," he said. "Mr. Calducci helped me, and he can help you too."

It sounded crazy, but I had to admit Bob had aroused my curiosity. So Saturday morning I hopped on my bike and pedaled down to River Road.

Calducci's Clothing Shop certainly wasn't much to look at. The shop window was dirty, and the sign above it looked as if it would fall apart if you breathed on it. But then I saw it in the window-the most awesome jacket I had ever laid eyes on. It was made of black leather with fringe the colors of the rainbow and beaded cuffs. Across the back in glowing letters were written the words "KING OF THE MOUNTAIN."

"Like to try it on?" someone spoke quietly. I looked up and saw a balding, middle-aged man with a black mustache. He was standing in the doorway.

"Are you Mr. Calducci?" I asked.

"That's me," he said smiling. "Come on inside and I'll show you the jacket."

I hesitated. "I'm sure it's too expensive for me," I mumbled.

"Let's not talk about money," said the man, ushering me into the store. "One thing at a time."

So I tried on the jacket. It was a perfect fit. This was strange, because in the window it looked several sizes bigger. My skin tingled when I put it on. It felt like there was a current of electricity running through me. It was exciting and a little scary at the same time.

"This jacket was made for you, young man," said Mr. Calducci.

"Maybe," I said, "but it wasn't made for my allowance. I'm sure I can't afford it."

"So, don't buy it," replied the store owner. "I'll tell you what. You can take it on loan."

I never heard of a clothing store loaning clothes, but I wasn't going to argue with him. "You mean like a rental?" I asked.

"Yes, something like that," said Mr. Calducci. "See how you like it and we'll talk later."

I thanked him and left wearing the jacket.

That night, I joked and talked at dinner more than I can ever remember. I actually felt completely at ease with my parents and we didn't have one argument. My parents even believed my story about the jacket! It was truly amazing. I couldn't explain it, but the new jacket gave me a confidence that I'd never felt before.

The next day I woke up feeling full of enthusiasm. I actually looked forward to going to school. That was a switch! I put on my jacket over my school clothes and looked in the mirror. I wondered what the other kids would think of it.

You might say my taste in clothes before this was definitely on the nerdish side. What I wore pretty much reflected my personality. No one seemed to notice me much, which is just the way I liked it.

But did they ever notice me now! I was the center of attention the moment I strolled into class. And the amazing part was I thoroughly enjoyed it!

Our teacher, Ms. Bateman, gave us a surprise quiz that morning. I normally get so flustered during quizzes that I automatically get half the answers wrong. Or else I fret so long over one question that I never finish in time. But not now. I felt cool as a cucumber in my new jacket and answered every question with ease. When Ms. Bateman returned the corrected quizzes just before lunchtime, I had a perfect 100.

"Good work, Walter," said Ms. Bateman. "I'm pleased to see your study habits are improving."

How could I tell her my study habits had nothing to do with it—that it was all the jacket's doing?

In the lunch line, everyone wanted to get a closer look at my jacket. Kids who never noticed I was alive before were suddenly treating me like their best friend. That's when Gorilla Gordon made his appearance.

"Where'd you get the cool threads, punk?" Gorilla sneered. "The Army and Navy Store?"

I looked at Gorilla and then at the other kids. No one said a word. I suddenly realized I wasn't scared of this bully one bit.

"Look, Gorilla," I said, looking him right in the eye, "why don't you find a nice tall tree to climb up into, and leave the jungle floor to us intelligent humans?"

You should've seen the expression on Gorilla's face! Once he got over the shock of having Walter the Nerd talk back to him, however, he got good and angry. He reached out and grabbed me by the front of my jacket.

Before I knew what I was doing, I pulled his hands away and flipped him over my shoulder. He let out a groan as he hit the floor and just lay there stunned for a moment. The circle of students cheered. "Guess that'll teach you to mess with the king!" yelled one boy.

Gorilla got up to the sound of jeering laughter, gave me a nasty look, and stalked away. That day I didn't have any problem finding company for lunch. Nearly everyone wanted to sit at my table and talk with me. In one day, I had gone from being Mr. Nobody to the Personality Kid.

At one point, I glanced up and saw Bob sitting across at another table. I smiled at him and he winked back at me. We were the only two people in school who knew the secret of my success.

From then on, I wore my jacket everywhere. At school, at home. I even slept in it. I quickly became the best student in my class and the top athlete on the playing field during recess. Everyone was my friend—everybody but Gorilla Gordon—and when the time came to elect a class president for all the sixth grades, I was the leading candidate.

The day before the election was to be held, each candidate was supposed to give a short speech in a special assembly. I wrote my speech the night before. (It was brilliant, of course!) When I'd finished, I folded the speech and put it in my jacket pocket.

The next morning at school, all my friends were congratulating me as if I had already won the election. Before the assembly, I took my place backstage with the other three candidates.

Ms. Bateman asked me if I'd carry the wooden speakers' podium from backstage to center stage. It must have weighed fifty tons, and it was tough trying to lift it with my jacket on. So I took off the jacket and carefully folded it over a chair backstage. Then I lugged the podium out to the middle of the stage as the students took their seats in the auditorium.

Imagine my surprise when I came backstage and found my jacket was gone! Who could've taken it? I immediately thought of Gorilla Gordon. This was his revenge for showing him up in the cafeteria that day! I had to find him and get it back.

But just then Ms. Bateman appeared. "We're ready to begin, Walter," she said. "You'll speak second, all right?"

"But I can't," I stammered.

"What do you mean?" asked the teacher.

"My jacket's gone!" I told her.

"It is?" she said. "Maybe you just misplaced it. I'm sure it's around here someplace."

"You don't understand," I said. "My speech was in the pocket of my jacket."

"Oh," said Ms. Bateman. "Well, I'm sure you can improvise. You're such an excellent public speaker."

Now, the King of the Mountain was an excellent public speaker. But without that jacket, I wasn't king of anything. The moment of truth had come.

"Well," I said to myself, trying to be philosophical, "it was fun while it lasted."

The first candidate finished her speech. Ms. Bateman gave me the signal to come out on stage. That twenty-foot walk to the podium was the longest walk of my life.

I gazed out over the expectant faces of my classmates. They looked eager, anxious to hear what I was going to say. Just realizing they already liked me, even before I opened my mouth, was comforting. Maybe all wasn't lost yet, I thought to myself.

"Fellow students," I began at last. "You've all noticed a big change in me over these past few weeks. Well, it wasn't really me that changed, but the way I felt about myself. My jacket says 'King of the Mountain.' I think we're all kings of the mountain in our own ways. Maybe all anyone needs is a little confidence to scale the mountain. If you elect me your class president, I'll make it my goal to help you reach the top. If we work together, I think we can make our school number one. Thank you."

That was it. Short and sweet. There was a long moment of silence. I really blew it, I thought to myself. Then suddenly the applause started. Everybody in the auditorium was clapping and shouting. Some kids were even giving me a standing ovation. It was incredible!

As I made way for the next speaker, I noticed Gorilla Gordon down in front, clapping right along with everyone else. He didn't look like someone who had just stolen my jacket, but then maybe he was a better actor than I thought.

That afternoon, I looked all over school for the jacket. But it was nowhere to be found. I went home a worried wreck. The next day at school I had even more reason to worry. The votes were counted and I won the election by a landslide. Now I really felt like a fake. How was I ever going to make good as class president without my jacket to give me confidence?

After class, I rushed down to River Road to Calducci's Clothing Shop. I figured whatever kind of wizard Mr. Calducci was, he could make me another jacket like the first one. But to my amazement, there was my jacket in the window where I had first seen it!

"Hello, young man," said Mr. Calducci when I entered the shop. "I'm surprised to see you back here."

"Not as surprised as I am," I told him. "How on earth did my jacket get back here?"

"That's simple," he explained. "I picked it up backstage before your speech. I told you it was only a loan."

I was stunned. "But why did you take it at the very moment I needed it most?"

Mr. Calducci smiled and shook his head. "You had no more use for it—as your speech proved. Frankly, I think it was a big improvement over the one you wrote. You made a discovery about yourself in that speech. The jacket was just a way to show you what you had inside all along."

It was beginning to sink in. Mr. Calducci was right. The jacket helped me to realize my potential. Now that I had confidence in myself, I didn't need it anymore.

"So the jacket always comes back to you?" I asked.

"Of course," he said. "All my clothes are strictly on short-term loan."

"I don't know how to thank you," I told him.

"The best way you can thank me is to tell someone else about my shop—someone else who needs a shot of self-confidence," said Mr. Calducci.

I said I would do that. Before I left, I took one last look at the jacket in the window. It didn't look so special anymore. It looked just like any other jacket.

That was a week ago. I haven't found anyone yet who needs Mr. Calducci's help. Maybe you know someone who could use a little self-confidence? Say, you look a little down in the dumps yourself. Why don't you take this card I have here? I know you won't be sorry . . .

> CALDUCCI'S CLOTHING SHOP
> 19 River Road
> "Clothes that give confidence"

Extending Comprehension

(The following Extending Comprehension activities can be presented after students finish reading the story. The activities also appear in the *Literature Anthology*.)

1. (Students can answer the Story Questions either orally or in writing. If the questions are presented orally, use the script below.)
2. (Students can select one or more Discussion Topics. Discussions can take place in small groups or with the entire class.)
3. (Students can use the Writing Ideas to respond to the story in writing.)

Story Questions

1. How did Walter feel about himself before he got the jacket?
   - (Ideas: *He thought he was a nerd; he thought he was a coward; he didn't like to be noticed.*)
2. How did wearing the jacket make Walter feel?
   - (Ideas: *Confident; cool; brave; like he had a new personality.*)
3. Name at least three things that were different for Walter after he started wearing the jacket.
   - (Ideas: *He wasn't afraid of Gorilla; he didn't get nervous about the surprise quiz; people at school noticed him; he went from "Mr. Nobody" to the "Personality Kid"; he was athletic; he was the leading candidate for class president.*)

4. Do you think the jacket had magical powers? Use evidence from the story to support your answer.
   - (Ideas for Yes answers: *the jacket was a perfect fit, even though it looked too big in the window; Walter's skin tingled when he put on the jacket the first time; Walter's life changed for the better at school and at home; the jacket disappears.*)
   - (Ideas for No answers: *Walter's improvised speech was better than the one he wrote while wearing the jacket; the jacket didn't disappear—Mr. Calducci came and got it; when Walter saw the jacket in the window at the end of the story, it looked like an ordinary jacket.*)
5. Mr. Calducci said that Walter discovered something about himself. What did Walter discover?
   - (Ideas: *He discovered he was responsible for the changes in his life, not the jacket; he discovered he had the power to change his life within himself.*)

Discussion Topics

1. An old saying tells us that "you're only as good as you think you are." Discuss this saying with your classmates. During your discussion, try to answer the following questions:
   - How does this saying apply to Walter?
   - How does this saying apply to you?
2. The jacket plays an important role in this story; it is almost like a character. Discuss whether or not the jacket has magical powers.
   - What parts of the story make you think the jacket has magical powers?
   - What parts of the story make you think the jacket does not have magical powers?
3. This story ends with Walter offering Mr. Calducci's card to you. Why do you think the author ended the story this way? During your discussion, try to answer the following questions:
   - In what kinds of situations do most students need a little more confidence?
   - Do you like the way this story ended? Explain your answer.

Writing Ideas

1. Tell three things you would do if you had a jacket from Mr. Calducci's store. Also, tell how you would feel if you were wearing the jacket.
2. When you improvise, you are doing something without preparing to do it. When you are philosophical about something that happened, you accept what happened even though you are not happy about it. Write about a time you had to improvise something. Or, write about a time you tried to be philosophical about something that happened to you.

Story 4

Ginger's Challenge

New Vocabulary Words

Everybody, take out your *Literature Anthology.* Turn to page 48. ✔
What is the title of this story? (Signal.) *"Ginger's Challenge."*
Who is the author? (Signal.) *Josephine Noyes Felts.*
   1. First we'll read some words from the story, and then we'll talk about what they mean.
   2. Word 1 is **rebellious.** What word? (Signal.) *Rebellious.* (Repeat for every numbered word.)
   3. It's your turn to read all the words.
   4. Word 1. (Signal.) *Rebellious.*
      • (Repeat for every numbered word.)

1. rebellious	4. barbed wire	7. stile
2. loafing	5. tousled	8. cutoff
3. mounted up	6. smoldering	9. clapper
		10. indignant

Definitions

(For each definition, call on a student to read the definition aloud; then, present the tasks that go with that definition to the group.)
   1. *When you are **rebellious,** you resist doing what you are asked to do.*
      • Everybody, what do we call children who resist doing what they are asked to do? (Signal.) *Rebellious children.*
   2. *When you are **loafing,** you are wasting time.*
      • Everybody, what's another way of saying **The boys were wasting time on the playground?** (Signal.) *The boys were loafing on the playground.*
   3. *Things that are **mounting up** are piling up.*
      • Everybody, what's another way of saying **The clouds piled up behind the mountains?** (Signal.) *The clouds mounted up behind the mountains.*
   4. *Wire fence with small, sharp pieces sticking out is called a **barbed wire** fence.*
      • **Barbed wire** can be dangerous. If people and animals fall on **barbed wire** they get cuts on their bodies.
      • Everybody, what would happen if you fell on a **barbed wire** fence? (Ideas: *I would cut myself; I would rip my clothes.*)
      • Everybody, what would happen if a horse bumped into a **barbed wire** fence? (Idea: *The horse would get cut.*)

5. When you look **tousled,** you look messy.
   - Everybody, what's another way of saying **After getting caught in the wind storm, he looked messy?** (Signal.) *After getting caught in the wind storm, he looked tousled.*
6. When a fire **smolders,** it burns with little smoke and no flame.
   - Everybody, what's another way of saying **The fire burned with little smoke and no flame?** (Signal.) *The fire smoldered.*
7. Steps that are built next to a wall or a fence are called a **stile.**
   - Everybody, what's another way of saying **Terry climbed the steps to get over the fence?** (Signal.) *Terry climbed the stile to get over the fence.*
8. A **cutoff** is a shortcut.
   - Everybody, what's another way of saying **Maria saved time by taking the shortcut through the park?** (Signal.) *Maria saved time by taking the cutoff through the park.*
9. The **clapper** of a bell is the piece of metal that makes a noise when it hits the bell.
   - The **clapper** hangs down inside the bell.
10. **Indignant** is another word for angry.
    - Everybody, what's another way of saying **The children were angry because they had to stay home?** (Signal.) *The children were indignant because they had to stay home.*

Story Background

1. (Call on individual students to read two or three sentences.)
2. (After students complete a section, ask the questions for that section.)

Many people are fascinated by the beauty and power of horses. And why not? Horses are fascinating animals. Long ago, people discovered that horses could be trained to do the kind of work that required strength and speed. Horses pulled the plows that farmers used to prepare the land for planting seeds. Horses pulled big wagons loaded with heavy supplies. A single horse could carry one person from one place to another much faster than that person could walk. Teams of horses pulled the big carriages and stagecoaches that carried people from one place to another. Knights in armor even rode horses into battles.

- How did horses help farmers? (Ideas: *They pulled plows; they pulled wagons full of supplies.*)
- How did horses help people get from one place to another? (Ideas: *They went faster than people could walk; they pulled carriages and stage coaches.*)
- Can you think of other ways that horses worked for people? (*Accept all reasonable ideas.*)

Horses are no longer needed to do this kind of work. Most farmers do not need horses to pull their plows. They use tractors to plow their fields and trucks to carry their supplies. People don't ride on horses or sit in horse-drawn carriages to get from one place to another. Instead, they use cars, buses, trains, and airplanes. Horses no longer carry knights in armor into battles.

- Give some reasons that tell why horses do not do this kind of work any more. (Idea: *Modern machines do the jobs that horses used to do.*)

In some places, however, horses still work for people. Men and women who work on cattle ranches use horses to help them round up cattle, and in some cities, police officers ride horses to help them direct crowds of people. But today, most horses are used for pleasure. Some people ride horses because they like to be outside riding on trails that go through fields and woods. Others train horses to compete in horse shows. Still other people train horses to run in races. You read about one kind of race in "A Horse to Remember."

- Name some ways horses are still used to help people work. (Ideas: *Ranchers use them to round up cattle; police officers ride horses to control crowds; accept other reasonable ideas.*)
- Name some things people who ride horses for pleasure do with horses. (Ideas: *They ride because they like to be outside; they train horses to compete in horse shows; they train horses for horse races; accept other reasonable ideas.*)

Many writers have written stories about horses and about the people who take care of and ride horses. Some young people love horse stories and read as many of them as they can get their hands on. As they read these stories, they learn some of the special "horse" words that people who work with horses use and that writers like to use in the stories they write about horses. In "Ginger's Challenge," you will come across words that name the parts of a horse, words that describe how horses move, and words that name the equipment people use to control horses.

In the section below, some of these words are defined. Read these definitions before you start reading the story. You may also want to look back and read the definitions as you need them to help you better understand the story.

Some words that name parts of a horse:
- The **muzzle** is the front part of a horse's head.
- **Hooves** are the hard, tough coverings of the feet of a horse.
- The **flanks** are the sides of a horse.
- The **withers** are located between the horse's shoulder bones at the bottom of its neck.

Some words that describe how horses move:
- When a horse **prances,** it moves proudly and in a lively way.
- When a horse **bolts,** it suddenly runs away, sometimes because it has been frightened.
- When a horse **gallops,** it goes very fast.
- When a horse **canters,** it is going a little slower than a gallop.
- When a horse **rears,** it stands up on its hind legs.
- When a horse **throws off** a rider, it jumps up and down, or rears, so that the rider falls off the saddle.
- When a horse **shies,** it stops suddenly or moves away quickly because something has frightened it.

Some words that name equipment used to control horses:
- A **lunge line** is a long rope used to exercise a horse.
- A **harness** is the leather strap a horse wears when hitched to a cart or wagon.
- The **bridle** is the leather strap a horse wears on its head while being ridden or driven.

- The **reins** are the straps attached to the bridle that the rider uses to control the horse.
- The **saddle** is the leather seat that is strapped to the body of the horse. A rider sits on the saddle.
- The **stirrups** are made of metal and are attached by straps to the saddle. Riders place their feet in the stirrups.

Some other words used in stories about horses:
- When a horse is **tethered,** it is tied up with a short rope so that it can move only a short distance.
- A **horsewoman** is a woman who knows a lot about riding and who is a very good rider.
- When a rider wants her horse to jump, she leans forward, stands in the stirrups, and holds up her body. When she does this, she is **lifting to jump.** She does not interfere with the horse's movement as it jumps.
- Each time a rider and a horse go around a racetrack, they complete a **lap.**
- When a rider and a horse practice together, the horse gets a **workout.**

Focus Questions

1. (Call on individual students to read the Focus Questions aloud.)
2. (Remind students to think about those questions as they read the story.)
   - *At the beginning of the story, why does Tommy talk about the barbed wire fence at the farm of Mr. and Mrs. Zigafoos?*
   - *Why does Ginger decide to go for help?*
   - *How does the author write about bad weather, and how does the bad weather make Ginger's trip even more difficult?*
   - *Why does Ginger decide to take the cutoff?*
   - *What are Ginger's doubts and worries as she rides to the village?*

Ginger's Challenge
by Josephine Noyes Felts
Illustrated by Sandy Rabinowitz

"I don't believe it. I just don't believe it!" whispered Ginger Grey to herself as she watched Dark Boy, the beautiful black steeplechaser, going round and round on the lunge, the training rope to which he was tethered in the O'Malley's yard. She was stroking him with her eyes, loving every curve, every flowing muscle of his slender, shining body.

But the voice of Tim O'Malley, Dark Boy's owner, still echoed in her ears. "You're a brave little horsewoman, Ginger, but Dark Boy would kill you. I'm getting rid of him next week. He's thrown three experienced men and run away twice since I've had him. You are not to get on him!"

Ginger wiped a rebellious tear from her cheek, looking quickly around to make sure that neither ten-year-old Tommy nor the two younger children had seen her. She was alone at the O'Malley farm, several miles away from home, looking after the O'Malley children while their father and mother were in town. Why couldn't she have had the exercising and training of this glorious horse! Her heart ached doubly, for she longed to ride him next week in the horse show at Pembroke.

Ginger glanced now at the two little girls playing in the yard. They needed their noses wiped. She took care of this, patted them gently, and went back to where Dark Boy was loafing at the end of the lunge. He didn't seem to mind the light saddle she had put on him. The reins of the bridle trailed the ground. She must go soon and take it off. He'd had a good workout today, she thought with satisfaction. Exercise was what he needed. And now with nobody riding him . . .

She shivered suddenly and noticed how much colder it had turned. A great bank of black clouds had mounted up over the woods behind the meadow. She studied the clouds anxiously. Bad storms sometimes rose quickly out of that corner of the sky. The air seemed abnormally still, and there was a weird copper light spreading from the west.

If it was going to storm she'd better get the children in the house, put Dark Boy in the barn, and find Tommy. Here came Tommy now, dirty, tousled, one leg of his jeans torn and flapping as he walked.

"Barbed wire," he explained cheerfully, pointing to his pants. "Zigafoos has fenced his fields with it!"

A sharp gust of wind rounded the house. Tommy flapped in it like a scarecrow. A shutter on the house banged sharply; the barn door creaked shrilly as it slammed. Dark Boy reared and thudded to the ground.

"Look!" yelled Tommy suddenly. "What a close funny cloud!"

A thin spiral of smoke was rising from behind the O'Malley's barn. Ginger's heart froze within her. Fire! She raced around the barn. Then she saw with horror that the lower part of that side was burning. The wind must have blown a spark from a smoldering trash pile. Already the blaze was too much for anything she and Tommy could do. She'd have to get help at once!

As she tore back toward the house, pictures flashed through her mind. The big red fire truck was in the village six miles down the road. There were no phones. Any cars in the scattered neighborhood would be down in the valley with the men who used them to get to work at the porcelain factory. She'd have to get to the village and give the fire alarm herself immediately. Perhaps on Dark Boy . . .

She dashed over to him and caught his bridle. He tossed his head and sidled away from her, prancing with excitement. As she talked quietly to him, with swift fingers she loosened the lunge, letting it fall to the ground. She felt sure that she could guide him if only she could get on him and stay on him when he bolted. She thrust her hand deep in her pocket and brought out two of the sugar lumps she had been saving for him.

"Sugar for a good boy," she panted and reached up for his muzzle. Dark Boy lipped the sugar swiftly, his ears forward.

With a flying leap Ginger was up, had swung her right leg over him and slipped her right foot in the stirrup. She sat lightly forward as jockeys do. Would he resent her? Throw her off? Or could she stick?

Indignant, Dark Boy danced a wide circle of astonishment. The wind was whistling furiously now around the house, bending the trees. Ginger held the reins firmly and drew Dark Boy to a prancing halt. Then, suddenly, he reared. She clung with her lithe brown knees and held him tight. Precious minutes were flying. She thought of the bright tongues of flame licking up the side of the barn.

"Tommy! Take care of the children!" she shouted over her shoulder as Dark Boy angrily seized the bit between his teeth and whirled away. "I'll get help!"

Ginger's light figure in a red blob of sweater flashed down the road through the twisting trees. Fast as Dark Boy's bright hooves beat a swift rhythm on the hard clay road, Ginger's thoughts raced ahead. She glanced at her watch. By the road it was six miles to the town. At Dark Boy's throbbing gallop they might make it in fifteen minutes. By the time the fire department got back, it might well be much too late.

There was a crash like thunder off in the woods to her left as the first dead tree blew down. Dark Boy shied violently, almost throwing her headlong, but she bent lower over his neck and clung. Suddenly her heart stiffened with dread. What had she done! She'd been wrong to leave the children. Suppose Tommy took them into the house, and the house caught fire from the barn! She hadn't thought of the wind and the house. She'd only thought of saving the barn!

Desperately she pulled at Dark Boy's mouth. But he was going at a full runaway gallop, the bit between his teeth. Stop now? Go back? No!

There was one way that she might save precious seconds: take him across the fields, the short cut, the way the children went to school. That way it was only two miles! There were fences between the fields, but Dark Boy was a steeplechaser and trained to jump. She'd have to take a chance on jumping him now. They thundered toward the cutoff.

Peering ahead for fallen trees as the branches groaned and creaked above her, she guided him into the little lane that ran straight into a field where the main road turned sharply. Now he was responding to her touch, his great muscles flowing under his glossy coat like smoothly running water. She held him straight toward the stile at the far end of the field. Here was the place to take their first jump. Would he shy before it and make them lose the moments they were saving? Or would he take it smoothly?

She leaned anxiously forward and patted Dark Boy's silky neck. "Straight into it, beautiful! Come on, Boy!"

Dark Boy laid back an ear as he listened. A few yards ahead of the stile, she tightened the reins, lifted his head, and rose lightly in the stirrups. Dark Boy stretched out his neck, left the ground almost like a bird, she thought. His bright hooves cleared the stile.

"Wonderful, beautiful Boy!" Ginger cried as they thudded on.

Now to the second fence! Over it they went, smooth as silk. Her heart lifted.

Down below them in the valley the little town of Honeybrook flashed in and out of sight behind the tortured trees. She thought briefly of the steep bank from the lower field onto the road below. What would Dark Boy do there? Would he go to pieces and roll as horses did sometimes to get down steep banks? Or could she trust him, count on his good sense, hold him firmly while he put his feet together and slid with her safely to within reach of the fire alarm?

They were headed now across a rounded field. Dark Boy lengthened his glistening neck, stretched his legs in a high gallop. Just then, irrelevantly, Tommy flashed into Ginger's mind, his torn jeans flapping in the wind. "Barbed wire! Oh, Dark Boy!"

Here was a danger she had not considered, a danger that stretched straight across their path, one she could not avoid! The lower end of Zigafoos' field, the one they were crossing now at such headlong speed, was fenced with it. Dark Boy couldn't possibly see it! This time she would be helpless to lift him to the jump. He'd tear into it, and at this pace, he would be killed. She would never give her warning. Her heart beating wildly, she pulled the reins up to her chest.

"This way, Boy!" turning his head.

He curved smoothly. There weren't two of them now; horse and rider were one. They made the wide circle of the field. First at a gallop, then dropping to a canter and a walk. She stopped him just in time. He was quivering, shaking his head, only a few feet from the nearly invisible, vicious wire. As she slid to her feet, the wind threw her against him.

"Here, Boy, come on," she urged breathlessly. Dark Boy, still trembling, followed her. She skinned out of her sweater and whipped its brilliant red over the barbed wire, flagging it for him. "There it is, Boy, now we can see it!"

Dark Boy was breathing heavily. Without protest this time, he let her mount. She dug her heels into his flanks and put him into a gallop for the jump. Amid a thunder of hooves she took him straight for the crimson marker. Dark Boy lifted his feet almost daintily, stretched out his head, and they were clear!

He galloped now across the sloping field. "Good Boy, good Boy!" she choked, patting his foaming withers as he stretched out on the last lap of their race against fire and time.

The wind was still sharp in her face, but the terrifying black clouds had veered to the south, traveling swiftly down the Delaware valley. She could see distinctly the spire of the old church rising above the near grove of trees. How far beneath them it still seemed! That last fifty feet of the trail they would have to slide.

"Come on!" she urged, holding the reins firmly, digging her heels into his flanks to get one last burst of speed from his powerful frame. They flew along the ledge. Ahead in the clearing she could see the long bank that dropped to the road leading into the town. Just under top runaway speed but breathing hard, Dark Boy showed that the race was telling on him. With gradual pressure she began to pull him in.

"Slow, Boy, slow," she soothed. "You're doing fine! Don't overshoot the mark. Here we are, old fellow. Slide!"

His ears forward, his head dipped, looking down, quivering in every inch of his spent flanks, Dark Boy responded to the pressure of her knees and hands. Putting his four feet together, he half slid, half staggered down the bank and came to a quivering stop on the empty village street not ten feet from the great iron ring that gave the fire alarm. He was dripping and covered with foam.

As Ginger's hand rose and fell with the big iron clapper, the clang of the fire alarm echoed, and people ran to their doors. The alarm boomed through the little covered bridge up to Smith's machine shop. The men working there heard it, and dropping their tools, came running, not bothering to take off their aprons. It rang out across Mrs. Harnish's garden. Mr. Harnish and the oldest Harnish boy heard it and vaulted lightly over the fence, then ran, pulling on their coats.

While the big red engine roared out of the Holms' garage and backed up toward the canal bridge to get under way, Ginger called out the location of the fire. She fastened Dark Boy securely to a fence and climbed into the fire truck. They roared away up the hill.

Ginger looked at her watch again. In just eight minutes, she and Dark Boy had made their race through the storm. It seemed eight hours! A few more minutes would tell whether or not they had won.

"Please, God," Ginger whispered, "take care of Tommy and the girls!"

They slowed briefly at Erwin's corner to pick up two more volunteers, then sent the big red truck throbbing up Turtle Hill. Tears trickled down between Ginger's fingers. Ned Holm threw an arm gently around her shoulders.

"Good girl!" he said smiling at her reassuringly. "We go the hill up! We get there in time!"

Ginger shook the tears from her eyes and thanked him with a smile. But at the wheel Rudi set his lips in a grim line as he gave the truck all the power it had and sent it rocking over the rough road. The siren screamed fatefully across the valley. A barn can burn in little time and catch a house, too, if the wind is right, and this wind was right! "How'd you come?" he growled.

"Across the fields—on Dark Boy."

"Dark Boy!" Rudi's eyes narrowed and he held them fixed on the road as he steered.

Ned Holm gasped. "You mean that steeplechaser nobody can stay on?"

"I stayed on!"

They rounded the turn at the top of the hill. Now they could see the great black cloud of smoke whirling angrily over the O'Malley's trees. As they came to a throbbing stop in the O'Malley's yard and the men set up the pump at the well, a corner of the house burst into flames. Five minutes more and . . . !

Tommy ran panic-stricken toward them. The barn was blazing fiercely now and in a little while all that would be left of it would be the beautiful Pennsylvania Dutch stonework. A stream of water played over the house. Sparks were falling thick and fast but the stream was soaking the shingles.

Ginger caught Tommy in her arms. "Where are the kids?" she shouted.

"In—in the house. I carried them up and then put the fence at the stairs. They don't like it much!"

Ned Holm ran with Ginger up the steep, narrow stairs and helped her carry out the squirming, indignant children.

That night when the fire was out and the big O'Malleys were home, and the little O'Malleys safely in bed, Ginger at home told her mother all about the day. She was a little relieved that nobody scolded her about riding Dark Boy. Her mother just cried a little and hugged her.

Next morning they saw Tim O'Malley riding Dark Boy up the Greys' lane. Ginger raced out to meet him. Tim swung down and led the black horse up to Ginger.

"Here's your horse," he said simply. "You've won him!"

Ginger stared at him speechless.

Tim went on. "I want you to ride Dark Boy next week in the Pembroke show. And I expect you to win!"

"We'll try, sir," said Ginger.

Extending Comprehension

(The following Extending Comprehension activities can be presented after students finish reading the story. The activities also appear in the *Literature Anthology*.)

1. (Students can answer the Story Questions either orally or in writing. If the questions are presented orally, use the script below.)
2. (Students can select one or more Discussion Topics. Discussions can take place in small groups or with the entire class.)
3. (Students can use the Writing Ideas to respond to the story in writing.)

Story Questions

1. At the beginning of the story, how did Ginger feel about Dark Boy? Support your answer with information from the story.
   - (Ideas: *She loved to look at him; she admired him; she wanted to exercise and train him; she wanted to ride him in the horse show.*)
2. When Tommy O'Malley comes home from visiting Mr. and Mrs. Zigafoos' fields, he says his pants are torn because of the barbed wire. Why is the author telling you about that barbed wire fence?
   - (Idea: *Because the dangerous fence that Dark Boy later has to jump over is that same barbed wire fence.*)
3. List at least three things Ginger worries about as she rides Dark Boy to the village.
   - (Ideas: *She doesn't know if she will be able to get help in time to save the barn; she doesn't know if Dark Boy can make all of the jumps; she worries about the children.*)
4. Why did Mr. O'Malley give Dark Boy to Ginger?
   - (Ideas: *Because Ginger showed everyone a rider could stay on Dark Boy; because she and Dark Boy had saved Mr. and Mrs. O'Malley's house from burning down.*)

Discussion Topics

1. At the beginning of the story, Ginger's problem was that she wanted to ride Dark Boy but couldn't. She had another problem when the barn caught on fire. She had to decide what to do. Discuss how she resolved these two problems. Then think about the problem that was facing Dark Boy at the beginning of the story. During your discussion, try to answer the following questions:
   - What were the two problems that Ginger and Dark Boy faced at the beginning of the story?
   - How did Ginger resolve those two problems?
   - How did she and Mr. O'Malley resolve the problems of Dark Boy?
2. When Dark Boy was galloping to the village, he faced many challenges. Ginger, who was a good horsewoman, helped him meet those challenges. During your discussion, try to answer the following questions:
   - What were some of the challenges that Dark Boy faced in his race to the village?
   - What did Ginger do to help Dark Boy meet each one of his challenges?

3. While she was riding on Dark Boy to the village, Ginger had some worries and doubts about what she was doing. During your discussion, try to answer the following questions:
   - What were Ginger's worries and doubts about leaving the farm?
   - What would you do if you had to choose between going for help or staying with the children and watching the barn burn?

Writing Ideas

1. Find some of the "horse words" in the story and use as many of them as you can to write a description of a horse you would like to own. Or write an entire story about a horse.

2. In this story, Ginger faced an emergency. She chose to do something dangerous to get help. To carry out her decision, she had to leave the children in the house. She told their brother to take care of them. Do you think she did the right thing to ride away for help? Write her a letter explaining your answer.

3. The bad weather plays an important role in this story. In some places, the author uses vivid words and sentences to describe the bad weather. Find at least two places in which the author describes the weather. Write down some of her words and then write a paragraph that tells how those words helped you imagine what the weather was like in the story.

4. If you are particularly interested in horses, ask your teacher or your librarian to help you find more books about horses. You can start a horse dictionary that includes the words you read in "Ginger's Challenge" and "A Horse to Remember." When you read more books about horses, you can add more words to your horse dictionary.

Story 5

Brown Wolf

New Vocabulary Words

Take out your *Literature Anthology.* Turn to page 69. ✔
What is the title of this story? (Signal.) *"Brown Wolf."*
Who is the author? (Signal.) *Jack London.*

1. First we'll read some words from the story, and then we'll talk about what they mean.
2. Word 1 is **cottage.** What word? (Signal.) *Cottage.*
   - (Repeat for every numbered word.)
3. It's your turn to read all the words.
4. Word 1. What word? (Signal.) *Cottage.*
   - (Repeat for every numbered word.)

1. cottage
2. cliff
3. gliding effortlessly
4. spring

5. fangs
6. bristle
7. miracle
8. hardships

9. dog sounds:
- snarl
- bark
- growl
- cry
- howl
- whine
- pant

Definitions

(For each definition, call on a student to read the definition aloud; then, present the tasks that go with that definition to the group.)

1. *A* **cottage** *is a small house.*
   - Everybody, what's another way of saying **They lived at the beach in a small house?** (Signal.) *They lived at the beach in a cottage.*
2. *A* **cliff** *is a very steep side of a hill or mountain.*
   - Everybody, what's another way of saying **We looked at the very steep side of the hill?** (Signal.) *We looked at the cliff.*
3. *An animal that is running smoothly and easily is* **gliding effortlessly.**
   - Everybody, tell me another way of saying **The cat is running smoothly and easily?** (Signal.) *The cat is gliding effortlessly.*
4. *A* **spring** *is a place where fresh water comes out of the ground.*
   - Everybody, what's the name of a place where fresh water comes out of the ground? (Signal.) *A spring.*
5. ***Fangs*** *are the four pointed teeth that many animals have.*
   - Everybody, you have very tiny fangs. Touch them.

6. *When a dog **bristles,** the fur on its back stands on end.*
   - Everybody, what's another way of saying **The dog was so angry that its fur stood on end?** (Signal.) *The dog was so angry that it bristled.*
7. *A **miracle** is an event that cannot be explained.*
   - Listen: When a sudden rainstorm put out the forest fire, people said, "That rain was . . . (Signal.) *a miracle."*
8. *When you put up with difficulties, you put up with **hardships.***
   - Everybody, what's another way of saying **On their long journey, the dogs put up with many difficulties?** (Signal.) *On the long journey, the dogs put up with many hardships.*
9. **Dog sounds: Snarl, bark, growl, cry, howl, whine,** and **pant.** (Ask individual students to snarl, bark, growl, cry, howl, whine, or pant like a dog.)

Story Background

1. (Call on individual students to read two or three sentences.)
2. (After students complete a section, ask the questions for that section.)

> The author of "Brown Wolf," Jack London, was born in San Francisco, California, in 1876. His family was poor. He left school to earn money and find adventure. He worked on fishing boats in San Francisco Bay and then shipped out as a sailor on a ship that went to Japan. When he returned to the San Francisco Bay area, he decided to see his own country. He hitched rides on railroad trains and visited and worked in many parts of the United States.

   - Where was Jack London born? (Idea: *San Francisco, California.*)
   - What kind of work did he do? (Ideas: *He worked on fishing boats; he shipped out as a sailor.*)
   - Where did he travel? (Ideas: *Japan; many parts of the United States.*)

> He came back to the San Francisco area and went to high school. He was very smart, and he worked hard. He was able to do most of his four years of high school studies in one year. After that year, he went to the University of California and began to write stories about his travels. He left the university to travel to Alaska during the gold rush of 1897. The winter he spent there inspired much of his writing, including "Buck," the Jack London story you read in your textbook.

   - When he returned to San Francisco, what did he do? (Ideas: *Went back to high school; started at the university.*)
   - When he left the university, where did he go? (Idea: *To the gold rush in Alaska.*)

Jack London did not settle in one place for very long. He always wanted to visit new places. When he left Alaska, he went to England, to Russia, and then to the South Pacific. Everywhere he went, he wrote about what he saw and heard.

He finally settled in northern California. He bought land near a small town called Glen Ellen and built a house that he named "Wolf House." He wrote "Brown Wolf" while he was living in Glen Ellen. Because Jack London liked to write about where he was living, he wrote about the land surrounding Glen Ellen in this story. Jack London died in Glen Ellen in 1916. He was only forty years old, but he had written fifty books.

- What other parts of the world did Jack London visit? (Ideas: *England; Russia; the South Pacific.*)
- Where did he live at the end of his life? (Ideas: *In Wolf House; in Glen Ellen; in California.*)
- How many books had he written? (Signal.) *Fifty.*

To better appreciate the strength of "Brown Wolf," you should know that the distance from the town of Glen Ellen to the southern border of Oregon is about 300 miles. You should also know that the state of Washington is another 250 miles from southern Oregon. Finally, the Yukon Territory is over 2,000 miles from Glen Ellen.

Let's see if we remember those distances.

- About how many miles is it from Glen Ellen to the Oregon border? (Signal.) *About 300 miles.*
- How many more miles is it to the state of Washington? (Signal.) *250 miles.*
- How many miles is it from Glen Ellen to Alaska? (Signal.) *Over 2000 miles.*

Focus Questions

1. (Call on individual students to read the Focus Questions aloud.)
2. (Remind students to think about those questions as they read the story.)
   - *Who are the main characters in this story?*
   - *What are the many things Marge and Walt do to win Wolf's love?*
   - *What do we learn about Wolf that makes people think he is from the north?*
   - *How does Wolf treat Skiff Miller? How does he treat other strangers?*
   - *The author keeps reminding us of the differences between California and the Yukon— how does he do that?*
   - *Why is it important that Madge, Walter, and Skiff Miller trust each other?*

Brown Wolf*
by Jack London
Illustrated by Joel Snyder

Madge Irvine put on her walking shoes and walked to the front door of the small mountain cottage. Her husband Walt was waiting for her outside, enjoying the warm California sun. Madge looked at the forest that surrounded the cottage, then turned to her husband.

"Where's Wolf?" she asked.

"He was here a moment ago," said Walt. "He was chasing a rabbit the last I saw of him."

*Story is adapted for young readers

"Wolf! Wolf! Here, Wolf!" she called, as they left the cottage and took the trail that led down through the forest to the county road.

Walt put the little finger of each hand between his lips and began to whistle loudly. Madge and Walt heard a crashing in the bushes and then, forty feet above them, on the edge of a cliff, a large animal appeared.

His body and coat and tail were like a huge timber wolf's, but his color showed that he was really a dog. No wolf was ever colored like him. He was brown, deep brown, redbrown, brown in every way. His back and shoulders were a warm brown, and his belly was a brownish yellow. His throat and paws were light brown, and his eyes were golden.

Wolf's front legs knocked a pebble loose, and he watched the fall of the pebble with pointed ears and sharp eyes until it struck at the Irvine's feet. Then he looked right at them and seemed to laugh.

"Come here, Wolf," Walt called out to him.

His ears flattened back and down at the sound as if an invisible hand was patting him on the head. They watched him scramble into the forest. Then they proceeded on their way. He joined them several minutes later, but he did not stay for long. A pat and a rub around the ears from the man, and a longer hug from the woman, and he was far down the trail in front of them, gliding effortlessly over the ground like a true wolf.

The man and woman loved the dog very much, but it had been hard for them to win his love. He had drifted in about three years ago. Tired and hungry, he had killed a rabbit right next to their cottage, and then crawled away and slept by the spring at the foot of the blackberry bushes. He had snarled at Walt the next morning, and he had snarled at Madge when she gave him a large pan of bread and milk.

Wolf continued to be an unfriendly dog, and refused to let them lay hands on him. Every time they came near, he would show his fangs and his hair would bristle. But he remained by the blackberry bushes, sleeping and resting, and eating the food they gave him. He remained because he was weak, and several days later, when he felt better, he disappeared.

And that should have been the end of him. But, the very next day, Walt had to take a business trip north, to Oregon. Riding along on the train, near the California-Oregon border, he happened to look out of the window and saw his unfriendly guest moving along the road, tired, dust-covered, and soiled from two hundred miles of travel.

Walt got off the train at the next station, bought a piece of meat, and captured the dog on the outskirts of the town. Walt transported Wolf back to Glen Ellen in the baggage car, and took him back to the mountain cottage. Wolf was tied up for a week, and the Irvines tried everything to make him happy. But he only snarled at their soft-spoken love words.

They soon discovered that he never barked. In all the time they had him, he never barked.

To win Wolf's affection became a problem. Walt liked problems. He had a metal tag made, on which was stamped: "Return to Walt Irvine, Glen Ellen, California." This tag was put on a collar and strapped around the dog's neck. Then Wolf was turned loose, and he promptly disappeared. A day later, a telegram came from a county over one hundred miles north. In twenty hours, the dog had gone over a hundred miles and was still going north when he was captured.

Wolf was sent back by train. The Irvines tied him up for three days, and he was let loose on the fourth, and he left once again. This time he got all the way north to Oregon when he was caught and returned. Always, as soon as he received his freedom, he fled—and always he fled north.

Another time, the dog crossed all of Oregon, and most of Washington, before he was picked up and returned. The speed with which he traveled was remarkable. On the first day's run he was known to cover as much as a hundred and fifty miles, and after that he would go a hundred miles a day until caught. He always arrived back lean and hungry and mean, and always left fresh and lively, making his way northward for some reason that no one could understand.

But at last, after a year of running away, he accepted the Irvines and decided to remain at the cottage where he had killed the rabbit and slept by the spring. After he decided to stay, a long time went by before he allowed the man and woman to pet him. He only liked the Irvines and no guest at the cottage could ever make friends with him. A low growl greeted every approach. If anyone was foolish enough to come nearer, the naked fangs appeared, and the growl became a snarl.

The Irvines could only guess at his past life. They figured that he must have come up from the south when he first came to their cottage. Mrs. Johnson, their nearest neighbor, thought he was a Yukon dog. She said that her brother, who was looking for gold up there, had told her about dogs like Wolf.

The Irvines agreed with Mrs. Johnson. The tips of Wolf's ears had obviously been so severely frozen at some time that they would never quite heal again. Besides, he looked like the photographs of the Yukon dogs they saw in magazines and newspapers. They often wondered about his past, and tried to imagine what his Yukon life had been like. They knew that the north still drew him, for at night they sometimes heard him crying softly; and when the north wind blew and the bite of frost was in the air, he would let out a sad cry like a long wolf howl. Yet he never barked; nothing could make him bark.

Part 2
* * *

Wolf paused by Madge and Walt for a quick pat on the head. Then he glided quickly ahead of them. Both Madge and Walt seemed to be thinking about Wolf as they followed him down the path. It was a long way to the county road, and when they came to a clearing, they sat down on a log.

A tiny stream flowed out of the forest, dropped over a slippery stone, and ran across the path at their feet. From the valley arose the song of meadowlarks, while around them great yellow butterflies fluttered in and out, through sunshine and shadow.

They heard a sound from the path. It was a crunching of heavy feet. As Walt and Madge looked at each other, a man came into view around the turn of the trail. He was sweaty. With a handkerchief in one hand he mopped his face, while in the other hand he carried a new hat. He was a well-built man, and his muscles seemed on the point of bursting out of the new black clothes he wore.

"Warm day," said Walt.

The man paused and nodded. "I guess I ain't much used to the warmth," he said. "I'm used to cold weather."

"You don't find any of that in this country," Walt laughed.

"Should say not," the man answered. "And I ain't lookin' for it either. I'm trying to find my sister. Maybe you know where she lives. Her name's Johnson, Mrs. William Johnson."

"You must be her Yukon brother!" Madge cried, her eyes bright with interest. "We've heard so much about you."

"Yes ma'am, that's me," he answered. "My name's Miller, Skiff Miller. I just thought I'd surprise her."

Madge stood up to show Skiff Miller the way to his sister's house. "Do you see that redwood?" she said, pointing up the canyon. "Take the little trail that turns off to the right. It's the shortcut to her house. You can't miss it."

"Yes'm, thank you, ma'am," he said.

"We'd like to hear you tell about the Yukon," Madge said. "Could we come over one day while you are at your sister's? Or, better yet, won't you come over and have dinner with us?"

"Yes'm, thank you, ma'am," he mumbled. Then he continued, "I ain't stopping long. I have to be pulling north again. I go out on tonight's train."

Madge was about to say that it was too bad, when Wolf trotted into the clearing.

Skiff Miller froze. He had eyes only for the dog, and a great wonder came into his face. "Well, I'll be hanged," he said, slowly and solemnly.

He sat down on the log, leaving Madge standing. At the sound of his voice, Wolf's ears had flattened down, then his mouth had opened in a laugh. He trotted slowly up to the stranger and first smelled his hands, then licked them.

Skiff Miller patted the dog's head and slowly and solemnly repeated, "Well, I'll be hanged."

"Excuse me, ma'am," he said the next moment. "I was just surprised, that's all."

"We're surprised, too," she answered slowly. "We never saw Wolf act friendly toward a stranger."

"Is that what you call him—Wolf?" Miller asked.

Madge nodded. "But I can't understand his friendliness toward you—unless it's because you're from the Yukon. He's a Yukon dog, you know."

"Yes'm," Miller said, working away. He lifted one of Wolf's forelegs and examined the footpads, pressing them and denting them with his thumb. "Kind of soft," he remarked. "He ain't been on a trail for a long time."

"I say," Walt broke in, "it's remarkable the way he lets you handle him."

Skiff Miller got up and asked, sharply, "How long have you had him?"

But just then the dog, squirming and rubbing against the newcomer's legs, opened his mouth and barked. It was a loud bark, brief and joyous, but a bark.

Walt and Madge stared at each other. The miracle had happened. Wolf had barked.

"It's the first time he ever barked," Madge said.

"First time I ever heard him, too," Miller replied.

Madge smiled at Miller. "Of course," she said, "since you have only seen him for five minutes."

Skiff Miller looked at her. "I thought you understood," he said slowly. "I thought you'd figured it out from the way he acted. He's my dog. His name ain't Wolf. It's Brown."

"Oh, Walt!" Madge cried to her husband.

Walt demanded, "How do you know he's your dog?"

"Because he is," was the reply.

"That's no proof," Walt said sharply.

In his slow way, Skiff Miller looked at the dog, then said, "The dog's mine. I raised him and I guess I ought to know. Look here. I'll prove it to you."

Skiff Miller turned to the dog. "Brown!" His voice rang out sharply, and at the sound the dog's ears flattened down. "Gee!" The dog made a swinging turn to the right. "Now mush on!" Abruptly the dog stopped turning and started straight ahead, halting obediently at command.

"I can do it with whistles," Skiff Miller said proudly. "He was my lead dog. Somebody stole him from me three years ago, and I've been looking for him ever since."

Madge's voice trembled as she asked, "But—but are you going to take him away with you?"

The man nodded.

Madge asked, "Back into that awful Yukon?"

He nodded and added, "Oh, it ain't so bad as all that. Look at me. Pretty healthy man—ain't I?"

"But the dogs! The terrible hardship, the heartbreaking work, the starvation, the frost! Oh, I've read about it and I know."

Miller said nothing.

Madge paused a moment, then said, "Why not leave him here? He is happy. He'll never suffer from hunger—you know that. He'll never suffer from cold and hardship. Everything is soft and gentle here. He will never feel a whip again. And as for the weather—why, it never snows here."

"Yes, it's hot here," Skiff Miller said and laughed.

"But answer me," Madge continued. "What do you have to offer him in that Yukon life?"

"Food, when I've got it, and that's most of the time," came the answer.

"And the rest of the time?"

"No food."

"And the work?"

"Yes, plenty of work," Miller blurted out impatiently. "Work without end, and hunger, and frost, and all the rest of the hardships—that's what he'll get when he comes with me. But he likes it. He's used to it. He knows that life. He was born to it and brought up in it. And you don't know anything about it—you don't know what you're talking about. That's where the dog belongs, and that's where he'll be happiest."

"The dog doesn't go," Walt announced "So there is no need for any more talk."

"What's that?" Skiff Miller demanded. His brows lowered and his face became flushed.

"I said, the dog doesn't go, and that settles it," Walt said. "I don't believe he's your dog. You may have seen him sometime. You may have sometimes driven him for his owner. But his obeying the ordinary driving commands of the trail doesn't prove that he is yours. Any dog in the Yukon would obey you as he obeyed. Besides, he is probably a valuable dog, and that might explain why you want to have him."

Skiff Miller's huge muscles bulged under the black cloth of his black coat as he carefully looked Walt up and down. His face hardened, then he said, "I reckon there's nothing in sight to prevent me from taking the dog right here and now."

Walt's face flushed, and the striking muscles of his arms and shoulders seemed to stiffen and grow tense. Madge quickly stepped between the two men.

"Maybe Mr. Miller is right," she said. "I am afraid that he is. Wolf does seem to know him, and certainly he answers to the name of 'Brown.' He made friends with him instantly, and you know that's something he never did with anybody before. Besides, look at the way he barked. He was just bursting with joy."

"Joy over what?" asked Walt.

"Finding Mr. Miller, I think," answered Madge.

Walt's striking muscles relaxed, and his shoulders seemed to droop with hopelessness.

"I guess you're right, Madge," he said. "Wolf isn't Wolf, but Brown. He must belong to Mr. Miller."

Part 3

*   *   *

The three people were silent for a moment, then Madge brightened up and said, "Perhaps Mr. Miller will sell us the dog. We can buy him."

Skiff Miller shook his head. "I had five dogs," he said. "Wolf was the leader. Somebody once offered me twelve hundred dollars for him. I didn't sell him then, and I ain't selling him now. Besides, I think a mighty lot of that dog. I've been looking for him for three years. I couldn't believe my eyes when I saw him just now. I thought I was dreaming. It was too good to be true."

"But the dog," Madge said quickly. "You haven't considered the dog."

Skiff Miller looked puzzled.

"Have you thought about him?" she asked.

"I don't know what you're driving at," Miller said.

"Maybe the dog has some choice in the matter," Madge went on. "Maybe he has his likes and dislikes. You haven't considered him. You give him no choice. It hasn't even entered your mind that he might prefer California to Alaska. You consider only what you like. You treat him like a sack of potatoes."

This was a new way of looking at it, and Miller's face hardened as he started to think to himself.

"If you really love him," Madge continued, "you would want him to be happy, no matter where he is."

Miller asked, "Do you think he'd sooner stay in California?"

Madge nodded her head. "I'm sure of it."

Skiff Miller started thinking out loud. "He was a good worker. He's done a lot of work for me. He never loafed on me, and he was great at getting a new team into shape. He's got a head on him. He can do everything but talk. He knows we're talking about him."

The dog was lying at Skiff Miller's feet, his head down close to his paws, his ears erect and listening. His eyes were quick and eager to follow the sounds of one person and then the other.

Miller went on. "There's a lot of work in him yet. He'll be good for years to come."

Skiff Miller opened his mouth and closed it again without speaking. Finally he said, "I'll tell you what I'll do. Your remarks, ma'am, make sense. He has worked hard, and maybe he's earned a soft place and has got a right to choose. Anyway, we'll leave it up to him. Whatever he says, goes. You people stay right here sitting down. I'll say goodbye, and I'll walk off. If he wants to stay, he can stay. If he wants to come with me, let him come. I won't call him to come and don't you call him to come back."

Miller paused a moment, then added, "Only, you must play fair. Don't call him after my back is turned."

"We'll play fair," Madge said. "I don't know how to thank you."

"I don't see that you've got any reason to thank me," he replied. "Brown ain't decided yet. Now you won't mind if I go away slow? It's only fair, since I'll be out of sight in a hundred yards."

Madge agreed, and added, "and I promise you that we won't do anything to try to change his mind."

"Well, then, I might as well be getting along," Skiff Miller said. And he got ready to leave.

Wolf lifted his head quickly, and still more quickly got to his feet when Miller shook hands with Madge. Wolf sprang up on his hind legs, resting his forepaws on Madge's hip and at the same time, licking Skiff Miller's hand. When Miller shook hands with Walt, Wolf repeated his act, resting his weight on Walt and licking both men's hands.

"It ain't no picnic, I can tell you that," Miller said. These were his last words, as he turned and went slowly up the trail.

Wolf watched him go about twenty feet, as though waiting for the man to turn and come back. Then, with a quick, low whine, Wolf sprang after him, caught up to him, gently grabbed Miller's hand between his teeth, and tried gently to make him stop.

But Miller did not stop. Wolf raced back to where Walt Irvine sat, catching his coat sleeve in his teeth and trying to drag him toward Miller.

Wolf wanted to be in two places at the same time, with the old master and the new, but the distance between them was increasing. He sprang about excitedly, making short nervous leaps and twists, now toward one person, now toward the other, not knowing his own mind, wanting both and unable to choose, uttering quick, sharp whines and beginning to pant.

He sat down, thrust his nose upward, and opened his mouth wide. He was ready to howl.

But just as the howl was about to burst from his throat, he closed his mouth and looked long and steadily at Miller's back. Suddenly Wolf turned his head, and looked just as steadily at Walt. The dog received no sign, no suggestion and no clue as to what he should do.

As Wolf glanced ahead to where the old master was nearing the curve of the trail, Wolf became excited again. He sprang to his feet with a whine, and then, struck by a new idea, turned toward Madge. He had ignored her up to now, but now, he went over to her and snuggled his head in her lap, nudging her arm with his nose—an old trick of his when begging for favors. He backed away from her and began to twist playfully.

All his body, from his twinkling eyes and flattened ears to the wagging tail, begged her to tell him what to do. But Madge did not move.

The dog stopped playing. He was saddened by the coldness of these people who had never been cold before.

He turned and gently gazed after the old master. Skiff Miller was rounding the curve. In a moment he would be gone from view. Yet he never turned his head, plodding straight onward, as though he had no interest in what was occurring behind his back.

And then he went out of view. Wolf waited for him to reappear. He waited a long minute, silently, without movement, as though turned to stone. He barked once, and waited. Then he turned and trotted back to Walt Irvine. He sniffed his hand and dropped down heavily at his feet, watching the trail where it curved from view.

The tiny stream that slipped down the stone seemed to gurgle more loudly than before. Except for the meadowlarks, there was no other sound. The great yellow butterflies drifted silently through the sunshine and lost themselves in the sleepy shadows. Madge smiled at her husband.

A few minutes later Wolf got on his feet. His movements were decisive. He did not glance at the man and woman. His eyes were fixed on the trail. He had made up his mind. They knew it. And they knew that they had lost.

Wolf started to trot away, and Madge had to force herself not to call him back. She remembered the promise she had made to Skiff Miller. Walt's solemn look showed that he also remembered the promise.

Wolf's trot broke into a run. He made leaps that were longer and longer. Not once did he turn his head. He cut sharply across the curve of the trail and was gone.

Extending Comprehension

(The following Extending Comprehension activities can be presented after students finish reading the story. The activities also appear in the *Literature Anthology*.)

1. (Students can answer the Story Questions either orally or in writing. If the questions are presented orally, use the script below.)

2. (Students can select one or more Discussion Topics. Discussions can take place in small groups or with the entire class.)

3. (Students can use the Writing Ideas to respond to the story in writing.)

Story Questions

1. Is Wolf one of the main characters in the story? Tell why or why not. (Ideas: *Yes, Wolf is the most important character in the story; he is the character that the other characters value; he has to make a difficult decision at the end of the story. No, Wolf is just a dog; he doesn't say anything.*)

2. Describe at least three of the many things that Madge and Walt did to win Wolf's love. (Ideas: *They gave him food; they let him stay near the cottage; Walt brought him back on the train; Walt had an identification tag made asking that Wolf be sent back to Glen Ellen.*)

3. What do we learn about Wolf that makes people think he is from the north? (Ideas: *The neighbor said he looked like a dog from the Yukon; the tips of his ears had been frozen; he looked like photographs of Yukon dogs; he cried at night when the wind blew from the north; he howled when it got cold.*)

4. Compare how Wolf treats Skiff Miller to how he treats other strangers. (Ideas: *When Skiff Miller arrived, Wolf's ears flattened down; he laughed, licked Skiff's hands, and barked; When other strangers approached the cottage, Wolf growled and showed his fangs.*)

5. Why does Madge think Wolf will be happier in California? (Ideas: *Wolf will get enough food; the weather isn't cold; he won't have to work.*)

6. Why was it so necessary for Madge, Walter, and Skiff Miller to trust each other? (Idea: *They wanted Wolf to have the opportunity to make up his mind.*)

7. Why do you think Wolf decided to go with Skiff Miller? (Accept all reasonable answers.)

8. Why is "Brown Wolf " a good title for the story? (Idea: *It combines the name that Madge and Walter gave him with the name that Skiff Miller gave him.*)

Discussion Topics

1. Wolf has to choose between the easy life in California and the hard life in the Yukon. Discuss the advantages of living in each place. During you discussion, think about the answers to the following questions:
   - What kind of life did Wolf have in California? What was the weather like? When did he eat? Did he work?
   - What kind of life did he have in the Yukon? What was the weather like? When did he eat? What kind of work did he do?

2. Wolf treated Skiff Miller differently than he treated other strangers. He also responded to Skiff Miller's commands. Discuss the different responses Wolf made to Skiff Miller. During your discussion, attempt to answer the following questions:
   - How did Wolf first respond? How did he respond to Skiff Miller after that?
   - At what point in the story were you convinced that the dog belonged to Skiff?
   - Would a California dog know to respond to the commands "gee" and "now mush on"? Explain your answer.

3. Discuss the events at the end of the story that let you know how undecided Wolf was. During your discussion, try to answer the following questions:
   - What things did Wolf do that let you know he was struggling to make up his mind?
   - Where do you think Wolf should have gone?

Writing Ideas

1. The author doesn't tell you some important things about this story. He doesn't tell you how Wolf got from the Yukon to California. He only tells you that he was stolen from Skiff Miller. Write down your idea of what happened. Tell who stole Brown, how that person and Brown got to California, and how Brown got away from that person.

2. You have read two stories by Jack London. Strong dogs that are very loyal to their owners are important characters in these stories. Write your own story about a strong and loyal dog. It can be about a dog you know or about a dog you wish you knew.

3. Madge, Walt, and Skiff Miller had to trust each other to not call out to Wolf. Did they keep their trust? Write about a time in your life that it was particularly important for you to be trusted and what would have happened if you hadn't kept your trust.

Story 6

Like Jake & Me

New Vocabulary Words

Everybody, take out your *Literature Anthology.* Turn to page 88. ✔

What is the title of this story? (Signal.) *"Like Jake & Me."*

Who is the author? (Signal.) *Mavis Jukes.*

1. First we'll read some words from the story, and then we'll talk about what they mean.
2. The words in line 1 are **Stetson hat.** What words? (Signal.) *Stetson hat.*
   - (Repeat for every numbered word.)
3. It's your turn to read all the words.
4. Line 1. What words? (Signal.) *Stetson hat.*
   - (Repeat for every numbered word.)

1. Stetson hat
2. raven
3. nectar

4. steer
5. entomologist
6. landscape

7. cautiously
8. grapple
9. swagger

Definitions

(For each definition, call on a student to read the definition aloud; then, present the tasks that go with that definition to the group.)

1. *A **Stetson hat** is a particular brand of hat that always looks the same. A **Stetson** is made out of felt, has a wide brim and a high crown. Cowboys often wear **Stetsons.***
   - What part of a hat is the brim? (Idea: *The part that sticks out and circles your head.*)
   - What part of a hat is the crown? (Idea: *The part that covers the top of your head.*)
   - Where have you seen a **Stetson hat?** (Ideas: *In the movies; on TV; know someone who owns one.*)
2. *A **raven** is a large black bird that makes a loud, unpleasant noise.*
   - Everybody, what do we call a large black bird that makes a loud, unpleasant noise? (Signal). *A raven.*
3. ***Nectar** is the juice from a fruit.*
   - Everybody, here's another way of saying **I drank the juice from a peach: I drank peach nectar.**
   - Everybody, what's another way of saying **She filled the jar with the juice from a pear?** (Signal.) *She filled the jar with pear nectar.*

4. A **steer** is a male cow that is raised for beef.
   - Everybody, what do we call a male cow that is raised for beef? (Signal.) *A steer.*
5. An **entomologist** is a scientist who studies insects.
   - Everybody, what do we call a scientist who studies insects? (Signal.) *An entomologist.*
6. Another word for scenery is **landscape.**
   - Pretend you are on a farm. Describe what the **landscape** would look like. (Ideas: *farmhouses; crops; trees; hills.*)
7. When you do something **cautiously,** you do it with caution and care.
   - Everybody, here's another way of saying **With care and caution, she picked up the bits of glass: Cautiously, she picked up the bits of glass.**
   - Everybody, what's another way of saying **With care and caution, he put the vase on the shelf?** (Signal.) *Cautiously, he put the vase on the shelf.*
8. When you **grapple** with something, you struggle with that thing.
   - Everybody, here's another way of saying **She struggled with the knots in her shoelaces: She grappled with the knots in her shoelaces.**
   - Everybody, what's another way of saying **He struggled with the tight fitting glove?** (Signal.) *He grappled with the tight fitting glove.*
9. When you **swagger,** you walk like you think you are very important.
   - (Call on a student.) Show me how you would swagger to the door.

Story Background

1. (Call on individual students to read two or three sentences.)
2. (After students complete a section, ask the questions for that section.)

> The author of "Like Jake and Me," Mavis Jukes, lives in northern California. Her house is in the country. She is a lawyer, but she writes books for young people. She likes to write **realistic fiction** stories about regular people involved in everyday situations. Her story, "Like Jake and Me," is a good example of this kind of fiction.
>
> "Like Jake and Me" is about a young boy, Alex, his mother, and his stepfather. These characters may remind you of people you know. Although the story is about a serious topic, the relationship between Alex and his stepfather is very funny as well.
>
> Mavis Jukes also writes realistically about the setting of the story. Most of "Like Jake and Me" takes place outdoors in a setting with lots of trees. We can imagine how those trees look if we know something about them. The story begins near a cypress grove, which is a small woods of cypress trees. Cypress trees are evergreens, which means that their leaves are green all year long. Later in the story, you will read about poplar trees growing on the distant hills. Poplar trees are tall and narrow. They lose their leaves in the winter. The story takes place in the fall, so the leaves of poplar trees are yellow. We know the leaves will soon fall off these trees. You will also read about a pear tree that has pears growing in an unusual way.

- What do we call stories written about regular people involved in everyday situations? (Idea: *Realistic fiction.*)
- What is the serious topic of "Like Jake and Me"? (Idea: *The relationship between Alex and his stepfather.*)

Focus Questions

1. (Call on individual students to read the Focus Questions aloud.)
2. (Remind students to think about these questions as they read the story.)
   - *Why does Alex think he is so different from Jake?*
   - *Why does Jake think he is so different from Alex?*
   - *Why do you think the story is titled "Like Jake and Me"?*

Like Jake and Me
by Mavis Jukes
Illustrated by James Watling

The rain had stopped. The sun was setting. There were clouds in the sky the color of smoke. Alex was watching his stepfather, Jake, split wood at the edge of the cypress grove. Somewhere a toad was grunting.

"Jake!" called Alex.

Jake swung the axe, and wood flew into the air.

"Jake!" Alex called again. "Need me?" Alex had a loose tooth in front. He moved it in and out with his tongue.

Jake rested the axe head in the grass and leaned on the handle. "What?" he said. He took off his Stetson hat and wiped his forehead on his jacket sleeve.

Alex cupped his hands around his mouth. "Do . . . you . . . need . . . me . . . to . . .help?" he hollered. Then he tripped over a pumpkin, fell on it, and broke it. A toad flopped away.

Jake adjusted the raven feather behind his hatband. "Better stay there!" he called. He put his hat back on. With powerful arms, he sunk the axe blade into a log. It fell in half.

"Wow," thought Alex. "I'll never be able to do that."

Alex's mother was standing close by, under the pear tree. She was wearing fuzzy woolen leg warmers, a huge knitted coat with pictures of reindeer on the back, and a red scarf with the name *Virginia* on it. "I need you," she said.

Alex stood up, dumped the pumpkin over the fence for the sheep, and went to Virginia.

"I dropped two quarters and a dime in the grass. If I bend down, I may never be able to get up again," she said. Virginia was enormous. She was pregnant with twins, and her belly blocked her view to the ground. "I can't even see where they fell."

"Here!" said Alex. He gave her two quarters. Then he found the dime. He tied her shoe while he was down there.

"Thanks," said Virginia. "I also need you for some advice." She pointed up. "Think it's ready?"

One of the branches of the pear tree had a glass bottle over the end of it. Inside were some twigs and leaves *and* two pears. In the spring, Virginia had pushed the bottle onto the branch, over the blossoms. During the summer, the pears had grown and sweetened inside the bottle. Now they were fat and crowding each other.

The plan was that when the pears were ripe, Virginia would pull the bottle from the tree, leaving the fruit inside. Then she'd fill the bottle with pear nectar and trick her sister, Caroline. Caroline would never guess how Virginia got the pears into the bottle!

"Shall we pick it?" asked Virginia.

"Up to you!" said Alex.

Months ago, Virginia had told him that the pears, and the babies, would be ready in the fall. Alex looked away at the hills. They were dusky gray. There were smudges of yellow poplars on the land. Autumn was here.

Alex fiddled with his tooth. "Mom," he asked, "do you think the twins are brothers or sisters?"

"Maybe both," said Virginia.

"If there's a boy, do you think he'll be like Jake or like me?"

"Maybe like Jake *and* you," said Virginia.

"Like Jake *and* me?" Alex wondered how that could be possible.

"Right," said Virginia.

"Well, anyway," said Alex, "would you like to see something I can do?"

"Of course," she said.

Alex straightened. Gracefully he lifted his arms and rose up on his toes. He looked like a bird about to take off. Then he lowered his arms and crouched. Suddenly he sprang up. He spun once around in midair and landed lightly.

Virginia clapped. "Great!"

Alex did it again, faster. Then again, and again. He whirled and danced around the tree for Virginia. He spun until he was pooped. Jake had put down the axe and was watching.

"Ballet class!" gasped Alex. "Dad signed me up for lessons, remember?"

"Of course I remember," said Virginia. "Go show Jake!"

"No," panted Alex. "Jake isn't the ballet type."

"He might like it," said Virginia. "Go see!"

"Maybe another time," said Alex. He raced across the field to where Jake was loading his arms with logs. "Jake, I'll carry the axe."

"Carry the axe?" Jake shook his head. "I just sharpened that axe."

Alex moved his tooth with his tongue and squinted up at Jake. "I'm careful," he said.

Jake looked over at the sheep nosing the pumpkin. "Maybe another time," he told Alex.

Alex walked beside him as they headed toward the house. The air was so cold Jake was breathing steam. The logs were stacked to his chin.

Virginia stood under the pear tree, watching the sunset. Alex ran past her to open the door.

Jake thundered up the stairs and onto the porch. His boots were covered with moss and dirt. Alex stood in the doorway.

"Watch it!" said Jake. He shoved the door open farther with his shoulder, and Alex backed up against the wall. Jake moved sideways through the door.

"Here, I'll help you stack the wood!" said Alex.

"Watch it!" Jake came down on one knee and set the wood by the side of the woodstove. Then he said kindly, "You've really got to watch it, Alex. I can't see where I'm going with so big a load."

Alex wiggled his tooth with his tongue. "I just wanted to help you," he said. He went to Jake and put his hand on Jake's shoulder. Then he leaned around and looked under his Stetson hat. There was bark in Jake's beard. "You look like a cowboy in the movies."

"I have news for you," said Jake. "*I am* a cowboy. A real one." He unsnapped his jacket. On his belt buckle was a silver longhorn steer. "Or was one." He looked over at Alex.

Alex shoved his tooth forward with his tongue.

"Why don't you just pull out that tooth?" Jake asked him.

"Too chicken," said Alex. He closed his mouth.

"Well, everybody's chicken of something," said Jake. He opened his jacket pocket and took out a wooden match. He chewed on the end of it and looked out the windows behind the stove. He could see Virginia, still standing beneath the tree. Her hands were folded under her belly.

Jake balled up newspaper and broke some sticks. He had giant hands. He filled the woodstove with the wadded paper and the sticks and pushed in a couple of logs.

"Can I light the fire?" Alex asked.

"Maybe another time," said Jake. He struck the match on his rodeo belt buckle. He lit the paper and threw the match into the fire.

Just then Alex noticed that there was a wolf spider on the back of Jake's neck. There were fuzzy babies holding on to her body. "Did you know wolf spiders carry their babies around?" said Alex.

"Says who?" asked Jake.

"My dad," said Alex. He moved his tooth out as far as it would go. "He's an entomologist, remember?"

"I remember," said Jake.

"Dad says they only bite you if you bother them, or if you're squashing them," said Alex.

"But still, I never mess with wolf spiders." He pulled his tooth back in with his tongue.

"Is that what he says, huh," said Jake. He jammed another log into the stove, then looked out again at Virginia. She was gazing at the landscape. The hills were fading. The farms were fading. The cypress trees were turning black.

"I think she's pretty," said Alex, looking at the spider.

"I do, too," said Jake, looking at Virginia.

"It's a nice design on her back," said Alex, examining the spider.

"Yep!" said Jake. He admired the reindeer coat, which he'd loaned to Virginia.

"Her belly sure is big!" said Alex.

"It has to be, to carry the babies," said Jake.

"She's got an awful lot of babies there," said Alex.

Jake laughed. Virginia was shaped something like a pear.

"And boy! Are her legs woolly!" said Alex.

Jake looked at Virginia's leg warmers. "Itchy," said Jake. He rubbed his neck. The spider crawled over his collar.

"She's in your coat!" said Alex. He backed away a step.

"We can share it," said Jake. He liked to see Virginia bundled up. "It's big enough for both of us. She's got to stay warm." Jake stood up.

"You sure are brave," Alex said. "I like wolf spiders, but I wouldn't have let that one into my coat. That's the biggest, hairiest wolf spider I've ever seen."

Jake froze. "Wolf spider! Where?"

"In your coat getting warm," said Alex.

Jake stared at Alex. "What wolf spider?"

"The one we were talking about, with the babies!" said Alex. "And the furry legs."

"Wolf spider!" Jake moaned. "I thought we were talking about Virginia!" He was holding his shoulders up around his ears.

"You never told me you were scared of spiders," said Alex.

"You never asked me," said Jake in a high voice. "Help!"

"How?" asked Alex.

"Get my jacket off!"

Alex took hold of Jake's jacket sleeve as Jake eased his arm out. Cautiously, Alex took the jacket from Jake's shoulders. Alex looked in the coat.

"No spider, Jake," said Alex. "I think she went into your shirt."

"My shirt?" asked Jake. "You think?"

"Maybe," said Alex.

Jake gasped. "Inside? I hope not!"

"Feel anything furry crawling on you?" asked Alex.

"Anything *furry* crawling on me?" Jake shuddered. "No!"

"Try to get your shirt off without squashing her," said Alex. "Remember, we don't want to hurt her. She's a mama."

"With babies," added Jake. *"Eek!"*

"And," said Alex, "she'll bite!"

"Bite? Yes, I know!" said Jake. "Come out on the porch and help me! I don't want her to get loose in the house!"

Jake walked stiffly to the door. Alex opened it. They walked out onto the porch. The sky was thick gray and salmon colored, with blue windows through the clouds.

"Feel anything?" asked Alex.

"Something . . ." said Jake. He unsnapped the snaps on his sleeves, then the ones down the front. He opened his shirt. On his chest was a tattoo of an eagle that was either taking off or landing. He let the shirt drop to the floor.

"No spider, back or front," reported Alex.

They shook out the shirt.

"Maybe your jeans," said Alex. "Maybe she got into your jeans!"

"Not my *jeans!*" said Jake. He quickly undid his rodeo belt.

"Your boots!" said Alex. "First you have to take off your boots!"

"Right!" said Jake. He sat down on the boards. Each boot had a yellow rose and the name *Jake* stitched on the side. "Could you help?" he asked.

"Okay," said Alex. He grappled with one boot and got it off. He checked it. He pulled off and checked the sock. No spider. He tugged on the other boot.

"You've got to pull harder," said Jake, as Alex pulled and struggled. "Harder!"

The boot came off and smacked Alex in the mouth. "Ouch!" Alex put his tongue in the gap. "Knocked my tooth out!" He looked in the boot. "It's in the boot!"

"Yikes!" said Jake.

"Not the spider," said Alex. "My tooth." He rolled it out of the boot and into his hand to examine it.

"Dang," said Jake. "Then hurry up." Alex dropped the tooth back into the boot. Jake climbed out of his jeans and looked down each leg. He hopped on one foot to get the other sock off.

"She won't be in your sock," said Alex. "But maybe—"

"Don't tell me," said Jake. "Not my shorts!"

Alex stared at Jake's shorts. There were pictures of mallard ducks on them. "Your shorts," said Alex.

"I'm afraid to look," said Jake. He thought he felt something creeping just below his belly button.

"Someone's coming!" said Alex. "Quick! Give me your hat! I'll hold it up and you can stand behind it."

"Help!" said Jake in a small voice. He gave Alex the hat and quickly stepped out of his shorts. He brushed himself off in the front.

"Okay in the back," said Alex, peering over the brim of the hat.

Jake turned his shorts inside out, then right side in again. No spider. When he bent over to put them on, he backed into his hat, and the raven feather poked him. Jake howled and jumped up and spun around in midair.

"I didn't know you could do ballet!" said Alex. "You dance like me!"

"I thought I felt the spider!" said Jake. He put on his shorts.

"What on *earth* are you doing?" huffed Virginia. She was standing at the top of the stairs, holding the bottle with the pears inside.

"We're hunting for a spider," said Jake.

"Well!" said Virginia. "I like your hunting outfit. But aren't those *duck*-hunting shorts, and aren't you cold?"

"We're not hunting for spiders," explained Jake. "We're hunting for a spider."

"A big and hairy one that *bites!*" added Alex.

"A wolf spider!" said Jake, shivering. He had goose bumps.

"Really!" said Virginia. She set the bottle down beside Jake's boot. "Aha!" she cried, spying Alex's tooth inside. "Here's one of the spider's teeth!"

Alex grinned at his mother. He put his tongue where his tooth wasn't.

Jake took his hat from Alex and put it on.

"Hey!" said Virginia.

"What?" said Jake.

"The spider!" she said. "It's on your hat!"

"Help!" said Jake. "Somebody help me!"

Alex sprang up into the air and snatched the hat from Jake's head.

"Look!" said Alex.

"Holy smoke!" said Jake.

There, hiding behind the black feather, was the spider.

Alex tapped the hat brim. The spider dropped to the floor. Then off she swaggered with her fuzzy babies, across the porch and into a crack.

Jake went over to Alex. He knelt down. "Thanks, Alex," said Jake. It was the closest Alex had ever been to the eagle. Jake pressed Alex against its wings. "May I have this dance?" Jake asked.

Ravens were lifting from the blackening fields and calling. The last light had settled in the clouds like pink dust.

Jake stood up holding Alex, and together they looked at Virginia. She was rubbing her belly. "Something is happening here," she told them. "It feels like the twins are beginning to dance."

"Like Jake and me," said Alex. And Jake whirled around the porch with Alex in his arms.

Extending Comprehension

(The following Extending Comprehension activities can be presented after students finish reading the story. The activities also appear in the *Literature Anthology.*)

1. (Students can answer the Story Questions either orally or in writing. If the questions are presented orally, use the script below.)
2. (Students can select one or more Discussion Topics. Discussions can take place in small groups or with the entire class.)
3. (Students can use the Writing Ideas to respond to the story in writing.)

Story Questions

1. In the beginning of the story, what would Jake say when Alex offered to help him do something?
   - (Ideas: *"Maybe another time"; Jake wouldn't let Alex help him.*)
2. Why did Alex think he was so different from Jake?
   - (Ideas: *Because Alex liked ballet and Jake didn't; because Jake was big and strong and Alex wasn't.*)
3. Jake and Alex each had something they were afraid of. What were those things?
   - (Idea: *Jake was afraid of spiders and Alex was afraid of pulling his tooth.*)
4. After Jake lit the fire, some funny things happened. Name at least three things that were funny.
   - (Ideas: *They both thought they were talking about the same thing but they weren't; Jake had to keep taking off more and more of his clothes until he didn't have any on; Jake felt his feather and thought it was the spider; Alex's tooth was knocked out by Jake's boot; Alex reminded Jake the spider had babies and that it would bite him.*)
5. Why do you think the story is titled "Like Jake and Me"?
   - (Ideas: *Because by the end of the story, Alex realized that he and Jake were alike in some ways; because Alex learned that both he and Jake were afraid of things and that Jake did like to dance.*)

Discussion Topics

1. Alex and Jake have a very funny conversation. Discuss what made this conversation so funny. During your discussion, try to answer the following questions:
   - Why did Jake and Alex think they were talking about the same topic?
   - The author uses imagery during this part of the story. This means the author's words helped you picture what was happening. Describe the picture you imagined during this funny part of the story.
2. Even though this story has a very funny part, it also has a serious message. The title of the story gives you a clue about its message. Talk about why you think this story is called "Like Jake and Me." During your discussion, try to answer the following questions:
   - At the beginning of the story, Alex and Jake thought they were very different from each other. In what ways did they think they were different?
   - The experience with the spider helped Alex and Jake realize they were alike in some ways. How were they alike?

Writing Ideas

1. Pretend you are Virginia. Describe what you see when you get to your porch after Jake and Alex still haven't found the wolf spider. Be sure to tell what Jake looks like, what Alex is missing and what things are on the porch. Tell what your reaction is when you see this situation.

2. Both Jake and Alex are afraid of certain things. Tell about something that frightens you. Tell why it frightens you and what you have tried to do so you aren't as afraid of it.

Story 7

Thank You, M'am

New Vocabulary Words

Everybody, take out your *Literature Anthology.* Turn to page 103. ✔

What is the title of this story? (Signal.) *"Thank You, M'am."*

Who is the author? (Signal.) *Langston Hughes.*

1. First we'll read some words from the story, and then we'll talk about what they mean.
2. Word 1 is **cocoa.** What word? (Signal.) *Cocoa.*
   - (Repeat for every numbered word.)
3. It's your turn to read all the words.
4. Word 1. What word? (Signal.) *Cocoa.*
   - (Repeat for every numbered word.)

1. cocoa
2. contact
3. frail

4. kitchenette
5. latching
6. mistrusted

7. presentable
8. roomers
9. suede

Definitions

(For each definition, call on a student to read the definition aloud; then, present the tasks that go with that definition to the group.)

1. ***Cocoa*** *is a hot drink made with milk and chocolate.*
2. *When things are in* ***contact,*** *they touch each other.*
   - Everybody, make your hand **contact** the top of your head.
3. *Something that is very weak or delicate is* ***frail.***
   - Everybody, what's another way of saying **The sick child looked weak?** (Signal.) *The sick child looked frail.*
4. *A* ***kitchenette*** *is a very small kitchen.*
5. *When you are* ***latching*** *onto something, you are grabbing it and hanging onto it.*
   - Everybody, show me how you would **latch** onto your book.
6. ***Mistrusted*** *means not trusted.*
   - Everybody, what's another way of saying **The child was not trusted by her classmates?** (Signal.) *The child was mistrusted by her classmates.*
7. *A person who is neat and clean is* ***presentable.***
   - What are some things you do so you will look **presentable?** (Ideas: *Brush my teeth; comb my hair; wash my face.*)
8. ***Roomers*** *are people who live in a rented room in a house.*

9. *Suede is leather that has a soft surface.*

- What are some things that are made out of **suede?** (Ideas: *Shoes; purses; belts.*)

Story Background

1. (Call on individual students to read two or three sentences.)
2. (After students complete the passage, ask the questions.)

> "Thank You, M'am" is another example of realistic fiction. It was written by a famous African American author from Missouri named Langston Hughes. When he was 22 years old, Langston Hughes moved to Harlem in New York City. Harlem was and still is a neighborhood where black writers, musicians, and artists live and work. During the 1920s and 1930s in Harlem, Langston Hughes was one of the leaders in a group of creative people who celebrated their black traditions through writing and music. People refer to the work of this group as the Harlem Renaissance.
>
> Langston Hughes is well known for his short stories, novels, plays, and poetry about the everyday experiences of black people. Even though the short story you will read was written in 1958, its message still rings true today.

- Everybody, who is the author of the story you are going to read? (Signal.) *Langston Hughes.*
- Who are some of the people who live and work in Harlem? (Ideas: *Black writers; black musicians; black artists.*)
- Langston Hughes was a leader of a group of creative people.
- How did this group honor their black culture? (Idea: *Through their writings and music.*)
- What is Langston Hughes best known for? (Ideas: *His short stories, novels, plays, poetry; his writings about the experiences of black people.*)

Focus Questions

1. (Call on individual students to read the Focus Questions aloud.)
2. (Remind students to refer to these questions as they read the story.)
   - *What unexpected things does Mrs. Jones do for Roger?*
   - *What do the two main characters have in common?*
   - *What do you think Roger learns from Mrs. Jones?*
   - *Why do you think the story is called, "Thank You, M'am"?*

> **Thank You, M'am**
> by Langston Hughes
> Illustrated by Donald Cook
>
> She was a large woman with a large purse that had everything in it but a hammer and nails. It had a long strap, and she carried it slung across her shoulder. It was about eleven o'clock at night, dark, and she was walking alone, when a boy ran up behind her and tried to snatch her purse. The strap broke with the sudden single tug the boy gave it from behind. But the boy's weight and the weight of the purse combined caused him to lose his balance. Instead of taking off full blast as he had hoped, the boy fell on his back on the sidewalk, and his legs flew up. The large woman simply turned around and kicked him

right square in his blue-jeaned sitter. Then she reached down, picked the boy up by his shirt front, and shook him until his teeth rattled.

After that the woman said, "Pick up my pocketbook, boy, and give it here."

She still held him tightly. But she bent down enough to permit him to stoop and pick up her purse. Then she said, "Now ain't you ashamed of yourself?"

Firmly gripped by his shirt front, the boy said, "Yes'm."

The woman said, "What did you want to do it for?"

The boy said, "I didn't aim to."

She said, "You a lie!"

By that time two or three people passed, stopped, turned to look, and some stood watching.

"If I turn you loose, will you run?" asked the woman.

"Yes'm," said the boy.

"Then I won't turn you loose," said the woman. She did not release him.

"Lady, I'm sorry," whispered the boy.

"Um-hum! Your face is dirty. I got a great mind to wash your face for you. Ain't you got nobody home to tell you to wash your face?"

"No'm," said the boy.

"Then it will get washed this evening," said the large woman, starting up the street, dragging the frightened boy behind her.

He looked as if he were fourteen or fifteen, frail and willow-wild, in tennis shoes and blue jeans.

The woman said, "You ought to be my son. I would teach you right from wrong. Least I can do right now is to wash your face. Are you hungry?"

"No'm," said the being-dragged boy. "I just want you to turn me loose."

"Was I bothering you when I turned that corner?" asked the woman.

"No'm."

"But you put yourself in contact with me," said the woman. "If you think that that contact is not going to last a while, you got another thing coming. When I get through with you, sir, you are going to remember Mrs. Luella Bates Washington Jones."

Sweat popped out on the boy's face, and he began to struggle. Mrs. Jones stopped, jerked him around in front of her, put a half nelson around his neck, and continued to drag him up the street. When she got to her door, she dragged the boy inside, down a hall, and into a large kitchenette-furnished room at the rear of the house. She switched on the light and left the door open. The boy could hear other roomers laughing and talking in the large house. Some of their doors were open, too, so he knew he and the woman were not alone. The woman still had him by the neck in the middle of her room.

She said, "What is your name?"

"Roger," answered the boy.

"Then, Roger, you go to that sink and wash your face," said the woman, whereupon she turned him loose—at last. Roger looked at the door—looked at the woman— looked at the door—and went to the sink.

"Let the water run until it gets warm," she said. "Here's a clean towel."

"You gonna take me to jail?" asked the boy, bending over the sink.

"Not with that face, I would not take you nowhere," said the woman. "Here I am trying to get home to cook me a bite to eat, and you snatch my pocketbook! Maybe you ain't been to your supper either, late as it be. Have you?"

"There's nobody home at my house," said the boy.

"Then we'll eat," said the woman. "I believe you're hungry—or been hungry—to try to snatch my pocketbook!"

"I want a pair of blue suede shoes," said the boy.

"Well, you didn't have to snatch my pocketbook to get some suede shoes," said Mrs. Luella Bates Washington Jones. "You could have asked me."

"M'am?"

The water dripping from his face, the boy looked at her. There was a long pause. A very long pause. After he had dried his face, and not knowing what else to do, dried it again, the boy turned around, wondering what next. The door was open. He could make a dash for it down the hall. He could run, run, run, run!

The woman was sitting on the daybed. After a while she said, "I were young once, and I wanted things I could not get."

There was another long pause. The boy's mouth opened. Then he frowned, not knowing he frowned.

The woman said, "Um-hum! You thought I was going to say *but*, didn't you? You thought I was going to say *but I didn't snatch people's pocketbooks.* Well, I wasn't going to say that." Pause. Silence. "I have done things, too, which I would not tell you, son—neither tell God, if He didn't already know. Everybody's got something in common. So you set down while I fix us something to eat. You might run that comb through your hair so you will look presentable."

In another corner of the room behind a screen was a gas plate and an icebox. Mrs. Jones got up and went behind the screen. The woman did not watch the boy to see if he was going to run now, nor did she watch her purse, which she left behind on the daybed.

But the boy took care to sit on the far side of the room, away from the purse, where he thought she could easily see him out of the corner of her eye if she wanted to. He did not trust the woman *not* to trust him. And he did not want to be mistrusted now.

"Do you need somebody to go to the store," asked the boy, "maybe to get some milk or something?"

"Don't believe I do," said the woman, "unless you just want sweet milk yourself. I was going to make cocoa out of this canned milk I got here."

"That will be fine," said the boy.

She heated some lima beans and ham she had in the icebox, made the cocoa, and set the table. The woman did not ask the boy anything about where he lived, or his folks, or anything else that would embarrass him. Instead, as they ate, she told him about her job in a hotel beauty shop that stayed open late, what the work was like, and how all kinds of women came in and out, blondes, redheads, and Spanish. Then she cut him a half of her ten-cent cake.

"Eat some more, son," she said.

When they were finished eating, she got up and said, "Now here, take this ten dollars and buy yourself some blue suede shoes. And next time, do not make the mistake of latching onto *my* pocketbook nor *anybody else's*—because shoes got by devilish ways will burn your feet. I got to get my rest now. But from here on in, son, I hope you will behave yourself."

She led him down the hall to the front door and opened it. "Good night! Behave yourself, boy!" she said, looking out into the street as he went down the steps.

The boy wanted to say something other than, "Thank you, m'am," to Mrs. Luella Bates Washington Jones, but although his lips moved, he couldn't even say that as he turned at the foot of the barren stoop and looked up at the large woman in the door. Then she shut the door.

Extending Comprehension

(The following Extending Comprehension activities can be presented after students finish reading the story. The activities also appear in the *Literature Anthology*.)

1. (Students can answer the Story Questions either orally or in writing. If the questions are presented orally, use the script below.)
2. (Students can select one or more Discussion Topics. Discussions can take place in small groups or with the entire class.)
3. (Students can use the Writing Ideas to respond to the story in writing.)

Story Questions

1. What unexpected things did Mrs. Jones do for Roger? (Ideas: *She took him to her home instead of calling the police; she fed him; she gave him money so he could buy the shoes he wanted.*)
2. Why do you think Roger decided against running away, even though he had the chance? (Ideas: *Because Mrs. Jones acted as if she cared about him; because Mrs. Jones's behavior made him curious about her; because Mrs. Jones was going to feed him; because Mrs. Jones told him he could have asked her for money instead of trying to steal her pocketbook.*)
3. What did the two main characters have in common? (Ideas: *They both wanted things they couldn't get; they both had hard times; they both had done things they were ashamed of.*)
4. What do you think Roger learned from Mrs. Jones? (Ideas: *Strangers can be kind and helpful; people should treat each other with respect; some adults do understand what it's like to want something so badly that you'd steal to get it; having people trust you is important.*)
5. Why do you think the story is titled "Thank You, M'am"? (Ideas: *Because Roger had many reasons to be thankful to Mrs. Jones; because saying "thank you" shows respect and appreciation after someone helps you; because Roger wanted to say more than just "thank you."*)

Discussion Topics

1. This story is titled "Thank You, M'am" but these words are never said in the story. During your discussion, try to answer the following questions:
   - Why do you think Roger couldn't say the words "Thank You, M'am" at the end of the story?
   - Why do you think the author chose that title but never had a character speak those words?

2. Mrs. Jones treated Roger differently than you might have expected, considering he had tried to steal her pocketbook. What would you have done to Roger if you were Mrs. Jones? During your discussion, try to answer the following questions:
   - What would you have said to Roger?
   - Would you have called the police? Explain your answer.

Writing Ideas

1. You've probably heard the expression, "you can't judge a book by its cover." Explain what this means and tell how it relates to Roger's experience with Mrs. Jones.

2. Pretend you are Roger. You are now grown up and have a teenage son of your own. Write a conversation between your son and you that explains how that day with Mrs. Jones changed your life. Be sure to include questions your son would ask you.

Story 8

The Circuit

New Vocabulary Words

Take out your *Literature Anthology.* Turn to page 114. ✔
What is the title of this story? (Signal.) *"The Circuit."*
Who is the author? (Signal.) *Francisco Jiménez.*

1. First we'll read some words from the story, and then we'll talk about what they mean.
2. Word 1 is **sharecropper.** What word? (Signal.) *Sharecropper.*
   - (Repeat for every numbered word.)
3. It's your turn to read all the words.
4. Word 1. What word? (Signal.) *Sharecropper.*
   - (Repeat for every numbered word.)

1. sharecropper 2. pickers 3. shack	4. jalopy 5. vineyard 6. savor	7. cities in California: • Fresno • Santa Maria • Santa Rosa

Definitions

(For each definition, call on a student to read the definition aloud; then, present the tasks that go with that definition to the group.)

1. *A **sharecropper** is someone who rents land from a farmer.*
   - To pay the rent, he gives the farmer a part, or share, of the food he grows.
   - Everybody, does a **sharecropper** own the land he works on? (Signal.) *No.*
   - Does he rent the land he grows food on? (Signal.) *Yes.*
   - What does he use to pay the rent? (Idea: *A share of the food he grows.*)
2. *People who harvest fruits and vegetables are sometimes called **pickers.***
   - Everybody, what's another way of saying **The people harvested the grapes?** (Signal.) *The pickers harvested the grapes.*
3. *A house that needs lots of fixing up is a **shack.***
   - Everybody, what do we call a house that needs fixing up? (Signal.) *A shack.*
4. *Another way of saying an **old car that needs lots of fixing up** is **jalopy.***
   - Everybody, what do we call an old car that needs a lot of fixing up? (Signal.) *A jalopy.*
5. *A **vineyard** is a field where grapevines grow.*
   - Everybody, what do we call fields where grapevines grow? (Signal.) *Vineyards.*
   - Everybody, what's another way of saying **Look at all the grapevines in that field?** (Signal.) *Look at all the grapevines in that vineyard.*

6. *Savor* is another word for appreciate.
- Everybody, what's another way of saying **Shawn appreciated the wonderful music?**
(Signal.) *Shawn savored the wonderful music.*

7. *Cities in California:* **Fresno, Santa Maria,** and **Santa Rosa.**

Story Background

1. (Call on individual students to read two or three sentences.)

2. (After students complete a section, ask the questions for that section.)

The author of "The Circuit," Francisco Jiménez, wrote the story to tell about the lives of California farm workers. The narrator is a young boy. As you read the story, you will learn about the narrator's family and the work that he, his brother, and his father do. You will also learn about the food his mother cooks for the family and the places they live.

Even though the story takes place in California during the 1950s, it is a story that could be told about many places today. Like many farm workers who come to work in the United States, the narrator's family is from Mexico. California farmers need extra workers to help them with planting and harvesting their crops. Like many farm workers today, the narrator's family stays in one place and then, when the crops have been harvested in that place, they move to another place. Sometimes families stay in as many as six different places in one year. They live in labor camps, old houses, and sometimes, like the family of the narrator, garages.

During the harvest season, farm workers work for many long hours every day. Sometimes they work seven days a week. The crops must be harvested when they are ready. The work is very hard, and usually the sun is very hot. Children often work alongside their parents. In the story, the oldest children work in the fields with their father instead of going to school.

The story opens near the end of the strawberry harvest. Ito, the Japanese sharecropper, is in charge of the workers. Ito is unhappy because the best part of the strawberry season is over. Read the story to see what happens to some of the workers.

Many people have worked over the years to improve the working and living conditions of the farm workers who come to work in California and other states.

- When does this story take place? (Idea: *In the 1950s.*)
- Why did the narrator's father bring his family to California? (Idea: *To find work so they could earn money.*)
- Why did the farmers in California want people from Mexico to work on their farms?
(Ideas: *They needed help to get their crops planted and harvested; they didn't have to pay them a lot of money.*)

The family in the story speaks Spanish. The author uses some Spanish and Spanish-sounding words to make his story seem more real. The Spanish words are in italics. The author gives the translation for some of these words in parentheses. For example, he writes *es todo* (that's it) and *mi olla* (my pot). Other times you will see Spanish words in italics without a translation.

You can sometimes figure out the meaning of these words from the other words in the sentence.

Here are some words to try to figure out. The sentences that the words are in may help you. If you already speak Spanish, this will be easy for you!

- The *braceros* came from Mexico to work on the big farms of California.
- He came from *Jalisco* in Mexico. She came from Arizona in the United States.
- When the bell rang, the teacher said, "*Ya esora.* Get your things together and line up."
- I like to listen to Mexican *corridos* as much as I like to listen to rap. *Corridos* singers tell true stories about people or horses or ranches.
- When the game was over, my brother said, "*Vámonos,*" and we walked home.

- How can you tell you are reading a Spanish word? (Idea: *Spanish and Spanish-sounding words are printed in italics.*)
- What do you think *braceros* means? (Idea: *A farm worker from Mexico.*)
- What do you think *Jalisco* is? (Idea: *A state in Mexico*)
- What do you think *ya esora* means? (Idea: *It's time to go.*)
- What do you think *vámonos* means? (Idea: *Let's go.*)
- What do you think *corridos* is? (Ideas: *A kind of music; songs that tell true stories.*)

Focus Questions

1. (Call on individual students to read the Focus Questions aloud.)
2. (Remind students to think about those questions as they read the story.)
   - *What kind of work do the father and his sons do? Where do they work and how long do they work each day?*
   - *What kinds of places does the family live in?*
   - *Why does the family have to move from one place to another? How does the narrator feel about moving?*
   - *Why does the narrator like school?*
   - *What do packed cardboard boxes mean to the narrator?*
   - *Why does the story have the title, "The Circuit"?*

The Circuit
By Francisco Jiménez
Illustrated by Meryl Henderson

It was that time of year again. Ito, the strawberry sharecropper, did not smile. It was natural. The peak of strawberry season was over and the last few days the workers, most of them *braceros,* were not picking as many boxes as they had during the months of June and July.

As the last days of August disappeared, so did the number of braceros. Sunday, only one—the best picker came to work. I liked him. Sometimes we talked during our half-hour lunch break. That is how I found out he was from Jalisco, the same state in Mexico my family was from. That Sunday was the last time I saw him.

When the sun had tired and sunk behind the mountains, Ito signaled us that it was time to go home. *"Ya esora,"* he yelled in his broken Spanish. Those were the words I waited for twelve hours a day, everyday, seven days a week, week after week. And the thought of not hearing them again saddened me.

As we drove home Papa did not say a word. With both hands on the wheel, he stared at the dirt road. My older brother, Roberto, was also silent. He leaned his head back and closed his eyes. Once in a while he cleared from his throat the dust that blew in from outside.

Yes, it was that time of year. When I opened the front door to the shack, I stopped. Everything we owned was neatly packed in cardboard boxes. Suddenly I felt even more the weight of hours, days, weeks, and months of work. I sat down on a box. The thought of having to move to Fresno and knowing what was in store for me there brought tears to my eyes.

That night I could not sleep. I lay in bed thinking about how much I hated this move.

A little before five o' clock in the morning, Papa woke everyone up. A few minutes later, the yelling and screaming of my little brothers and sisters, for whom the move was a great adventure, broke the silence of dawn. Shortly, the barking of dogs accompanied them.

While we packed the breakfast dishes, Papa went outside to start the "Carcanchita." That was the name Papa gave his old '38 Plymouth. He bought it in a used-car lot in Santa Rosa in the winter of 1949. Papa was very proud of his little car. *"Mi Carcanchita,"* my little jalopy, he called it. He had a right to be proud of it. He spent a lot of time looking at other cars before buying this one. When he finally chose "Carcanchita," he checked it thoroughly before driving it out of the car lot. He examined every inch of the car. He listened to the motor, tilting his head from side to side like a parrot, trying to detect any noises that spelled car trouble. After being satisfied with the looks and sounds of the car, Papa then insisted on knowing who the original owner was. He never did find out from the car salesman. But he bought the car anyway. Papa figured the original owner must have been an important man because behind the rear seat of the car he found a blue necktie.

Papa parked the car out in front and left the motor running. *"Listo"* (ready), he yelled. Without saying a word, Roberto and I began to carry the boxes out to the car. Roberto carried the two big boxes and I carried the two smaller ones. Papa then threw the mattress on top of the car and tied it with ropes to the front and rear bumpers.

Everything was packed except Mama's pot. It was an old large galvanized pot she had picked up at an army surplus store in Santa Maria the year I was born. The pot was full of dents and nicks, and the more dents and nicks it had, the more Mama liked it. *"Mi olla"* (my pot), she used to say proudly.

I held the front door open as Mama carefully carried out her pot by both handles, making sure not to spill the cooked beans. When she got to the car, Papa reached out to help her with it. Roberto opened the rear car door and Papa gently placed it on the floor behind the front seat. Papa sighed, wiped the sweat off his forehead with his sleeve, and said wearily, *"Es todo"* (that's it.)

As we drove away, I felt a lump in my throat. I turned around and looked at our little shack for the last time.

At sunset we drove into a labor camp near Fresno. Since Papa did not speak English, Mama asked the camp foreman if they need any more workers. "We don't need no more," said the foreman, scratching his head. "Check with Sullivan down the road. Can't miss him. He lives in a big white house with a fence around it."

When we got there, Mama walked up to the house. She went through a white gate, past a row of rose bushes, up the stairs to the front door. She rang the doorbell. The porch light came on and a tall husky man came out. They exchanged a few words. After the man went in, Mama clasped her hands and hurried back to the car. "We have work! Mr. Sullivan said we can stay there the whole season," she said gasping and pointing to an old garage near the stables.

The garage was worn out by the years. It had no windows. The walls, eaten by termites, strained to support the roof full of holes. The loose dirt floor, populated by earthworms, looked like a gray road map.

That night, by the light of a kerosene lamp, we unpacked and cleaned our new home. Roberto swept away the loose dirt, leaving the hard ground. Papa plugged the holes in the walls with old newspapers and tin cap tops. Mama fed my little brothers and sisters. Papa and Roberto then brought in the mattress and placed it on the far corner of the garage. "Mama, you and the little ones sleep on the mattress. Roberto, Panchito, and I will sleep outside under the trees," Papa said.

Early next morning Mr. Sullivan showed us where his crop was, and after breakfast, Papa, Roberto, and I headed for the vineyard to pick.

Around nine o' clock the temperature had risen to almost one hundred degrees. I was completely soaked in sweat and my mouth felt as if I had been chewing on a handkerchief. I walked over to the end of the row, picked up the jug of water we had brought, and began drinking. "Don't drink too much; you'll get sick," Roberto shouted. No sooner had he said that than I felt sick to my stomach. I dropped to my knees and let the jug roll off my hands. I remained motionless with my eyes glued on the hot sandy ground. All I could hear was the drone of insects. Slowly I began to recover. I poured water over my face and neck and watched the black mud run down my arms and hit the ground.

I still felt a little dizzy when we took a break to eat lunch. It was past two o' clock and we sat underneath a large walnut tree that was on the side of the road. While we ate, Papa jotted down the number of boxes we had picked. Roberto drew designs on the ground with a stick. Suddenly I noticed Papa's face turn pale as he looked down the road. "Here comes the school bus," he whispered loudly in alarm. Instinctively, Roberto and I hid in the vineyards. We did not want to get in trouble for not going to school. The yellow bus stopped in front of Mr. Sullivan's yard. Two neatly dressed boys about my age got off. They carried books under their arms. After they crossed the street, the bus drove away. Roberto and I came out from hiding and joined Papa. *"Tienen que tener cuidado"* (you have to be careful), he warned us.

After lunch we went back to work. The sun kept beating down. The buzzing insects, the wet sweat, and the hot dry dust made the afternoon seem to last forever. Finally the mountains around the valley reached out and swallowed the sun. Within an hour it was too dark to continue picking. The vines blanketed the grapes, making it difficult to see the bunches. *"Vámonos,"* said Papa, signaling to us that it was time to quit work. Papa then took out a pencil and began to figure out how much we had earned our first day. He wrote down numbers, crossed some out, wrote down some more. *"Quince"* (fifteen dollars), he murmured.

When we arrived home, we took a cold shower underneath a waterhose. We then sat down to eat dinner around some wooden crates that served as a table. Mama had cooked a special meal for us. We had rice and tortillas with *carne con chile,* my favorite dish.

The next morning I could hardly move. My body ached all over. I felt little control over my arms and legs. This feeling went on every morning for days until my muscles finally got used to the work.

It was Monday, the first week of November. The grape season was over and I could now go to school. I woke up early that morning and lay in bed, looking at the stars and savoring the thought of not going to work and of starting sixth grade for the first time that year.

Since I could not sleep, I decided to get up and join Papa and Roberto at breakfast. I sat down at the table across from Roberto, but I kept my head down. I did not want to look up and face him. I knew he was sad. He was not going to school today. He was not going tomorrow, or next week, or next month. He would not go until the cotton season was over, and that was sometime in February. I rubbed my hands together and watched the dry, acid-stained skin fall to the floor in little rolls.

When Papa and Roberto left for work, I felt relief. I walked to the top of a small grade next to the shack and watched the "Carcanchita" disappear in the distance in a cloud of dust.

Two hours later, around eight o' clock, I stood by the side of the road waiting for school bus number twenty. When it arrived I climbed in. No one noticed me. Everyone was busy either talking or yelling. I sat in an empty seat in the back.

When the bus stopped in front of the school, I felt very nervous. I looked out the bus window and saw boys and girls carrying books under their arms. I felt empty. I put my hands in my pants pockets and walked to the principal's office. When I entered I heard a woman's voice say: "May I help you?" I was startled. I had not heard English for months. For a few seconds I remained speechless. I looked at the lady who waited for an answer. My first instinct was to answer in Spanish, but I held back. Finally, after struggling for English words I managed to tell her that I wanted to enroll in the sixth grade. After answering many questions, I was led to the classroom.

Mr. Lema, the sixth-grade teacher, greeted me and assigned me a desk. He then introduced me to the class. I was so nervous and scared at that moment when everyone's eyes were on me that I wished I were with Papa and Roberto picking cotton. After taking roll, Mr. Lema gave the class the assignment for the first hour. "The first thing we have to do this morning is finish reading the story we began yesterday," he said enthusiastically. He walked up to me, handed me an English book, and asked me to read. "We are on page 125," he said politely. When I heard this, I felt blood rush to my head; I felt dizzy. "Would you like to read?" he asked hesitantly. I opened the book to page 125. My mouth was dry. My eyes began to water. I could not begin. "You can read later," Mr. Lema said understandingly.

For the rest of the reading period I kept getting angrier and angrier with myself. I should have read, I thought to myself.

During recess I went into the restroom and opened my English book to page 125. I began to read in a low voice, pretending I was in class. There were many words I did not know. I closed the book and headed back to the classroom.

Mr. Lema was sitting at his desk correcting papers. When I entered he looked up at me and smiled. I felt better. I walked up to him and asked if he could help me with the new words. "Gladly," he said.

The rest of the month I spent my lunch hours working on English with Mr. Lema, my best friend at school.

One Friday during lunch hour Mr. Lema asked me to take a walk with him to the music room. "Do you like music?" he asked me as we entered the building.

"Yes, I like Mexican *corridos*," I answered. He then picked up a trumpet, blew on it and handed it to me. The sound gave me goose bumps. I knew that sound. I heard it in many Mexican corridos. "How would you like to learn how to play it?" he asked. He must have read my face because before I could answer, he added: "I'll teach you how to play it during our lunch hours."

That day I could hardly wait to get home to tell Papa and Mama the great news. As I got off the bus, my little brothers and sisters ran up to meet me. They were yelling and screaming. I thought they were happy to see me, but when I opened the door to our shack, I saw that everything we owned was neatly packed in cardboard boxes.

Extending Comprehension

(The following Extending Comprehension activities can be presented after students finish reading the story. The activities also appear in the *Literature Anthology*.)

1. (Students can answer the Story Questions either orally or in writing. If the questions are presented orally, use the script below.)
2. (Students can select one or more Discussion Topics. Discussions can take place in small groups or with the entire class.)
3. (Students can use the Writing Ideas to respond to the story in writing.)

Story Questions

1. What were some of the difficulties the narrator, his father, and his brothers faced when they went to work in the fields? (Ideas: *They had to work 12 hours a day, seven days a week; they worked week after week; the sun was hot, and they got very hot; their muscles ached from the hard work.*)

2. Name two places the family lived. Describe what the second place looked like when they moved in. Then describe how the family worked to improve that place. (Ideas: *They lived in a shack and a garage; the garage was very dirty; the family swept away the dirt; they filled up the holes in the walls.*)

3. Tell how the author lets us know that the narrator doesn't like to move. (Ideas: *He was sad when he knew that they were leaving the strawberry fields; he couldn't sleep the night before they moved.*)

4. Who made school a happy place for the narrator? Tell two things this person did that made the narrator feel good. (Ideas: *His teacher helped the narrator learn English; he said he would help the narrator learn to play the trumpet.*)

5. How do you think the narrator feels at the end of the story? Tell why he feels that way. (Ideas: *He feels sad; he regrets that he can't continue learning English from his teacher; he is upset that he can't learn to play the trumpet.*)

6. Explain why the title of the story is "The Circuit." Hint: a circuit is a circle. (Ideas: *The narrator ends up where he starts, moving from one place to another; the family has to keep on moving.*)

Discussion Topics

1. The author uses interesting words and sentences to describe what the narrator sees and how he feels. Here are four sentences from the book. Discuss the meaning of each sentence. Tell which words make the sentences more interesting.

- "When the sun had tired and sunk behind the mountains, Ito signaled us it was time to go."
- "The mountains around the valley reached out and swallowed the sun."
- "Suddenly, I felt even more the weight of hours, weeks, and months of work."
- "I woke up early that morning and lay in bed, looking at the stars and savoring the thought of not going to work . . ."

2. Do you think the children who work in this story should be going to school? During your discussion, try to answer the following questions:

- Why does the father make his boys hide when the school bus arrives?
- Why doesn't the mother make the father let the boys go to school?
- Why do you think the narrator finally got to go to school but his brother didn't?
- Why do you think the narrator liked school so much?

Writing Ideas

1. Although we learn a lot about the family in the story, some important facts are missing:

- The last name of the family
- The first name of the narrator
- The age of the narrator
- Where the mother learned English
- The number of little brothers and sisters in the family. From what you have learned about the narrator and his family, write a paragraph that tells about those missing facts. You can give the narrator a new first name, but see if you can find it in the story.

2. The narrator wants to write a letter to Mr. Lema to explain why he did not come back to school, but the narrator is working and the family has no paper. Write this letter for him. Tell Mr. Lema how grateful you are for his help. Explain to him why you are not in his classroom. Tell him what you are doing and how you feel about your life outside of school.

Story 9

Salmon Count

New Vocabulary Words

Everybody, take out your *Literature Anthology*. Turn to page 127. ✔
What is the title of this story? (Signal.) *"Salmon Count."*
Who is the author? (Signal.) *Clifford E. Trafzer.*

1. First we'll read some words from the story, and then we'll talk about what they mean.
2. Word 1 is **subside.** What word? (Signal.) *Subside.*
   • (Repeat for every numbered word.)
3. It's your turn to read all the words.
4. Word 1. What word? (Signal.) *Subside.*

   • (Repeat for every numbered word.)

1. subside	8. course of action	15. ritual
2. tipis	9. absorbed in	16. revolves around
3. blot out	10. arrogantly	17. retire to
4. abruptly	11. grudgingly	18. agonizing
5. welled up	12. strained	19. repress
6. elders	13. proposal	20. abandon
7. in accordance	14. moral support	

Definitions

(For each definition: call on a student to read the definition aloud; then, present the tasks that go with that definition to the group.)

1. *When something **subsides,** it becomes weaker.*
   • Everybody, what's another way of saying **The pain in my leg weakened?** (Signal.) *The pain in my leg subsided.*
2. ***Tipis** are tents that some Native Americans tribes use.*
   • You may have seen this word spelled t-e-e-p-e-e.
3. ***Blot out** is another way of saying **get rid of.***
   • Everybody, what's another way of saying **He wanted to get rid of the memory of his accident?** (Signal.) *He wanted to blot out the memory of his accident.*
4. ***Abruptly** is another way of saying **suddenly.***
   • Everybody, what's another way of saying **To avoid hitting the cat, she stopped the car suddenly?** (Signal.) *To avoid hitting the cat, she stopped the car abruptly.*

5. When a feeling is **welling up** in you, you are overcome with that feeling.
   - Everybody, here's another way of saying **I was overcome with joy: A feeling of joy welled up in me.**
   - Everybody, what's another way of saying **I was overcome with joy?** (Signal.) *A feeling of joy welled up in me.*
6. **Elders** are older people who are important in their community.
   - Everybody, here's another way of saying **In his family, John's grandfather is an important older person: In his family, John's grandfather is an elder.**
   - Everybody, what's another way of saying **In his family, John's grandfather is an important older person?** (Signal.) *In his family, John's grandfather is an elder.*
7. **In accordance** is another way of saying **in agreement.**
   - Everybody, what's another way of saying **Everyone should act in agreement with the rules?** (Signal.) *Everyone should act in accordance with the rules.*
8. A **course of action** is a way to do something.
   - Everybody, what's another way of saying **We have figured out a way to solve the problem?** (Signal.) *We have figured out a course of action.*
9. When you are **absorbed in** something, all your attention is focused on that thing.
   - Everybody, here's another way of saying **All his attention was focused on the ghost story: He was absorbed in the ghost story.**
   - Everybody, what's another way of saying **All his attention was focused on the ghost story?** (Signal.) *He was absorbed in the ghost story.*
10. When you act **arrogantly,** you act like you are more important than everyone else.
11. When you act **grudgingly,** you do something unwillingly.
    - Everybody, what's another way of saying **His mom unwillingly gave him permission to stay out late?** (Signal.) *His mom grudgingly gave him permission to stay out late.*
12. **Strained** is another word for **tense.**
    - Everybody, what's another way of saying **Their conversation was tense?** (Signal.) *Their conversation was strained.*
13. A **proposal** is a plan.
    - Everybody, what's another way of saying **I have a great plan?** (Signal.) *I have a great proposal.*
14. When you give someone **moral support,** you give that person encouragement.
    - Everybody, what's another way of saying **I appreciated the encouragement from my sister?** (Signal.) *I appreciated the moral support from my sister.*
15. A **ritual** is a customary way of doing something.
    - Everybody, here's another way of saying **He had a customary way of fixing his breakfast: He had a breakfast ritual.**
    - Everybody, what's another way of saying **The lawyers had a customary way of acting in the courtroom?** (Signal.) *The lawyers had a courtroom ritual.*
16. **Revolves around** is another way of saying **centers on.**
    - Everybody, what's another way of saying **The girl's life centers on ice skating?** (Signal.) *The girl's life revolves around ice skating.*
17. When you **retire to** a room, you go to that room to stay for a while.
    - Everybody, here's another way of saying **The judge went to her chambers to stay for a while: The judge retired to her chambers.**

- Everybody, what's another way of saying **The judge went to her chambers to stay for a while?** (Signal.) *The judge retired to her chambers.*

18. *Things that are **agonizing** cause agony and pain.*
    - Everybody, here's another way of saying **The decision caused agony and suffering: The decision was agonizing.**
    - Everybody, what's another way of saying **The long delay caused agony and suffering?** (Signal.) *The long delay was agonizing.*

19. ***Repress** is another way of saying **hold back.***
    - Everybody, what's another way of saying **The coach held back his anger?** (Signal.) *The coach repressed his anger.*

20. *When you **abandon** something, you give up that thing.*
    - Everybody, here's another way of saying **I promised my teacher I wouldn't give up playing the piano: I promised my teacher I wouldn't abandon playing the piano.**
    - Everybody, what's another way of saying **I told my grandfather I wouldn't give up our family traditions?** (Signal.) *I told my grandfather I wouldn't abandon our family traditions.*

Story Background

1. (Call on individual students to read two or three sentences each.)
2. (After students complete a section, ask the questions for that section.)

> "Salmon Count" is another example of realistic fiction. The story is about the efforts of the Nez Perce (pronounced "nez purse") Native American tribe to get back their salmon fishing rights. These rights had been established in the Nez Perce Treaty of 1863. This treaty was an agreement between the Nez Perce, who live in Idaho, and the United States government. The treaty stated that the Nez Perce could fish for salmon wherever they had done so in the past. A treaty with the United States government has priority over state laws. This means that if a state's law says something different from what a treaty agreement says, you obey the treaty with the United States government instead of the state law.

- What's a treaty? (Idea: *An agreement.*)
- A treaty is usually an agreement between two countries, but it can also be an agreement between a country and a group of people.
- What was the treaty the Nez Perce had with the United States government? (Idea: *The Nez Perce could fish for salmon whenever they wanted.*)
- If there is a difference between a treaty with the United States government and a state law, which one do you obey? (Signal.) *The treaty.*

> Salmon play an important role in the Nez Perce culture. The tribe has a long tradition of catching salmon. The Nez Perce depend on salmon as a main source of food. Of course, people other than the Nez Perce also like to eat salmon. As a result, other people fish for salmon to sell or to eat. This creates problems because too many people are fishing for salmon. One problem is that the Nez Perce count on having salmon to eat to survive. Another problem is that if too many people fish for salmon, there won't be enough left in the rivers and salmon will eventually become extinct.

- Name two reasons why salmon are important to the Nez Perce. (Ideas: *Salmon are a main source of food; the Nez Perce have been catching salmon for a long, long time.*)
- What two problems were created when people other than the Nez Perce started to fish for salmon? (Ideas: *There were less salmon available for the Nez Perce; the salmon might become extinct.*)

> In the story, the state of Idaho has a law that says when people can go fishing. The state law, however, is in conflict with the treaty the Nez Perce have with the United States government. According to the treaty, the Nez Perce can fish wherever they want. On the other hand, the state law says that people living in Idaho can only fish for salmon at certain times of the year.
>
> In the story, there is a preliminary trial in front of a judge because four of the Nez Perce have been arrested for breaking the state's fishing law. In a preliminary trial, a judge listens to both sides of a case and decides if there is enough evidence for a trial with a jury. In this story, the lawyer for the state, called the prosecutor, tries to prove that the four defendants are guilty because they broke the state law.

- What did the state do to make sure that the salmon would not become extinct? (Idea: *It made a law stating when people could fish for salmon.*)
- How was the state law different from the treaty the Nez Perce had with the United States government? (Idea: *The state law said people could only fish at certain times but the treaty said the Nez Perce could fish whenever they wanted.*)
- What's a preliminary trial? (Idea: *It's a type of trial in which a judge listens to both sides of a case and decides whether to bring it to a trial with a jury.*)
- What's the job of the prosecutor? (Idea: *To prove that the defendants are guilty.*)
- Who does the prosecutor work for? (Idea: *The state government.*)

> Many Native Americans have their own way of making important decisions. Members of the tribe gather together. These gatherings are called council meetings. In this story, the council holds a meeting to discuss what to do about the four tribal members who have been arrested and who must go to court. The council decides to hire a lawyer to prove that those who were arrested are innocent. The council wants the lawyer to prove that the four tribal members were following the treaty agreement. This lawyer is called the defense attorney because he defends those who have been arrested.

- What is it called when Native Americans gather together to make an important decision? (Signal.) *A council meeting.*
- In the story, what important decision did the Nez Perce make during their council meeting? (Idea: *To hire an attorney to prove the innocence of those who had been arrested.*)
- What do we call an attorney who is hired to prove the innocence of the defendants? (Signal.) *A defense attorney.*

Focus Questions

1. (Call on individual students to read the Focus Questions aloud.)
2. (Remind students to think about those questions as they read the story.)
   - *How did Matthew's mother set a good example when she found out her son had been arrested?*
   - *What was Grandfather's role in the story—what was his purpose?*
   - *What reasons did Matthew have to feel proud of himself, his mother, and his grandfather?*
   - *What evidence did Mr. Cohen present to the judge?*
   - *What important conversation occurred between Matthew and his grandfather at the end of the story?*

Salmon Count
by Clifford E. Trafzer
Illustrated by Alex Bloch

The sound of the handcuffs snapping shut around my brother's wrists echoed through the canyon. My stomach lurched and my throat closed into a dry lump. I was stunned by the sight of Matthew, wearing the red plaid shirt I had given him, being led away. That officer might as well have had no face. I remember only the brown uniform with bright brass buttons, the hat, and the silver-tinted sunglasses that hid the man's eyes. When Matthew tried to turn to say good-bye, he stumbled on the uneven ground. They passed out of view before I could move. Car doors slammed, the engine raced, and Matthew was gone.

The police also arrested Watie Jim, Wendell Scott, and Anna Hawk. They said our people were outlaws because they were fishing without a state fishing license. After that, our group stopped fishing. The camp was quiet for a time. Dazed, I walked along the Salmon River. I hiked a short distance to a rocky cliff overlooking the river. The pounding in my heart had subsided, but a dry lump still swelled in my throat. I sat down under a pine tree to collect my thoughts and wait for my mother's return. *She will be furious,* I thought.

Below me lay the six tipis we'd set up near the bank of the Salmon River. A group of small children played in the camp, shrieking and laughing as they chased each other. A few dogs added their sharp barks to the noise. Smoke drifted up from the smoldering campfires. I tried unsuccessfully to blot out the memory of police rushing toward us. The officers had yelled something, but we had not been able to make out their words over the roar of the river. Unsure of what to do, we had stood holding our fishing poles and watched them race forward.

"What happened, Andrew?" my mother asked when she returned, her arms filled with groceries. Her face wore that stern look that usually meant I had done something wrong.

"What happened here?"

"The police came. They arrested Matt. They took Watie, Wendell, and Anna, too," I blurted out. My voice was shaking. I worried that my mother blamed me for allowing the police to take Matt. She reached out her small, sun-darkened hand, brushing my black hair away from my eyes.

"I'm glad they didn't take you," she said. "But we need to think of a way to get Matt back." She turned abruptly and walked swiftly back to camp.

Everything was in a stir. A crowd had gathered in the center of camp, and people were voicing their opinions about the arrests.

"We don't have to put up with this," I heard one man say. "These people have been doing this to Native Americans for years. I say we've taken it too long." As the crowd murmured its agreement, I felt a cloud of angry power sweep over us. My mother broke the spell.

"No one wants to get them back any more than I do." Her calm voice silenced the crowd. "But we can't act in anger." To my surprise, the group turned toward my mother. A feeling of pride welled up in me as I noticed people quieting down to listen. She knew the power of words, and she used them well that day.

"What will we win by using violence? We must be as wise as the elders who have taught us. We are *Nee Me Poo,* Nez Perce people. We must act in accordance with our traditions. We should go home and eat our supper. Later, we can meet here in council to decide the best course of action."

People nodded and began walking back to their lodges. My mother placed her arm around my shoulder, and we joined my grandfather and little sister. Grandfather had already begun cooking our meal of salmon, corn, beans, and bread. My mother and grandfather poured cups of steaming coffee for themselves, while my sister and I sipped cans of cold juice. Of course we talked about the arrests, anger filling our hearts and our words.

My grandfather spoke in a voice of quiet strength. "There was a time," he said, gazing into his coffee, "when the Nez Perce people took too many salmon." I looked at him with surprise. For a moment, I thought he might be joking. The people had always fished for salmon. It was their life! But as I studied his thin frame, his long gray hair, and his stern, wrinkled face, I knew he was serious.

"The old people say that we got greedy and took more salmon than we needed. That's when the Salmon People got together to meet in council. The men and women, even the children, sat down to talk about the situation." Grandfather paused to eat a chunk of salmon.

"The Salmon People knew they needed strong power. What they decided to do," Grandfather continued, wiping his hands on a napkin, "was to send Salmon Chief to visit Rattlesnake." I must have looked puzzled, because Grandfather addressed me directly.

He motioned toward me with his hand. "The Salmon Chief went to Rattlesnake hoping to get some of his power—his poison. Native Americans didn't bother Rattlesnake People because the rattlesnake had poison that could kill them. The Salmon People believed they could use the poison power to defend themselves."

Grandfather stood up, absorbed in his own story. He was not a tall man, but he seemed to tower over us. "Salmon Chief found Rattlesnake stretched out along the banks of Salmon River, sunning himself. 'Hello, brother,' Salmon called out, 'we are having some trouble here with the *Nee Me Poo* taking too many of us. So I have come to you, brother, to ask for some of your power."

"At first Rattlesnake ignored Salmon Chief. Finally, he raised his head and looked down at Salmon Chief. 'I have no power to share with the Salmon People,' he said arrogantly. Salmon Chief was stung by the snake's refusal. In a fit of anger and frustration, the great chief lifted his tail and began beating Rattlesnake over the head.

"'Now will you give me some of your power?'" Grandfather imitated the Salmon Chief. "'No!' said Rattlesnake. Again, Salmon Chief beat him hard on the head. 'Now can we have some of your power?' Salmon Chief asked Rattlesnake. Again he was denied the poisonous power.

"Four times Salmon Chief asked Rattlesnake for his help," Grandfather continued with his story. "Only after the great Chief beat Rattlesnake five times on the head did the snake grudgingly give the Salmon People some of his power. That's why we are careful when we handle salmon. If he bites us, we will get infected with the poison given to Salmon People by Rattlesnake."

Grandfather smiled. "Have you ever wondered why the head of Rattlesnake is all smashed down?" he asked. "It is because of the time Salmon Chief beat Rattlesnake's head down flat."

My mother had listened to Grandfather's story respectfully. But when he finished, she said quietly, "Our people have always fished this river, Dad. No one can take that away from us." My grandfather nodded silently, but he directed a thoughtful glance my way. The strained exchange between my mother and my grandfather made me feel uncomfortable.

At the meeting everyone was given a chance to talk, even the young people like me. The woman next to me reminded us that the white man had destroyed the fish and that they now wanted to "protect" them. She told us that at the dams, the white people count every salmon that swims upriver, and that they want to decide how many fish we can catch. When she finished, it was my turn to speak. I was ready.

"In my class at school we have been studying Native American treaty rights. Our people made two treaties with the federal government, the Nez Perce Treaty of 1855 and the Nez Perce Treaty of 1863. I have read these treaties. We have talked about them in my class."

I paused for a moment to study the crowd. Men and women twice my age were listening carefully to my words. Encouraged by their attentiveness, I quickly continued. "Our first treaty says that the government guarantees our right to fish at all usual and accustomed areas. The government meant for us to catch fish as we always have, wherever we used to fish. Louis Cohen, a lawyer from Spokane, came to my class and told us so. I think we should call Mr. Cohen and ask him to defend my brother and his friends, and our treaty rights."

My words took the people by surprise. Even my mother seemed stunned by my proposal. I was beginning to feel a little embarrassed when Clarence Paul, one of our tribal leaders, stood up.

"Andrew's words are good," he announced. "I think he is on the right track. There is more at stake here than freeing our friends." Clarence's voice became louder. "We must make a stand against the state. They have no right, under our treaty, to stop us from fishing. Our agreement is with the United States, and the state government can't interfere. I know this Louis Cohen. He is a man of honor who works well with Native American people. I say, we should ask him for his help."

People nodded their heads in agreement, and a murmur of approval spread through the group. We invited Louis Cohen to defend my brother and his friends.

All along I was confident we would win the case. But on the day we went to the district court in Camasville, I was not so certain. Outside the courthouse on the rolling green lawn, five drums beat. Many singers gathered around the drums, singing some of the old songs. My heart soared hearing those songs. I was proud of the support these people were showing for my brother and the others.

The drumming finally ended, and everyone filed into the crowded courtroom. I sat nervously with the families of the defendants, in a row of seats located behind my brother and the others. Several people offered moral support by handing feathers and bundles to those on trial.

We all stood up when the judge entered the courtroom. Television made the routine seem eerily familiar, but this was not a TV show. My brother's freedom was at stake. Our freedom to live as we once lived was at stake. I watched nervously as the judge and attorneys began acting out the courtroom ritual. I knew this was only a preliminary trial, where the prosecuting attorney and the defense attorney would present their cases. The judge would determine if there was a need for a trial. The prosecutor made her case against the defendants, arguing that they were fishing off the reservation without a state fishing license. She said they had broken several laws.

Then, Mr. Cohen stood up, pausing dramatically before making his opening statement. He turned thoughtfully, gazing at the Native Americans filling the seats of the small courtroom. Slowly, he faced the judge, a white woman about 50 years old. The judge sat quietly throughout the opening statements by the prosecutor, now and then taking notes. An uneasy look passed over the judge's face. She squirmed slightly, swiveling her large leather chair. Mr. Cohen's hesitation seemed to be making her impatient and irritable.

Mr. Cohen finally spoke. "Your Honor," he began, "please allow me to offer a little background information that might clarify this matter." The judge nodded slightly, encouraging Mr. Cohen to continue. "Matthew George, Watie Jim, Wendell Scott, and Anna Hawk are Nez Perce Native Americans. Their people lived here on this land long before the arrival of Lewis and Clark or any other white people. Their lives, even their religion, revolve around their ties to this place. For centuries, the Nez Perce fished for salmon. Whenever they took the first salmon of the season, they held a thanksgiving ceremony called the First Salmon Ceremony. A strong bond exists between the defendants and the salmon."

Mr. Cohen paused and reached for several pieces of paper, holding them up for all to see. "Your Honor, I have in my hand the Nez Perce Treaty of 1855, a treaty offered by the national government to the Nez Perce. At the treaty council, Governor Isaac I. Stevens, who represented the United States, told the Nez Perce that forevermore the government would recognize their right to take fish at any time of year, on or off the reservation."

"Your Honor, I have offered to you this treaty and many other cases to show that the four defendants had a legal right to fish on the Salmon River. If you carefully consider the evidence and my arguments, you will find that the state has no case against the defendants. I hope you will then order their immediate release."

When the court session ended and the judge retired to her chambers, everyone remained seated. But when Mr. Cohen rose to leave the court, my mother and I stood up with the other Native Americans to show our respect for our attorney.

The days passed with agonizing slowness while we awaited the judge's decision. My family went through the motions of normal life, but my brother's legal battle remained foremost in our thoughts. Several days after the court hearing, I returned home hot and sweaty from a basketball game with some friends. My mother tried to look casual, but she couldn't repress her smile. I knew immediately that we had won.

As we hurried to the car to pick up Matthew, my mother turned to me. "You should be proud of yourself, Andrew," she said. "You helped us that day at the river."

Her words astonished me. "It was you who suggested that we call Mr. Cohen," my mother continued, "and it was you who said that our treaty rights were at stake. You helped us to see what we needed to do."

The glow from my mother's praise warmed me throughout the afternoon and into the evening. The family celebrated Matthew's homecoming with a meal of broiled salmon, green beans, boiled potatoes, and huckleberry pie. We talked long into the night, but Grandfather left shortly after supper. He slipped out of the house quietly, crossing our backyard to his little house. Dawn was breaking when I finally retired to my room. Peering out my window, I noticed Grandfather's light was on.

As I walked toward the tattered screen of his front door, I saw him sitting in an ancient wooden rocker. His gray hair gleamed in the lamplight, and long strands of hair reached below his narrow shoulders. Grandfather's dark eyes stared out a cracked window into the fading night. He turned when I came into his house, and his old face wore a sadness I could not understand. After all, Matthew had come home.

"What's wrong, Grandfather?" I asked. He bowed his head, staring at the floor. I waited patiently for the old man to speak.

"Are you glad that Matthew has come home?" he finally asked. Of course I was. He nodded. "I am happy too, that all four have been released."

"Then why do you look so sad?" I asked. His attitude almost made me angry. "This was a night to celebrate. You hardly said a thing at supper." Leaning forward in his chair, Grandfather motioned for me to sit down across from him.

"Andrew, throughout all of this legal business, I have been very worried," he said. "I feel sad because I think our people have forgotten an important point. I am an old man. I believe strongly in our fishing rights. But these rights were not given to us by the white man. The law that gives us the right to fish comes from the Creator, not the government. The old stories tell us that Coyote led the salmon upstream to spawn and die. Coyote brought us this gift, so that we might live. When we catch the fish, we stop and give thanks. We sing and celebrate with prayers and feasting. You have done it yourself."

I nodded. I was listening very hard.

"Because we are tied to this earth," Grandfather continued, "we have a special responsibility to the plants and animals. We must take care of them, so that they will take care of us." My grandfather sighed. "This is our way, Andrew. Through all of our fights for fishing rights, now and in the future, we must not forget the fish. The Salmon People are like our brothers and sisters, and we are their caretakers."

I moved closer to Grandfather, placing my hand on his shoulder. I assured the old man that I would not abandon the ways of the Nez Perce.

"That is good," he said, placing his hand on mine. "Tell your children and their children." He paused. "As long as there are young people like you, Andrew, I think our traditions will live for a long time."

We went outside and sat close together, quietly sharing the beginning of the new day.

Extending Comprehension

(The following Extending Comprehension activities can be presented after students finish reading the story. The activities also appear in the *Literature Anthology.*)

1. (Students can answer the Story Questions either orally or in writing. If the questions are presented orally, use the script below.)
2. (Students can select one or more Discussion Topics. Discussions can take place in small groups or with the entire class.)
3. (Students can use the Writing Ideas to respond to the story in writing.)

Story Questions

1. Why were the four Nez Perce arrested? (Idea: *Because they were fishing illegally; because they were fishing without a state license.*)
2. How did Matthew's mother react when she found out her son had been arrested? (Ideas: *Calmly and powerfully; she spoke about not acting in anger; she wanted to call a council meeting to decide what to do.*)
3. What were some of the messages in the story Grandfather told about the Salmon People and Rattlesnake? (Ideas: *It doesn't pay to be greedy; it doesn't pay to be arrogant; be careful when you handle salmon.*)
4. What did Andrew speak about at the council meeting? (Ideas: *The rights of the Nez Perce according to the treaty; he suggested hiring Louis Cohen to defend his brother and the others.*)
5. What course of action did the tribe decide to take? (Idea: *It decided to hire Louis Cohen.*)
6. What was the background information that Mr. Cohen, the defendants' attorney, presented to the judge? (Ideas: *There is a strong bond between the Nez Perce and the salmon; the treaty stated that the Nez Perce could fish anytime of year, on or off the reservation.*)
7. Why was Grandfather sad near the end of the story? (Idea: *Because he was worried that the tribe would forget its special responsibility to the plants and animals; because he was concerned that the tribe would forget the fish were like their brothers and sisters; because he felt the salmon were more important than the tribe's rights to fish for them.*)

Discussion Topics

1. Andrew's grandfather was a wise man. He felt deeply about Nez Perce traditions. What were some things Grandfather did to make sure his tribe's traditions weren't forgotten? During your discussion, try to answer the following questions:
   - What was the main message of the legend about the Salmon People and Rattlesnake?
   - What "special responsibility" did Grandfather want Andrew to understand and carry on?

2. Pretend you are not a Nez Perce and you have to follow the state's laws about when you can fish. Do you agree with the judge's decision? During your discussion, try to answer the following questions:
   - Why shouldn't treaties that are over 100 years old still be legal?
   - Why should treaties that are over 100 years old still be legal?

Writing Ideas

1. One theme in this story is the importance of protecting the environment. Write a legend that sends this message.
2. Even though Andrew is a child, the adults in the tribe listened to his ideas. Why do you think it is important for adults to listen to children?
3. Pretend you are the lawyer for the state, the prosecuting attorney. Write a plan for what you will say to the judge in court.
4. Pretend you are the defense attorney for the four Nez Perce Native Americans who were arrested. Write a plan for what you will say to the judge in court.

Story 10

The No-Guitar Blues

New Vocabulary Words

Everybody, take out your *Literature Anthology.* Turn to page 146. ✔
What is the title of this story? (Signal.) *"The No-Guitar Blues."*
Who is the author? (Signal.) *Gary Soto.*

1. First we'll read some words from the story, and then we'll talk about what they mean.
2. Word 1 is **warehouseman.** What word? (Signal.) *Warehouseman.*
   - (Repeat for every numbered word.)
3. It's your turn to read all the words.
4. Word 1. What word? (Signal.) *Warehouseman.*
   - (Repeat for every numbered word.)
5. What words? (Signal.) *Mexican food.* (If you have Spanish speaking students in your class, have them read and pronounce the words for the other students. If not, use the following pronunciation guide to help the students pronounce these words:)
   - *Tortillas*—tor TEE uz
   - *Papas*—PAW puz
   - *Chorizo con huevos*—cho REE so cone WAY vose
   - *Empanadas*—em puh NAH duz

1. warehouseman
2. muscular
3. perpetual
4. stash
5. deceitful

6. zombie
7. confess
8. wicker
9. wrongdoing
10. freeway

11. Mexican foods:
   - tortillas
   - papas
   - chorizo con huevos
   - empanadas

Definitions

(For each definition, call on a student to read the definition aloud; then, present the tasks that go with that definition to the group.)

1. *A **warehouseman** lifts and moves things in a warehouse.*
   - A warehouse is a building in which lots of things are stored.
   - Everybody, what's another way of saying **The man lifted and moved things in the warehouse?** (Signal.) *The warehouseman lifted and moved things in the warehouse.*
2. *Someone who is **muscular** has well developed muscles.*
   - Here's another way of saying **Marcy has very well developed muscles: Marcy is very muscular.**

- Everybody, what's another way of saying **Marcy has very well developed muscles?** (Signal.) *Marcy is very muscular.*

3. *If something is **perpetual,** it never stops.*
   - Everybody, what do you call a clock that never stops? (Signal.) *A perpetual clock.*

4. *To **stash** something away is to put it in a secret place.*
   - Everybody, what's another way of saying **he hid the money in the shoe box?** (Signal.) *He stashed the money in the shoe box.*

5. *A **deceitful** person misleads other people by telling lies.*
   - Everybody, what's another way of saying **Susan lied to her mother when she said she had finished her homework?** (Signal.) *Susan deceived her mother when she said she had finished her homework.*

6. *Someone who looks like a **zombie** looks like someone who is almost dead.*
   - Everybody, what's another way of saying **Tim felt so bad he looked almost dead?** (Signal.) *Tim felt so bad he looked like a zombie.*

7. *When you **confess** something, you admit you did that thing.*
   - Everybody, what's another way of saying **Marie admitted that she broke the bowl?** (Signal.) *Marie confessed that she broke the bowl.*

8. *In some churches, a basket made of **wicker** is passed around for people to put money in.*
   - **Wicker** is a very strong kind of straw. Some furniture is made of wicker.

9. *A **wrongdoing** is an action that is against the rules.*
   - Here's another way of saying **When Sam rode his bike into the playground, he broke the rules: When Sam rode his bike into the playground he committed a wrongdoing.**
   - Everybody, what's another way of saying **When Sam rode his bike into the playground he broke the rules?** (Signal.) *When Sam rode his bike into the playground, he committed a wrongdoing.*

10. *A **freeway** is a highway with many lanes of traffic.*
    - Everybody, what's another way of saying **You must drive fast on the highway?** (Signal.) *You must drive fast on the freeway.*

11. *The following are **Mexican foods: Tortillas** are like flat pancakes; **papas** are potatoes; **chorizo con huevas** is fried sausage with eggs; **empanadas** are little pies filled with meat.*

Story Background

1. (Call on individual students to read two or three sentences each.)
2. (After students complete a section, ask the questions for that section.)

"The No-Guitar Blues" is a story about a young Mexican American boy who wants a guitar. He and his family live in California. "The Circuit," another story about a Mexican American boy who lives in California, appears earlier in this book. The two boys in these stories and their families are similar in some ways but very different in other ways. One way they are similar is the city in which they live or live near. The family in "The No-Guitar Blues" lives in the city of Fresno. The family in "The Circuit" lives for a while in a garage on a farm near Fresno.

- Which state is the setting for these two stories? (Signal.) *California.*
- Which city in California do the boys and their families live in or near? (Signal.) *Fresno.*

Another way these families are similar is that they keep the culture of Mexico alive in their daily lives. Both boys enjoy eating the Mexican food their mothers prepare. Both boys are interested in learning to play musical instruments so they can play the kind of music that comes from Mexico.

When you read these stories you will find more similarities between the two boys and their families. You will find many differences as well. One difference is how the story is told. "The Circuit" is told *by* a young boy, but the story in "The No-Guitar Blues" is told *about* a young boy.

- What are some of the ways the two boys are similar? (Ideas: *They both like to eat their mothers' good Mexican food; they want to learn to play musical instruments.*)
- What is different in how the two stories are told? (Idea: *One story is told by a boy, the other story is told about a boy.*)

Music is important to people all over the world. Many people from Mexico bring musical instruments with them when they come to the United States. They play the music of Mexico in their new homes. Fausto, the young boy in "The No-Guitar Blues," wants to learn to play the guitar so he can play in a rock band. But he wants to play in a Mexicanstyle rock band. Still, he talks about the Mexican music his parents like. They like *conjunto* (con HUNE toe) music, which often includes *corridos* (core REE dos) or sad songs that tell stories.

The narrator in "The Circuit" wants to learn to play the trumpet. He loves the sound of a trumpet, and has heard it in many Mexican *corridos*.

- What kind of music group does Fausto want to play in? (Idea: *A Mexican rock band.*)
- What kind of music groups do his parents like? (Ideas: *Conjunto music; music from Mexico.*)
- What kind of music groups does the narrator of "The Circuit" love to hear? (Ideas: *Corridos groups; groups with trumpets.*)

Focus Questions

1. (Call on individual students to read the Focus Questions aloud.)
2. (Remind students to think about to those questions as they read the story.)
   - *Why did Fausto want to learn to play the guitar?*
   - *Why did Fausto want to earn money?*
   - *Why did Fausto always have doubts about his plans?*
   - *How did Fausto resolve his doubts?*

The No-Guitar Blues
by Gary Soto
Illustrated by Anni Mastik

The moment Fausto saw the group Los Lobos on "American Bandstand," he knew exactly what he wanted to do with his life—play guitar. His eyes grew large with excitement as Los Lobos ground out a song while teenagers bounced off each other on the crowded dance floor.

He had watched "American Bandstand" for years and had heard Ray Camacho and the Teardrops at Romain Playground, but it had never occurred to him that he too might become a musician. That afternoon Fausto knew his mission in life: to play guitar in his own band; to sweat out his songs and prance around the stage; to make money and dress weird.

Fausto turned off the television set and walked outside, wondering how he could get enough money to buy a guitar. He couldn't ask his parents because they would just say, "Money doesn't grow on trees" or "What do you think we are, bankers?" And besides, they hated rock music. They were into the *conjunto* music of Lydia Mendoza, Flaco Jimenez, and Little Joe and La Familia. And, as Fausto recalled, the last album they bought was *The Chipmunks Sing Christmas Favorites*.

But what the heck, he'd give it a try. He returned inside and watched his mother make tortillas. He leaned against the kitchen counter, trying to work up the nerve to ask her for a guitar. Finally, he couldn't hold back any longer.

"Mom," he said, "I want a guitar for Christmas."

She looked up from rolling tortillas. "Honey, a guitar costs a lot of money."

"How 'bout for my birthday next year," he tried again.

"I can't promise," she said, turning back to her tortillas, "but we'll see."

Fausto walked back outside with a buttered tortilla. He knew his mother was right. His father was a warehouseman at Berven Rugs, where he made good money but not enough to buy everything his children wanted. Fausto decided to mow lawns to earn money, and was pushing the mower down the street before he realized it was winter and no one would hire him. He returned the mower and picked up a rake. He hopped onto his sister's bike (his had two flat tires) and rode north to the nicer section of Fresno in search of work. He went door-to-door, but after three hours he managed to get only one job, and not to rake leaves. He was asked to hurry down to the store to buy a loaf of bread, for which he received a grimy, dirt-caked quarter.

He also got an orange, which he ate sitting at the curb. While he was eating, a dog walked up and sniffed his leg. Fausto pushed him away and threw an orange peel skyward. The dog caught it and ate it in one gulp. The dog looked at Fausto and wagged his tail for more. Fausto tossed him a slice of orange, and the dog snapped it up and licked his lips.

"How come you like oranges, dog?"

The dog blinked a pair of sad eyes and whined.

"What's the matter? Cat got your tongue?" Fausto laughed at his joke and offered the dog another slice.

At that moment a dim light came on inside Fausto's head. He saw that it was sort of a fancy dog, a terrier or something, with dog tags and a shiny collar. And it looked well fed and healthy. In his neighborhood, the dogs were never licensed, and if they got sick they were placed near the water heater until they got well.

This dog looked like he belonged to rich people. Fausto cleaned his juice-sticky hands on his pants and got to his feet. The light in his head grew brighter. It just might work. He called the dog, patted its muscular back, and bent down to check the license.

"Great," he said. "There's an address."

The dog's name was Roger, which struck Fausto as weird because he'd never heard of a dog with a human name. Dogs should have names like Bomber, Freckles, Queenie, Killer, and Zero.

Fausto planned to take the dog home and collect a reward. He would say he had found Roger near the freeway. That would scare the daylights out of the owners, who would be so happy that they would probably give him a reward. He felt bad about lying, but the dog was loose. And it might even really be lost, because the address was six blocks away.

Fausto stashed the rake and his sister's bike behind a bush, and, tossing an orange peel every time Roger became distracted, walked the dog to his house. He hesitated on the porch until Roger began to scratch the door with a muddy paw. Fausto had come this far, so he figured he might as well go through with it. He knocked softly. When no one answered, he rang the doorbell. A man in a silky bathrobe and slippers opened the door and seemed confused by the sight of his dog and the boy.

"Sir," Fausto said, gripping Roger by the collar. "I found your dog by the freeway. His dog license says he lives here." Fausto looked down at the dog, then up to the man. "He does, doesn't he?"

The man stared at Fausto a long time before saying in a pleasant voice, "That's right." He pulled his robe tighter around him because of the cold and asked Fausto to come in. "So he was by the freeway?"

"Uh-huh."

"You bad, snoopy dog," said the man, wagging his finger. "You probably knocked over some trash cans, too, didn't you?"

Fausto didn't say anything. He looked around, amazed by this house with its shiny furniture and a television as large as the front window at home. Warm bread smells filled the air and music full of soft tinkling floated in from another room.

"Helen," the man called to the kitchen. "We have a visitor." His wife came into the living room wiping her hands on a dishtowel and smiling. "And who have we here?" she asked in one of the softest voices Fausto had ever heard.

"This young man said he found Roger near the freeway."

Fausto repeated his story to her while staring at a perpetual clock with a bell-shaped glass, the kind his aunt got when she celebrated her twenty-fifth anniversary. The lady frowned and said, wagging a finger at Roger, "Oh, you're a bad boy."

"It was very nice of you to bring Roger home," the man said. "Where do you live?"

"By that vacant lot on Olive," he said. "You know, by Brownie's Flower Place."

The wife looked at her husband, then Fausto. Her eyes twinkled triangles of light as she said, "Well, young man, you're probably hungry. How about a turnover?"

"What do I have to turn over?" Fausto asked, thinking she was talking about yard work or something like turning trays of dried raisins.

"No, no, dear, it's a pastry." She took him by the elbow and guided him to a kitchen that sparkled with copper pans and bright yellow wallpaper. She guided him to the kitchen table and gave him a tall glass of milk and something that looked like an *empanada*. Steamy waves of heat escaped when he tore it in two. He ate with both eyes on the man and woman who stood arm-in-arm smiling at him. They were strange, he thought. But nice.

"That was good," he said after he finished the turnover. "Did you make it, ma'am?"

"Yes, I did. Would you like another?"

"No, thank you. I have to go home now."

As Fausto walked to the door, the man opened his wallet and took out a bill. "This is for you," he said. "Roger is special to us, almost like a son."

Fausto looked at the bill and knew he was in trouble. Not with these nice folks or with his parents but with himself. How could he have been so deceitful? The dog wasn't lost. It was just having a fun Saturday walking around.

"I can't take that."

"You have to. You deserve it, believe me," the man said.

"No, I don't."

"Now don't be silly," said the lady. She took the bill from her husband and stuffed it into Fausto's shirt pocket. "You're a lovely child. Your parents are lucky to have you. Be good. And come to see us again, please."

Fausto went out, and the lady closed the door. Fausto clutched the bill through his shirt pocket. He felt like ringing the doorbell and begging them to please take the money back, but he knew they would refuse. He hurried away, and at the end of the block, pulled the bill from his shirt pocket: it was a crisp twenty-dollar bill.

"Oh, man, I shouldn't have lied," he said under his breath as he started up the street like a zombie. He wanted to run to church for Saturday confession, but it was past four-thirty, when confession stopped.

He returned to the bush where he had hidden the rake and his sister's bike and rode home slowly, not daring to touch the money in his pocket. At home, in the privacy of his room, he examined the twenty-dollar bill. He had never had so much money. It was probably enough to buy a secondhand guitar. But he felt bad, like the time he stole a dollar from the secret fold inside his older brother's wallet.

Fausto went outside and sat on the fence. "Yeah," he said. "I can probably get a guitar for twenty. Maybe at a yard sale—things are cheaper."

His mother called him to dinner.

The next day he dressed for church without anyone telling him. He was going to go to eight o'clock mass.

"I'm going to church, Mom," he said. His mother was in the kitchen cooking *papas* and *chorizo con huevos*. A pile of tortillas lay warm under a dishtowel.

"Oh, I'm so proud of you, Son." She beamed, turning over the crackling *papas*.

His older brother, Lawrence, who was at the table reading the funnies, mimicked, "Oh, I'm so proud of you, my son," under his breath.

At Saint Theresa's he sat near the front. When Father Jerry began by saying we are all sinners, Fausto thought he looked right at him. Could he know? Fausto fidgeted with guilt. No, he thought. I only did it yesterday.

Fausto knelt, prayed, and sang. But he couldn't forget the man and the lady, whose names he didn't even know, and the *empanada* they had given him. It had a strange name but tasted really good. He wondered how they got rich. And how that dome clock worked. He had asked his mother once how his aunt's clock worked. She said it just worked, the way the refrigerator works. It just did.

Fausto caught his mind wandering and tried to concentrate on his sins. He said a Hail Mary and sang, and when the wicker basket came his way, he stuck a hand reluctantly in his pocket and pulled out the twenty-dollar bill. He ironed it between his palms, and dropped it into the basket. The grown-ups stared. Here was a kid dropping twenty dollars in the basket, while they gave just three or four dollars.

There would be a second collection for Saint Vincent de Paul, the lector announced. The wicker baskets again floated in the pews, and this time the adults around him, given a second chance to show their charity, dug deep into their wallets and purses and dropped in fives and tens. This time Fausto tossed in the grimy quarter.

Fausto felt better after church. He went home and played football in the front yard with his brother and some neighbor kids. He felt cleared of wrongdoing and was so happy that he played one of his best games of football ever. On one play, he tore his good pants, which he knew he shouldn't have been wearing. For a second, while he examined the hole, he wished he hadn't given the twenty dollars away.

Man, I coulda bought me some Levi's, he thought. He pictured his twenty dollars being spent to buy church candles. He pictured a priest buying an armful of flowers with *his* money.

Fausto had to forget about getting a guitar. He spent the next day playing soccer in his good pants, which were now his old pants. But that night during dinner, his mother said she remembered seeing an old bass guitarron the last time she cleaned out her father's garage.

"It's a little dusty," his mom said, serving his favorite enchiladas, "But I think it works. Grandpa says it works."

Fausto's ears perked up. That was the same kind the guy in Los Lobos played. Instead of asking for the guitar, he waited for his mother to offer it to him. And she did, while gathering the dishes from the table.

"No, Mom, I'll do it," he said, hugging her. "I'll do the dishes forever if you want."

It was the happiest day of his life. No, it was the second-happiest day of his life. The happiest was when his grandfather Lupe placed the guitarron, which was nearly as huge as a washtub, in his arms. Fausto ran a thumb down the strings, which vibrated in his throat and chest. It sounded beautiful, deep and eerie. A pumpkin smile widened on his face.

"OK, *hijo,* now you put your fingers like this," said his grandfather, smelling of tobacco and aftershave. He took Fausto's fingers and placed them on the strings. Fausto strummed a chord on the guitarron, and the bass resounded in their chests.

The guitarron was more complicated than Fausto imagined. But he was confident that after a few more lessons he could start a band that would someday play on "American Bandstand" for the dancing crowds.

Extending Comprehension

(The following Extending Comprehension activities can be presented after students finish reading the story. The activities also appear in the *Literature Anthology*.)

1. (Students can answer the Story Questions either orally or in writing. If the questions are presented orally, use the script below.)

2. (Students can select one or more Discussion Topics. Discussions can take place in small groups or with the entire class.)

3. (Students can use the Writing Ideas to respond to the story in writing.)

Story Questions

1. Why did Fausto want to learn to play the guitar? (Ideas: *He wanted to play in his own band; he wanted to be like the musicians he watched on television.*)

2. What are the first two ideas that Fausto had for earning money? (Ideas: *He would mow lawns; he would rake leaves.*)

3. What made Fausto think Roger belonged to rich people? (Ideas: *Roger looked like a fancy dog; he had dog tags and a fancy collar; he looked well fed and healthy.*)

4. Why did Fausto feel bad after the man gave him the money? (Ideas: *Fausto knew he hadn't been truthful; even though the man and the woman had been nice to him, Fausto had accepted their money.*)

5. Why did Fausto decide to go to confession? (Ideas: *He knew he had done the wrong thing; he felt bad because he had accepted money; he had not told the man and the woman the truth.*)

6. Tell why many people in the church put more money in the wicker basket the second time it went around. (Ideas: *They saw that a young boy had put in a lot of money, so they put in more money.*)

7. Give at least two reasons why Fausto was happy at the end of the story. (Ideas: *He had given away the money that he didn't feel right about having; he felt cleared of his wrongdoing; his grandfather gave him a guitarron and was helping him learn to play it.*)

Discussion Topics

1. "The No-Guitar Blues" begins and ends with descriptions of music and of playing musical instruments. Fausto wants to become a musician. Do you think he will succeed? Talk about what he would have to do to become a musician good enough to play in a group. During your discussion, try to answer the following questions:
   - What must people do to learn to play an instrument?
   - How do you think young people can learn to play in a group?
   - Would you like to be a musician? What kind?
   - Would you like to play in a group? In a band? In an orchestra?

2. After he took the $20 from the man, Fausto knew he had committed a wrongdoing. Before the story ends, Fausto finds a way to forgive himself. Discuss what he did and some other things he could have done. During your discussion, try to answer the following questions:
   - What does Fausto do to forgive himself?
   - What are some other things he could have done?
   - What would you have done?
   - Did Fausto learn something about himself by the end of the story?

Writing Ideas

1. Pretend a friend of Fausto's mother tells her that Fausto put $20 in the wicker basket at church. Fausto's mother asks him for an explanation. She wants to know where he got the $20 and why he gave it away. Pretend you are Fausto writing a letter of explanation to his mother. Tell why you needed money and the ideas you had for earning money. Then tell about Roger and what you decided to do with him. Describe the man and the woman and how the man gave you the $20. Then tell what made you decide that you shouldn't keep the $20 and what you decided to do so you would feel better.

2. Compare the families in "The Circuit" and "The No-Guitar Blues." Tell three ways the families are similar to each other, then tell three ways they are different from each other.

3. Write about a time you felt bad because you knew you had done something wrong. Then tell what you did to feel better.

4. The author says that the day that Fausto's grandfather placed the guitarron in his arms was the happiest day of Fausto's life. Write about one of the happiest days of your life. Tell what happened and why it made you feel happy.

Raymond's Run

New Vocabulary Words

Everybody, take out your *Literature Anthology*. Turn to page 157. ✔
What is the title of this story? (Signal.) *Raymond's Run.*
Who is the author? (Signal.) *Toni Cade Bambara.*

1. First we'll read some words from the story, and then we'll talk about what they mean.
2. Line 1 is **playing the dozens.** What words? (Signal.) *Playing the dozens.*
   • (Repeat for every numbered word.)
3. It's your turn to read all the words.
4. Line 1. What words? (Signal.) *Playing the dozens.*
   • (Repeat for every numbered word.)

1. playing the dozens	5. sidekicks	9. periscope
2. Mercury	6. May Pole	10. gesture
3. island	7. corsages	11. psyching up
4. prodigy	8. bongos	12. jutting out

Definitions

(For each definition: call on a student to read the definition aloud; then, present the tasks that go with that definition to the group.)

1. *When kids are **playing the dozens,** they are trying to outwit each other.*
   • **Playing the dozens** involves people criticizing or making fun of each other.
   • Everybody, what is another way of saying **The students were trying to outwit each other?** (Signal.) *The students were playing the dozens.*
2. **Mercury** *is the name of a Roman god who travels swiftly. He is sometimes called Quicksilver.*
   • Everybody, what is the name of the Roman god who travels swiftly? (Signal.) *Mercury.*
   • What's another name for Mercury? (Signal.) *Quicksilver.*
3. *In a city, an **island** is a safety zone in the middle of a busy street.*
   • Everybody, what is a safety zone in the middle of a busy street? (Signal.) *An island.*
4. *A young person with exceptional talent is a **prodigy.***
   • Everybody, what do you call a young person with exceptional talent? (Signal.) *A prodigy.*
5. *A **sidekick** is a very close friend.*
   • Everybody, what's another way of saying **Jason and his friends came to the party?** (Signal.) *Jason and his sidekicks came to the party.*

6. *A **May Pole** is a tall pole decorated with streamers. Children hold the streamers and dance around the pole.*
    - Everybody, what do you call a tall pole decorated with streamers? (Signal.) *A May Pole.*
7. *A **corsage** is a small bouquet of flowers worn by a woman.*
    - Everybody, what's another way of saying **Marsha was given a small bouquet of flowers to wear on her dress?** (Signal.) *Marsha was given a corsage to wear on her dress.*
8. ***Bongos** are a pair of connected drums that are beaten with the hands.*
    - Everybody, what do you call a pair of connected drums that are beaten with the hands? (Signal.) *Bongos.*
9. *A **periscope** is an instrument that contains lenses and mirrors. These are arranged so people can get a view of something that is not in their direct line of vision.*
    - Sailors in a submarine use a periscope to see things above the submarine.
    - Everybody, what is an instrument people can use to look at something that is not in their direct line of vision? (Signal.) *A periscope.*
10. *When people use hand or body movements to express an idea or a feeling, they are making **gestures**.*
    - Everybody, what is another way of saying **Mr. Pearson started the race with a hand movement?** (Signal.) *Mr. Pearson started the race with a gesture.*
11. *When a runner is **psyching up** for a race, she gets herself mentally ready for the race.*
    - Everybody, what is another way of saying **Mary is getting herself mentally ready for the race?** (Signal.) *Mary is psyching up for the race.*
12. *Something that **juts out,** sticks out.*
    - Everybody, what is another way of saying **Rosie's chin is sticking out?** (Signal.) *Rosie's chin is jutting out.*
    - Everybody, what is another way of saying **The dock stuck out into the lake?** (Signal.) *The dock jutted out into the lake.*

Story Background

1. (Call on individual students to read two or three sentences.)
2. (After students complete a section, ask the questions for that section.)

> The setting for "Raymond's Run" is New York City. Toni Cade Bambara, the author of this story, has spent most of her life in New York City. She writes stories and novels about people who live there. Her characters do things that people do every day in New York City, and they talk like many of the people who live there.
>
> New York City has the most people of any city in the United States. Over seven million people live in this city. If you look at a picture book of New York, you will see pictures of tall skyscrapers, big hotels, and beautiful parks. When you watch television shows that take place in New York, you sometimes see the beautiful offices of important people who are wearing expensive-looking clothes and the fancy apartments in which they live.

- Everybody, who is the author of the story you are going to read? (Signal.) *Toni Cade Bambara.*

- What city does she write about? (Signal.) *New York.*
- What are some of the things you see in picture books of New York and in television shows that take place in New York? (Ideas: *Tall skyscrapers; big hotels; beautiful parks; beautiful offices; fancy apartments; good looking people wearing expensive clothes.*)

When Toni Cade Bambara writes about New York, she doesn't write about tall buildings and people who wear expensive clothes. Rather, she writes about lesser known parts of the city and about the lives of the everyday people who live, work, and play in these places. Like Mavis Jukes, who wrote "Like Jake and Me," Toni Cade Bambara writes realistic fiction for young people. In their stories, these authors create characters who may remind us of people we know. They write about events that may be similar to our own experiences.

If you live in a big city, you may feel right at home as you read "Raymond's Run." If you don't live in a big city, you may learn about the lives of young people who live in a big city. As you read the story, pay attention to the narrator and what she says about her family and her teachers and how she deals with the kids in her neighborhood.

- Does Toni Cade Bambara write about tall buildings and people who wear expensive clothes? (Signal.) *No.*
- What kind of fiction does she write? (Signal.) *Realistic fiction.*

The title, "Raymond's Run," contains the name of the narrator's brother. Although Raymond is older than his sister, their family puts her in charge of him. She is in charge of him because, as she says, "He's not quite right." We don't learn much more about how or why Raymond is not quite right, except that his head is big. We do learn that he walks down the street in an odd way, but that his sister doesn't put up with anyone making fun of him. We also learn that he has a hidden talent, but we have to wait to the end of the story to find out what it is.

- Who are you going to pay particular attention to when you read the story? (Signal.) *The narrator.*
- What is the name of the narrator's brother? (Signal.) *Raymond.*
- What do you learn about him? (Ideas: *That he's not quite right; that he has a big head; that he walks down the street in an odd way; that she defends him.*)
- What are we going to find out about Raymond? (Idea: *That he has a hidden talent.*)

Focus Questions

1. (Call on individual students to read the Focus Questions aloud.)
2. (Remind students to refer to these questions as they read the story.)
   - *What is the narrator's nickname? Why does she have that name? What is her real name?*
   - *What does the narrator say and do to let you know she is serious about running?*
   - *Why is the narrator critical of Cynthia Proctor and the girls she meets on the sidewalk?*
   - *What is the narrator's attitude toward dressing up for the May Pole dance and wearing a strawberry costume?*
   - *What different things do you learn about Raymond as you read the story?*

- *How does what the narrator says about smiles at the end of the story change from what she said in the middle of the story?*
- *What happens at the end of the May Day race to make the narrator laugh out loud?*

Raymond's Run
by Toni Cade Bambara
Illustrated by Doris Ettlinger

I don't have much work to do around the house like some girls. My mother does that. And I don't have to earn my pocket money by hustling; George runs errands for the big boys and sells Christmas cards. And anything else that's got to get done, my father does. All I have to do in life is mind my brother Raymond, which is enough.

Sometimes I slip and say my little brother Raymond. But as any fool can see he's much bigger and he's older too. But a lot of people call him my little brother cause he needs looking after cause he's not quite right. And a lot of smart mouths got lots to say about that too, especially when George was minding him. But now, if anybody has anything to say to Raymond, anything to say about his big head, they have to come by me. And I don't play the dozens or believe in standing around with somebody in my face doing a lot of talking. I much rather just knock you down and take my chances even if I am a little girl with skinny arms and a squeaky voice, which is how I got the name Squeaky. And if things get too rough, I run. And as anybody can tell you, I'm the fastest thing on two feet.

There is no track meet that I don't win the first place medal. I used to win the twenty-yard dash when I was a little kid in kindergarten. Nowadays, it's the fifty-yard dash. And tomorrow I'm subject to run the quarter-meter relay all by myself and come in first, second, and third. The big kids call me Mercury cause I'm the swiftest thing in the neighborhood. Everybody knows that—except two people who know better, my father and me. He can beat me to Amsterdam Avenue with me having a two fire-hydrant headstart and him running with his hands in his pockets and whistling. But that's private information. Cause you can imagine some thirty-five-year-old man stuffing himself into PAL shorts to race little kids? So as far as everyone's concerned, I'm the fastest and that goes for Gretchen, too, who has put out the tale that she is going to win the first-place medal this year. Ridiculous. In the second place, she's got short legs. In the third place, she's got freckles. In the first place, no one can beat me and that's all there is to it.

I'm standing on the corner admiring the weather and about to take a stroll down Broadway so I can practice my breathing exercises, and I've got Raymond walking on the inside close to the buildings, cause he's subject to fits of fantasy and starts thinking he's a circus performer and that the curb is a tightrope strung high in the air. And sometimes after a rain he likes to step down off his tightrope right into the gutter and slosh around getting his shoes and cuffs wet. Then I get hit when I get home. Or sometimes if you don't watch him he'll dash across traffic to the island in the middle of Broadway and give the pigeons a fit. Then I have to go behind him apologizing to all the old people sitting around trying to get some sun and getting all upset with the pigeons fluttering around them, scattering their newspapers and upsetting the waxpaper lunches in their laps. So I keep Raymond on the inside of me, and he plays like he's driving a stage coach which is O.K. by me so long as he doesn't run me over or interrupt my breathing exercises, which I have to do on account of I'm serious about my running, and I don't care who knows it.

Now some people like to act like things come easy to them, won't let on that they practice. Not me. I'll high-prance down 34th Street like a rodeo pony to keep my knees strong even if it does get my mother uptight so that she walks ahead like she's not with me, don't know me, is all by herself on a shopping trip, and I am somebody else's crazy child. Now you take Cynthia Procter for instance. She's just the opposite. If there's a test tomorrow, she'll say something like, "Oh, I guess I'll play handball this afternoon and watch television tonight," just to let you know she ain't thinking about the test. Or like last week when she won the spelling bee for the millionth time, "A good thing you got 'receive,' Squeaky, cause I would have got it wrong. I completely forgot about the spelling bee." And she'll clutch the lace on her blouse like it was a narrow escape. Oh, brother. But of course when I pass her house on my early morning trots around the block, she is practicing the scales on the piano over and over and over and over. Then in music class she always lets herself get bumped around so she falls accidentally on purpose onto the piano stool and is so surprised to find herself sitting there that she decides just for fun to try out the ole keys. And what do you know— Chopin's waltzes just spring out of her fingertips and she's the most surprised thing in the world. A regular prodigy. I could kill people like that. I stay up all night studying the words for the spelling bee. And you can see me any time of day practicing running. I never walk if I can trot, and shame on Raymond if he can't keep up. But of course he does, cause if he hangs back someone's liable to walk up to him and get smart, or take his allowance from him, or ask him where he got that great big pumpkin head. People are so stupid sometimes.

So I'm strolling down Broadway breathing out and breathing in on counts of seven, which is my lucky number, and here comes Gretchen and her sidekicks: Mary Louise, who used to be a friend of mine when she first moved to Harlem from Baltimore and got beat up by everybody till I took up for her on account of her mother and my mother used to sing in the same choir when they were young girls, but people ain't grateful, so now she hangs out with the new girl Gretchen and talks about me like a dog; and Rosie, who is as fat as I am skinny and has a big mouth where Raymond is concerned and is too stupid to know that there is not a big deal of difference between herself and Raymond and that she can't afford to throw stones. So they are steady coming up Broadway and I see right away that it's going to be one of those Dodge City scenes cause the street ain't that big and they're close to the buildings just as we are. First I think I'll step into the candy store and look over the new comics and let them pass. But that's chicken and I've got a reputation to consider. So then I think I'll just walk straight on through them or even over them if necessary. But as they get to me, they slow down. I'm ready to fight, cause like I said I don't feature a whole lot of chit-chat, I much prefer to just knock you down right from the jump and save everybody a lotta precious time.

"You signing up for the May Day races?" smiles Mary Louise, only it's not a smile at all. A dumb question like that doesn't deserve an answer. Besides, there's just me and Gretchen standing there really, so no use wasting my breath talking to shadows.

"I don't think you're going to win this time," says Rosie, trying to signify with her hands on her hips all salty, completely forgetting that I have whupped her behind many times for less salt than that.

"I always win cause I'm the best," I say straight at Gretchen who is, as far as I'm concerned, the only one talking in this ventriloquist-dummy routine. Gretchen smiles, but it's not a smile, and I'm thinking that girls never really smile at each other because they don't know how and don't want to know how and there's probably no one to teach us how, cause grown-up girls don't know either. Then they all look at Raymond who has just brought his mule team to a standstill. And they're about to see what trouble they can get into through him.

"What grade you in now, Raymond?"

"You got anything to say to my brother, you say it to me, Mary Louise Williams of Raggedy Town, Baltimore."

"What are you, his mother?" sasses Rosie.

"That's right, Fatso. And the next word out of anybody and I'll be their mother too." So they just stand there and Gretchen shifts from one leg to the other and so do they. Then Gretchen puts her hands on her hips and is about to say something with her freckle-face self but doesn't. Then she walks around me looking me up and down but keeps walking up Broadway, and her sidekicks follow her. So me and Raymond smile at each other and he says, "Gidyap" to his team and I continue with my breathing exercises, strolling down Broadway toward the ice man on 145th with not a care in the world cause I am Miss Quicksilver herself.

I take my time getting to the park on May Day because the track meet is the last thing on the program. The biggest thing on the program is the May Pole dancing, which I can do without, thank you, even if my mother thinks it's a shame I don't take part and act like a girl for a change. You'd think my mother'd be grateful not to have to make me a white organdy dress with a big satin sash and buy me new white baby-doll shoes that can't be taken out of the box till the big day. You'd think she'd be glad her daughter ain't out there prancing around a May Pole getting the new clothes all dirty and sweaty and trying to act like a fairy or a flower or whatever you're supposed to be when you should be trying to be yourself, whatever that is, which is, as far as I am concerned, a poor Black girl who really can't afford to buy shoes and a new dress you only wear once a lifetime cause it won't fit next year.

I was once a strawberry in a Hansel and Gretel pageant when I was in nursery school and didn't have no better sense than to dance on tiptoe with my arms in a circle over my head doing umbrella steps and being a perfect fool just so my mother and father could come dressed up and clap. You'd think they'd know better than to encourage that kind of nonsense. I am not a strawberry. I do not dance on my toes. I run. That is what I am all about. So I always come late to the May Day program, just in time to get my number pinned on and lay in the grass till they announce the fifty-yard dash.

I put Raymond in the little swings, which is a tight squeeze this year and will be impossible next year. Then I look around for Mr. Pearson, who pins the number on. I'm really looking for Gretchen if you want to know the truth, but she's not around. The park is jam-packed. Parents in hats and corsages and breast-pocket handkerchiefs peeking up. Kids in white dresses and light-blue suits. The parkees unfolding chairs and chasing the rowdy kids from Lenox as if they had no right to be there. The big guys with their caps on backwards, leaning against the fence swirling the basketballs on the tips of their fingers, waiting for all these crazy people to clear out the park so they can play. Most of the kids in my class are carrying bass drums and glockenspiels and flutes. You'd think they'd put a few bongos or something for real like that.

Then here comes Mr. Pearson with his clipboard and his cards and pencils and whistles and safety pins and fifty million other things he's always dropping all over the place with his clumsy self. He sticks out in a crowd because he's on stilts. We used to call him Jack and the Beanstalk to get him mad. But I'm the only one that can out run him and get away, and I'm too grown for that silliness now.

"Well, Squeaky," he says, checking my name off the list and handing me number seven and two pins. And I'm thinking he's got no right to call me Squeaky, if I can't call him Beanstalk.

"Hazel Elizabeth Deborah Parker," I correct him and tell him to write it down on his board.

"Well, Hazel Elizabeth Deborah Parker, going to give someone else a break this year?" I squint at him real hard to see if he is seriously thinking I should lose the race on purpose just to give someone else a break. "Only six girls running this time," he continues, shaking his head sadly like it's my fault all of New York didn't turn out in sneakers. "That new girl should give you a run for your money." He looks around the park for Gretchen like a periscope in a submarine movie. "Wouldn't it be a nice gesture if you were . . . to ahhh . . ."

I give him such a look he couldn't finish putting that idea into words. Grownups got a lot of nerve sometimes. I pin number seven to myself and stomp away, I'm so burnt. And I go straight for the track and stretch out on the grass while the band winds up with "Oh, the Monkey Wrapped his Tail Around the Flag Pole," which my teacher calls by some other name. The man on the loudspeaker is calling everyone to the track and I'm on my back looking at the sky, trying to pretend I'm in the country, but I can't, because even grass in the city feels hard as sidewalk, and there's just no pretending you are anywhere but in a "concrete jungle" as my grandfather says.

The twenty-yard dash takes all of two minutes cause most of the little kids don't know no better than to run off the track or run the wrong way or run smack into the fence and fall down and cry. One little kid, though, has got the good sense to run straight for the white ribbon up ahead so he wins. Then the second-graders line up for the thirty-yard dash and I don't even bother to turn my head to watch cause Raphael Perez always wins. He wins before he even begins by psyching the runners, telling them they're going to trip on their shoelaces and fall on their faces or lose their shorts or something, which he doesn't really have to do since he is very fast, almost as fast as I am. After that is the forty-yard dash which I use to run when I was in first grade. Raymond is hollering from the swings cause he knows I'm about to do my thing cause the man on the loudspeaker announced the fifty-yard dash, although he might just as well be giving a recipe for angel food cake cause you can hardly make out what he's sayin for the static. I get up and slip off my sweat pants and then I see Gretchen standing at the starting line, kicking her legs out like a pro. Then as I get into place I see that ole Raymond is on line on the other side of the fence, bending down with his fingers on the ground just like he knew what he was doing. I was going to yell at him but then I didn't. It burns up your energy to holler.

Every time, just before I take off in a race, I always feel like I'm in a dream, the kind of dream you have when you're sick with fever and feel all hot and weightless. I dream I'm flying over a sandy beach in the early morning sun, kissing the leaves of the trees as I fly by. And there's always the smell of apples, just like in the country when I was little and used to think I was a choo-choo train, running through the fields of corn and chugging up the hill to the orchard. And all the time I'm dreaming this, I get lighter and lighter until I'm flying over the beach again, getting blown through the sky like a feather that weighs nothing at all. But once I spread my fingers in the dirt and crouch over the Get on Your Mark, the dream goes and I am solid again and am telling myself, Squeaky you must win, you must win, you are the fastest thing in the world, you can even beat your father up Amsterdam if you really try. And then I feel my weight coming back just behind my knees then down to my feet then into the earth and the pistol shot explodes in my blood and I am off and weightless again, flying past the other runners, my arms pumping up and down and the whole world is quiet except for the crunch as I zoom over the gravel in the track. I glance to my left and there is no one. To the right, a blurred Gretchen, who's got her chin jutting out as if it would win the race all by itself. And on the other side of the fence is Raymond with his arms down to his side and the palms tucked up behind him, running in his very own style, and it's the first time I ever saw that and I almost stop to watch my brother Raymond on his first run. But the white ribbon is bouncing toward me and I tear past it, racing into the distance till my feet with a mind of their own start digging up footfuls of dirt and brake me short. Then all the kids standing on the side pile on me, banging me on the back and slapping my head with their May Day programs, for I have won again and everybody on 151st Street can walk tall for another year.

"In first place . . ." the man on the loudspeaker is clear as a bell now. But then he pauses and the loudspeaker starts to whine. Then static. And I lean down to catch my breath and here comes Gretchen walking back, for she's overshot the finish line too, huffing and puffing with her hands on her hips taking it slow, breathing in steady time like a real pro and I sort of like her a little for the first time. "In first place . . ." and then three or four voices get all mixed up on the loudspeaker and I dig my sneaker into the grass and stare at Gretchen who's staring back, we both wondering just who did win. I can hear old Beanstalk arguing with the man on the loudspeaker and then a few others running their mouths about what the stopwatches say. Then I hear Raymond yanking at the fence to call me and I wave to shush him, but he keeps rattling the fence like a gorilla in a cage like in them gorilla movies, but then like a dancer or something he starts climbing up nice and easy but very fast. And it occurs to me, watching how smoothly he climbs hand over hand and remembering how he looked running with his arms down to his side and with the wind pulling his mouth back and his teeth showing and all, it occurred to me that Raymond would make a very fine runner. Doesn't he always keep up with me on my trots? And he surely knows how to breathe in counts of seven cause he's always doing it at the dinner table, which drives my brother George up the wall. And I'm smiling to beat the band cause if I've lost this race, or if me and Gretchen tied, or even if I've won, I can always retire as a runner and begin a whole new career as a coach with Raymond as my champion. After all, with a little more study I can beat Cynthia and her phony self at the spelling bee. And if I bugged my mother, I could get piano lessons and become a star. And I have a big rep as the baddest thing around. And I've got a roomful of ribbons and medals and awards. But what has Raymond got to call his own?

So I stand there with my new plans, laughing out loud by this time as Raymond jumps down from the fence and runs over with his teeth showing and his arms down to the side, which no one before him has quite mastered as a running style. And by the time he comes over I'm jumping up and down so glad to see him—my brother Raymond, a great runner in the family tradition. But of course everyone thinks I'm jumping up and down because the men on the loudspeaker have finally gotten themselves together and compared notes and are announcing, "In first place—Miss Hazel Elizabeth Deborah Parker." (Dig that.) "In second place—Miss Gretchen P. Lewis." And I look over at Gretchen wondering what the "P" stands for. And I smile. Cause she's good, no doubt about it. Maybe she'd like to help me coach Raymond; she obviously is serious about running, as any fool can see. And she nods to congratulate me and then she smiles. And I smile. We stand there with this big smile of respect between us. It's about as real a smile as girls can do for each other, considering we don't practice real smiling every day, you know, cause maybe we too busy being flowers or fairies or strawberries instead of something honest and worthy of respect . . . you know . . . like being people.

Extending Comprehension

(The following Extending Comprehension activities can be presented after students finish reading the story. The activities also appear in the *Literature Anthology*.)

1. (Students can answer the Story Questions either orally or in writing. If the questions are presented orally, use the script below.)

2. (Students can select one or more Discussion Topics. Discussions can take place in small groups or with the entire class.)

3. (Students can use the Writing Ideas to respond to the story in writing.)

Story Questions

1. In what ways does Squeaky watch out for Raymond? Describe three events from the story that show how she takes care of him.
   * (Ideas: *She has Raymond walk next to the buildings, away from the street; she makes sure he walks or runs near her; she won't let people take advantage of him; when they get to the race, she puts him in a swing; she decides she should coach him so that he can become a runner.*)

2. How does Squeaky let you know she is serious about running? Give two examples from the story.
   * (Ideas: *Squeaky says she always wins first place medals; she practices her breathing exercises; she keeps her knees strong by high prancing down the sidewalk; she has a lot of confidence in her ability to win races; she tells how she gets ready for a race.*)

3. Why is Squeaky critical of Cynthia Proctor and the girls she meets on the sidewalk?
   * (Ideas: *She thinks Cynthia Proctor is a phony; she thinks the girls on the sidewalk want to get the best of her; she thinks people want to tease Raymond and take advantage of him.*)

4. How does Squeaky feel about dressing up for the May Pole dance and wearing a strawberry costume? Tell how she feels and why she feels that way.
   - (Ideas: *She doesn't like to dress up; she thinks a poor girl shouldn't buy new shoes and a new dress that she wears only once; she thinks it's foolish to pretend to be a strawberry.*)
5. Describe one thing Raymond is doing at the beginning of the story and one thing he is doing at the end of the story.
   - (Ideas: *At the beginning of the story, Raymond is walking along the street pretending to drive a stage coach; at the end of the story, Raymond jumps over the fence and runs to his sister.*)
6. In the middle of the story, what does Squeaky say about the smiles of girls she knows? What does she say about smiles at the end of the story?
   - (Ideas: *In the middle of the story, girls don't know how to really smile at each other; at the end of the story, she and Gretchen are smiling real smiles—smiles of respect.*)
7. What happens at the May Day race to make Squeaky think about changing her plans?
   - (Ideas: *She sees that Raymond can run; she realizes that Gretchen is a good runner; she respects Gretchen.*)

Discussion Topics

1. Squeaky uses a lot of **colorful language** to describe the people she knows and the neighborhood in which she lives. Some quotations from the story appear below. Break up into groups. Take turns reading what Squeaky says. Then discuss what she is talking about.
   - "The big kids call me Mercury cause I'm the swiftest thing in the neighborhood."
   - "He can beat me to Amsterdam Avenue with a two fire-hydrant headstart."
   - "I've got Raymond walking on the inside close to the building, cause he's subject to fits of fantasy and starts thinking he's a circus performer and that the curb is a tightrope strung high in the air."
   - "I'll high-prance down 34th Street like a rodeo pony to keep my knees strong."
   - "Sometimes, if you don't watch him, he'll dash across traffic to the island in the middle of Broadway and give the pigeons a fit."
   - "I'm on my back, looking at the sky, trying to pretend I'm in the country, but I can't because even grass in the city feels hard as sidewalk, and there's just no pretending you are anywhere but in a 'concrete jungle' as my grandfather says."

   After you discuss the meanings of these quotations, look in the story to find at least one more colorful quotation. Each person should read a quotation and then lead a discussion of that quotation.
2. When Gretchen and her sidekicks meet Squeaky and Raymond on the sidewalk, Squeaky says that Gretchen smiles but that girls never really smile. She also says girls don't know how to smile because grown-ups don't know how to smile either. Discuss these observations. During your discussion, try to answer the following questions:
   - Why does Squeaky claim girls never really smile?
   - Do you think she is right? Tell why.
   - Why does she believe girls aren't taught to smile?

- Can you think of a time you had to smile but really didn't want to? Tell what happened.
- What causes Squeaky to think she and Gretchen gave each other real smiles at the end of the race?

Writing Ideas

1. Toni Cade Bambara writes as if the narrator, Squeaky, is talking to someone she knows. Squeaky lets you know what she thinks of herself and what she thinks of other people. Pretend it is the day after the race. Squeaky meets Cynthia Proctor. Write about their conversation. Include what Squeaky tells about the race and tell what she learned about herself. Then write about what you think Cynthia said, to her. Write so that it sounds like Squeaky and Cynthia are talking to each other.

2. You have been asked to write an article about the events of the May Day program for your school newspaper. Describe the park and the crowd of people who are there to watch the dancers and the racers. Tell about the May Pole dance, the little kids' run, the second-graders' run, and the 50-yard dash. Write about your interviews with Squeaky and Gretchen after the race.

3. Squeaky tells us what she thinks about just before she takes off in a race. Think about a time you were getting ready for something important. What did you think about just before you started? Write about what you did and how you got yourself ready to do it.

4. Write a story about next year's race. Raymond, Squeaky, and Gretchen are in the race as well as other runners. You can decide who is in the race, what happens during the race, and who wins the race.

Story 12

Without a Shirt

New Vocabulary Words

Everybody, take out your *Literature Anthology.* Turn to page 172. ✔
What is the title of this story? (Signal.) *"Without a Shirt."*
Who is the author? (Signal.) *Paul Jennings.*

1. First we'll read some words from the story, and then we'll talk about what they mean.
2. Word 1 is **smirk.** What word? (Signal.) *Smirk.*
   - (Repeat for every numbered word.)
3. It's your turn to read all the words.
4. Word 1. What word? (Signal.) *Smirk.*
   - (Repeat for every numbered word.)

1. smirk
2. rubbish

3. mussels
4. caretaker

5. pension
6. gale
7. spade

Definitions

(For each definition, first call on a student to read the definition aloud; then, present the tasks for that definition to the group.)

1. *A **smirk** is the kind of smile you give when you are making fun of someone or teasing someone in an unkind way.*
   - Everybody, show me a **smirk.** ✔
2. ***Rubbish** is another word for **garbage.***
   - Everybody, what's another way of saying **My dog loves to roll in garbage?** (Signal.) *My dog loves to roll in **rubbish.***
3. ***Mussels** are a type of seafood similar to clams.*
   - Usually, people eat **mussels.** In this story, **mussels** are used for bait.
4. *A **caretaker** is someone who takes care of a place or another person.*
   - What are some places that need a **caretaker?** (Ideas: *A park; a fancy garden; a campground; a cemetery.*)
   - Who are some people who need a **caretaker?** (Ideas: *Elderly people; sick people; young children.*)
5. *A **pension** is money you get from an employer when you stop working or when the person you are married to dies.*

6. *A **gale** is a very strong wind.*
   - Everybody, what's another way of saying **The sailboat got caught in a very strong wind?** (Signal.) *The sailboat got caught in a **gale**.*
7. *A **spade** is a type of shovel.*
   - Everybody, what's another way of saying **She used a shovel to dig in the sand?** (Signal.) *She used a **spade** to dig in the sand.*

Story Background

1. (Call on individual students to read two or three sentences.)
2. (After students complete a section, ask the questions for that section.)

"Without a Shirt" is a ghost story that takes place in Australia. Even though people from Australia speak English, they sometimes use different words than people from the United States use to describe the same thing. Some of these words are similar, like Mum for Mom. But some of the words are not at all similar. See if you can figure out what the words from Australia mean by reading the sentences that follow.

   - When our guests arrived, we invited them to come in and sit on the sofa in the lounge. What room do you think a lounge is? (**Idea:** *A living room.*)
   - George's mum is very rich. She wears very nice clothes and fancy jewelry and speaks in a posh voice. What kind of voice is a posh voice? (**Ideas:** *Snobby; stuck-up.*)
   - After we finished shopping, we put the big bags in the boot of our car so there would be room in the back seat. What part of a car do you think the boot is? (**Idea:** *The trunk.*) Everybody, what's the answer? (Signal.) *The trunk.*

You will probably notice something else that is different in this story that lets you know the author is Australian. There are no periods after abbreviations like Mr. and Mrs., so they look like this: Mr Bush and Mrs Featherstone.

   - What's another way we can tell this story wasn't written by an American author? (**Idea:** *No periods are used after abbreviations.*)

Focus Questions

1. (Call on individual students to read the Focus Questions aloud.)
2. (Remind students to think about to those questions as they read the story.)
   - *What extra words does Brian say before he stops talking?*
   - *What does Shovel start to find after Brian and his mom move to the house at the cemetery?*
   - *What happens the second time Brian tries to give his speech about his great-great-grandfather?*
   - *What happens so that Brian stops saying extra words at the end of his sentences?*

Without a Shirt
by Paul Jennings
Illustrated by Kate Flanagan

Mr Bush looked at the class. "Brian Bell," he said. "You can be the first one to give your History talk."

My heart sank. I felt sick inside. I didn't want to do it; I hated talking in front of the class. "Yes, Mr Bush without a shirt," I said. Sue Featherstone (daughter of the mayor) giggled. Slowly I walked out to the front of the class. I felt like death warmed up. My mouth was dry. "I am going to talk about my great great grandfather," I said. "He was a sailor. He brought supplies to Warrnambool in his boat without a shirt."

Thirty pairs of eyes were looking at me. Sue Featherstone was grinning. "Why didn't he wear a shirt?" she asked. She knew the answer. She knew all right. She just wanted to hear me say it.

"His name was Byron. People called him Old Ben Byron without a shirt."

"Why did they call him Old Ben Byron without a shirt?" Sue asked with a smirk. "That's a funny name."

"Don't tease him," said Mr Bush. "He is doing his best."

She was a mean girl, that Sue Featherstone. Real mean. She knew I couldn't help saying "without a shirt." After I had finished saying something I always said "without a shirt." All my life I had done it—I just couldn't help it. Don't ask me why. I don't know why; I just couldn't stop myself. I had been to dozens of doctors. None of them knew what caused it and none of them could cure me. I hated doing it. Everyone laughed. They thought I was a bit queer.

I looked at Sue Featherstone. "Don't be mean," I said. "Stop stirring. You know I can't stop saying 'without a shirt' without a shirt."

The whole grade cracked up. A lot of the kids tried not to laugh, but they just couldn't stop. They thought it was very funny. I went red in the face. I wished I was dead—and I wished that Sue Featherstone was dead too. She was the worst one in the form. She was always picking on me.

"Okay, Brian," said Mr Bush. "You can do your talk on Wednesday. You might be feeling a bit better by then." I went and sat down. Mr Bush felt sorry for me. They all felt sorry for me. Everyone except Sue Featherstone, that is. She never thought about anyone except herself.

Part 2

I walked home from school with Shovel. Shovel is my dog. He is called Shovel because he loves to dig holes. Nothing can stop him digging holes. He digs up old rubbish and brings it home and leaves it on the doorstep.

Once the man next door went fishing. He had a sack of mussels which he used for bait. When he got home he left them in the boot of his car and forgot about them. Two weeks later he found them—or I should say they found him. What a stink. Boy, were they on the nose! He had to bury them in his back yard. The next day Shovel dug them up and brought them home for me. He was always giving me presents like that. I didn't have the heart to punish him; he meant well. I just patted him on the head and said, "Good boy without a shirt."

Shovel was a great dog—terrific in fact. I am the first to admit that he didn't look much. He only had one eye, and half of one ear was gone. And he was always scratching. That wasn't his fault. It was the fleas. I just couldn't get rid of the fleas. I bought flea collars but they didn't work. I think that was because Shovel loved to roll in cow manure so much.

Apart from those few little things you wouldn't find a better dog than Shovel. He was always friendly and loved to jump up on you and give you a lick on the face. Mum and I would never give him up. He was all that we had left to remember Dad by. Shovel used to belong to Dad once. But Dad was killed in a car accident. So now there was just me, and Shovel and Mum.

When I reached home I locked Shovel in the back yard. It didn't look much like a back yard, more like a battle field with bomb holes all over it. Shovel had dug holes everywhere. It was no good filling them in; he would just dig them out again. I went into the kitchen to get a drink. I could hear Mum talking to someone in the lounge. It was Mrs Featherstone (wife of the mayor). She owned our house. We rented it from her. She was tall and skinny and had blue hair. She always wore a long string of pearls (real) and spoke in a posh voice.

"Mrs Bell," she was saying. "I'm afraid you will have to find another place to live. It just won't do. That dog has dug holes everywhere. The back yard looks like the surface of the moon. Either you get rid of the dog or you leave this house."

"We couldn't do that," said Mum. "Brian loves that dog. And it used to belong to his father. No, we couldn't give Shovel away."

Just then Shovel appeared at the window. He had something in his mouth. "There is the dreadful creature now," said Mrs Featherstone. "And what's that in its mouth?"

I rushed into the room. "Don't worry," I said. "It's only Tibbles without a shirt."

"Tibbles?" squeaked Mrs Featherstone. "What is Tibbles?"

"Our cat," I told her. "It died six months ago and I buried it at the bottom of the yard without a shirt."

Mrs Featherstone screamed and then she fainted. I don't know what all the fuss was about. It was only a dead cat. I know that Tibbles didn't look quite the same as when she was alive, but was that any reason to go and faint?

Anyhow, that is how we got kicked out of our house. And that is why we had to go and live in the cemetery.

Part 3

When I say that we had to live in a cemetery I don't mean that we lived in a grave or anything like that. No, we lived in a house in the middle of the cemetery. It was a big, dark old house. Once the caretaker lived there, but he was gone now and no one else wanted to live in it. That's why the rent was cheap. It was all that we could afford. Mum was on the pension and we didn't have much money.

"You'll be happy here," said the estate agent to Mum. "It's very quiet. And it's the cheapest house in town."

"I don't think that anyone can be happy in a graveyard," said Mum. "But it will have to do for now. It's all we can afford."

The agent walked off to his car. He was smiling about something. Then he looked at Shovel. "I hope your dog doesn't dig holes," he said. "It's not a good idea for dogs that live in cemeteries to dig holes." He thought that he had said something really funny. He was still laughing as he drove out of the gate.

"Big joke without a shirt," I called out after him.

The next day we moved in. I had a little room at the top of the house. I looked out over the graves. I could see the sea close by. The cemetery was next to the beach— we just had to walk over the sand dunes and there we were at Lady Bay Beach.

I went up to my room and started to work on my talk for school. I decided to write the whole thing out. That way I could make sure that I didn't have any "without a shirts" in it. I didn't want to give Sue Featherstone the chance to laugh at me again. The only trouble was that the last time I tried this it didn't work. I still said the "without a shirts" anyway. Still, it was worth a try—it might work this time. This is what I wrote.

OLD BEN BYRON

Old Ben Byron was my great great grandfather. He was the captain of a sailing ship. He sailed in with all sorts of goods for the town. He was one of the early settlers. This town is only here because of men like Ben Byron.

One day a man fell overboard. My great great grandfather jumped over to help him. The man was saved. But old Ben Byron was swept away. He drowned. His body was never found.

I know this might seem a bit short for a talk at school. It is. But something happened that stopped me writing any more.

Shovel had been gone for some time; I was starting to worry about him. I hoped he wasn't scratching around near any of the graves. I looked out the window and saw him coming. I ran downstairs and let him in. He ran straight up to my room and dropped something on the floor. It was a bone.

Part 4

I picked up the bone and looked at it. It was very small and pointed—just one little white bone. I could tell it was old. I knew I had seen a bone like that somewhere before, but I just couldn't think where. A funny feeling started to come over me. I felt lonely and lost, all alone. I felt as if I was dead and under the sea, rolling over and over.

My hand started to shake and I dropped the bone. I stared down at the bone on the floor. I was in bare feet and the bone had fallen right next to my little toe. Then I knew what sort of bone it was—it was a bone from someone's toe. It was a human toe bone.

"Oh no," I said to Shovel. "What have you done? Where have you been digging? You bad dog. You have dug up a grave. Now we are in trouble. Big trouble. If anyone finds out we will be thrown out of this house. We will have nowhere to live without a shirt."

I put on my shoes and ran outside. The strange feeling left me as soon as I closed the bedroom door. I only felt sad when I was near the bone. Outside it was cold and windy. I could hear the high seas crashing on the other side of the sand dunes. "Show me where you got it," I yelled at Shovel. "Show me which grave it was without a shirt." Shovel didn't seem to listen; he ran off over the sand dunes to the beach and left me on my own. I looked at all the graves. There were thousands and thousands of them. It was a very old cemetery and most of the graves were overgrown.

I started walking from one grave to the other trying to find signs of digging. I searched all afternoon. But I found nothing. I couldn't find the place where Shovel had dug up the bone.

In the end I walked sadly back to the house. I didn't know what to do with the bone. If anyone found it there would be a terrible fuss. We would be forced to leave the cemetery and would have nowhere to live.

When I reached the house Shovel was waiting for me. He was wagging his tail. He looked pleased with himself. He was covered in sand, and in his mouth he had another tiny bone. "The beach," I shouted. "You found it at the beach without a shirt." I snatched the bone from Shovel. As soon as I touched the bone the same sad feeling came over me. I felt lost and alone. I wanted something but I didn't know what it was.

It was another toe bone. I carried it up to my room and put it next to the other one. The feeling of sadness grew less. "That's strange without a shirt," I said to Shovel. I picked up the second bone and put it outside the door. The feeling came back. It was very strong. I opened the door and put the two bones together again. I didn't feel quite so sad. "These bones are not happy unless they are together," I said. "They want to be together without a shirt."

Part 5

I decided to have a serious talk to Shovel. I took his head between my hands. "Listen," I said. "You have to show me where you found these bones. I will have to fill in the hole. You can't go digging up dead bodies all over the place. You just can't without a shirt." Shovel looked at me with that big brown eye. I had the feeling that Shovel knew more about this than I did. He ran over to the door and started scratching at it. "Okay," I told him. "I'll come with you. But first I will hide these bones without a shirt." I put the two toe bones in a drawer with my socks. They still felt sad. So did I. As soon as I closed the drawer the feeling went.

We headed off to the beach. It was blowing a gale. The sand blew into my eyes and ears. I didn't know what to expect—maybe a big hole that Shovel had dug, with a skeleton in the bottom. Maybe a body washed up on the beach.

We climbed over the sand dunes and down to the shore. There was no one else on the beach. It was too cold. "Well," I said to Shovel, "show me where you got the bones without a shirt." He ran off into the sand dunes to a small hole. It was only as deep as my hand. There was no grave, just this small hole. I dug around with my hand but there were no other bones. "That's good," I told Shovel. "There is no grave, and there is no body. Just two toe bones. Tomorrow I will bury them and that will be the end of it without a shirt."

Shovel didn't listen. He ran off to the other end of the beach. It was a long way but I decided to follow him. When I reached him he was digging another hole. He found two more toe bones. I picked them up and straight away the sad, sad feeling came over me. "They want to be with the others," I said. "See if you can find any more without a shirt."

Shovel ran from one end of the beach to the other. He dug about thirty holes. In each hole he found one or two bones; some of them were quite big. I found an old plastic bag on the beach and put the bones in it. By the time it was dark the bag was full of unhappy bones. I felt like crying and I didn't know why. Even Shovel was sad. His tail was drooping. There wasn't one wag left in it.

I started to walk up the sand dunes towards home. Shovel didn't want to go; he started digging one more hole. It was a deep hole. He disappeared right inside it. At last he came out with something in his mouth, but it wasn't a bone. It was a shoe—a very old shoe. It wasn't anything like the shoes you buy in the shops. It had a gold buckle on the top. I couldn't see it properly in the dark. I wanted to take it home and have a good look at it.

"Come on, Shovel," I said. "Let's go home. Mum will be wondering where we are without a shirt." I picked up the bag and we walked slowly back to the house.

Part 6

I put the toe bones in the bag with the rest of them. Then I put the bag in my cupboard and shut the door. I felt much happier when the bones were locked away. They were unhappy and they made me unhappy. I knew what the trouble was; they wanted to be with all the other bones. I guessed that they were all buried in different places along the beach.

I looked at the shoe; it was all twisted and old. It had been buried in the sand dunes for a long time. I wondered whose it was. Then I noticed something—two initials were carved into the bottom. I could just read them. They were "B.B."

"Ben Byron," I shouted. "The bones belong to my great great grandfather without a shirt."

I suddenly thought of something—Ben Byron's shoe had reminded me. Tomorrow was Wednesday; I had to give my history talk at school. I groaned. I knew that I wouldn't be able to sleep worrying about it. And the more I worried the more nervous I would get. The more nervous I got the worse I would feel. The last time I gave a talk at school I got one out of ten. One out of ten. You couldn't get much lower than that.

Then I had an idea—I would take along the shoe. I would tell everyone I had found Ben Byron's shoe. That would make it interesting. I might even get three out of ten for my talk if I had the shoe. I put the shoe in my sock drawer and took the bag of bones out of the cupboard. I wanted to have a closer look at them.

I tipped the bones out into a pile on the floor. There were three long bones and a lot of small ones. The sad, lonely feeling came over me once more. I sat down on the bed and looked at the pile of sad bones. Then something happened that gave me a shock. The hair stood up on the back of my neck. I couldn't believe what I was seeing—the bones were moving. They were slowly moving around the floor. The bones were creeping around each other like a pile of snakes.

The bones sorted themselves out. They all fitted together. They formed themselves into a foot and a leg. All the bones were in the right order. I had the skeleton of Ben Byron's leg.

The leg didn't move. It just lay there on the floor. I sat on the bed looking at it for a long time. I can tell you I was scared—very scared. But I couldn't just leave the leg there; Mum might come in and see it. Anyway it was creepy having the skeleton of someone's leg lying on your bedroom floor. In the end I jumped up and swept all of the bones back into the bag and threw it into the corner of the room. Then I climbed into bed and put my head under the blanket. I tried to pretend that the bones weren't there.

Part 7

The next day I had to give my talk at school. It went worse than I thought. It was terrible. I stood in front of the class for ages without saying anything. I was so scared that my knees were knocking. The words just wouldn't come out. "What's up," said Sue Featherstone. "Haven't you got any shirts today?" A big laugh went up.

I managed to read the whole thing through to the end. I tried not to say anything else. I could feel it building up inside me—it was like a bomb waiting to go off. I kept my mouth closed tight but the words were trying to get out. My cheeks blew out and my face went red. "Look at him," laughed Sue Featherstone. "He's trying not to say it."

It was no good. The words exploded out. "Without a shirt."

I was embarrassed. I didn't know what to do. I grabbed the shoe. "This is Ben Byron's shoe," I said. "It was washed ashore without a shirt."

"It is not," said Sue Featherstone. "It's an old shoe that you found at the dump."

Everything was going wrong. I would probably get nought out of ten for this talk. Then something happened that changed everything. A feeling of sadness swept over me. Everyone in the room felt it—they all felt sad. Then someone screamed. It was the leg—it was standing there at the door. It hopped across the room. My hands were shaking so much that I dropped the shoe. The leg hopped across the platform and into the shoe. It wanted the shoe.

Sue Featherstone looked at the skeleton leg and started shouting out. "Get rid of it. Get rid of the horrible thing."

The leg started hopping towards her. It hopped right up onto her desk. She screamed and screamed. Then she ran for the door. Everyone else had the same idea—they all ran for the door at the same time. There was a lot of yelling and pushing. They were all trying to get out of the door at once. They were scared out of their wits.

The leg bones chased the whole class across the playground and down the street. I have never heard so much yelling and screaming in all my life.

I was left alone in the classroom with Mr Bush. He just sat there shaking his head. After a while he said, "I don't know how you did it, Brian. But it was a good trick. I give you ten out of ten for that talk. Ten out of ten."

"Thanks Mr Bush without a shirt," I said.

Part 8

When I got home from school the leg was waiting for me. It was just standing there in the corner of my room; it didn't move at all. But it was so sad and it made me sad. I felt as if I were a skeleton myself. I felt as if my bones were being washed away by the waves, as if they were being scattered along a long, sandy beach. I knew that this is what happened to Ben Byron. His bones had been washed up and scattered along Lady Bay Beach.

I looked at Shovel. "We have to find the rest of the bones," I said. "This leg will never have peace until all the bones are together again. We have to find the rest of the bones and we have to find them now without a shirt."

I took a spade and a sack and walked towards the beach. Shovel came with me and so did the leg. It hopped slowly behind us making a plopping sound as it came. It still had the shoe on. It was lucky that there was no one on the beach—they wouldn't have believed their eyes if they had seen a boy, a dog and a skeleton leg walking along the beach. I could hardly believe it myself.

I didn't know where to start looking. But the leg did. It hopped across the beach and stood still where it wanted us to dig. We spent all afternoon following the leg around and digging holes. In every hole we found some bones. I went as fast as I could; I wanted to get rid of the sad feeling. Tears were running down my face because I was so unhappy. Every time I found some more bones I put them in the sack. The bones were glad to be together; I could tell that. But they were still sad. They would not be happy until I found the last one.

After a long time I found the last bone. It was the skull. It was in a hole with an old shirt—a very old shirt. I had never seen one like it before. I put the skull and the shirt in the sack. Then I held open the top. The leg hopped into the sack with the other bones.

Part 9

The feeling of sadness went as soon as the leg joined the other bones. The bones were happy, I was happy and so was Shovel.

"Now," I said to Shovel. "We have a job to do. We have to bury all the bones in the same hole without a shirt."

I carried the bag of happy bones to a lonely place in the sand dunes, and Shovel and I started to dig a hole. We worked at it for hours and hours. At last it was deep enough. I took the bag of bones and tipped them into the grave. They fell into a pile out the bottom; then they started to move. They slithered around at the bottom of the hole. I should have felt scared but I didn't. I knew what was happening. The bones were joining up into a skeleton. After a while it was finished. The skeleton was whole. It lay still at the bottom of the grave looking up at me. It didn't look as if it was at peace. There was something else—it wanted something else. I looked in the sack. The shirt was still there.

I threw the shirt into the hole. "Don't worry," I said. "I won't bury you without a shirt."

The bones started to move for the last time. The skeleton moved onto its side with the shirt under its head. It was in a sleeping position. It was very happy. Music seemed to come up out of the grave—silent music. I could hear it inside my head.

We filled in the grave and smoothed down the sand. I decided to say a few words; after all, it was a sort of a funeral. I looked out to sea. I could feel tears in my eyes. This is what I said. "Here lie the bones of Ben Byron. At peace at last. Beside this beautiful bay."

Shovel looked up at me. He seemed to be smiling.

"Hey," I yelled. "I didn't mention a shirt. I didn't say it."

And I never did again.

Extending Comprehension

(The following Extending Comprehension activities can be presented after students finish reading the story. The activities also appear in the *Literature Anthology*.)

1. (Students can answer the Story Questions either orally or in writing. If the questions are presented orally, use the script below.)
2. (Students can select one or more Discussion Topics. Discussions can take place in small groups or with the entire class.)
3. (Students can use the Writing Ideas to respond to the story in writing.)

Story questions

1. What problem did Brian Bell have when he spoke? (Idea: *He would say "without a shirt" before he stopped talking.*)
2. Brian felt sad each time Shovel dug up a bone and gave it to him. How else did he feel when this happened? (Ideas: *Lonely; lost; like he was dead and under the sea rolling over and over.*)
3. What shocked Brian when he poured all the bones out of the bag and onto the floor of his room? (Ideas: *The bones moved; the bones sorted themselves out; the bones made the skeleton of a foot and a leg.*)
4. What happened the second time Brian gave his speech at school about his great-great-grandfather? (Ideas: *The skeleton leg came to get the shoe Brian brought to show the class; the skeleton leg jumped on Sue Featherstone's desk; Sue Featherstone started screaming; the class ran out the door after they saw the leg.*)
5. What did Brian do to make the bones happy? (Idea: *He buried all the bones together with the shirt.*)

Discussion Topics

1. Discuss why you think this story is called "Without a Shirt." During your discussion, try to answer the following questions:
   - Why do you think the author has Brian say "without a shirt" before he stops talking?
   - When and why does Brian stop saying "without a shirt"?
2. "Without a Shirt" is a ghost story. Ghost stories are supposed to scare you.
   - Discuss which parts you thought were the scariest.
   - Discuss why you thought those parts were scary.

Writing Ideas

1. Pretend you are Old Ben Byron. Write a letter to your great-great-grandson Brian explaining what happened the day you died trying to save the man who fell overboard. Also, tell Brian how you feel now that he has found your bones and properly buried them with a shirt.
2. Throughout most of the story, it seems very strange for Brian to say extra words before he stops talking. These words never made any sense to anyone, including Brian. The last time Brian says "without a shirt" is near the end of the story. Here is what he says, "Don't worry, I won't bury you without a shirt." Why is this the last time Brian ends a sentence with these words?

Bibliography of Correlated Trade Literature

Bibliography of Correlated Trade Literature

Note: Check the appropriateness of the vocabulary before making any selection for students to read independently.

Selection	Correlated Literature
Unit 1: No Place like Home	
"Ron's Summer Vacation" (Lessons 1–5)	• Blades, Ann **Back to the Cabin**—F • Enright, Elizabeth **Gone-Away Lake**—F • Pearce, A. Philippa **Minnow on the Say**—F
The Wonderful Wizard of Oz (Lessons 6–30)	• Carpenter, Angelica Shirley and Jean Shirley **L. Frank Baum: Royal Historian of Oz**—NF • Cleary, Beverly **Dear Mr. Henshaw**—F • Eager, Edward **The Time Garden**—F • Greenfield, Eloise **Sister**—F • Konigsburg, E. L. **From the Mixed-Up Files of Mrs. Basil E. Frankweiler**—F **Jennifer, Hecate, MacBeth, William McKinley, and Me, Elizabeth**—F* • Lowry, Lois **Anastasia Krupnik**—F, SP

F—Fiction; FO—Folktales/Fables; NF—Nonfiction; PI—Picture Book; PL—Play; PO—Poetry; *Supplementary Novel; SP—Available in Spanish

Bibliography of Correlated Trade Literature

Note: Check the appropriateness of the vocabulary before making any selection for students to read independently.

Selection	Correlated Literature
Unit 2: The World of Animals	
"Open Range" (Lesson 31)	• Frost, Robert *You Come Too: Favorite Poems for Young Readers*—PO • Harrison, David L *Wild Country: Outdoor Poems for Young People*—PO • Hopkins, Lee Bennett *My America: A Poetry Atlas of the United States*—PO • Yolen, Jane (Ed.) *Mother Earth Father Sky*—PO
"The Ugly Duckling" (Lessons 32–33)	• Holch, Gregory J. *The Things with Wings*—F • Park, Barbara *Almost Starring Skinnybones*—F • White, E. B. *The Trumpet of the Swan*—F*, SP
"A Horse to Remember" (Lessons 34–40)	• Goble, Paul *The Gift of the Sacred Dog*—F *The Girl Who Loved Wild Horses*—F • Henry, Marguerite *King of the Wind: The Story of the Godolphin Arabian*—F *Misty of Chincoteague*—F • Patent, Dorothy Hinshaw *Horses*—NF

F—Fiction; FO—Folktales/Fables; NF—Nonfiction; PI—Picture Book; PL—Play; PO—Poetry; *Supplementary Novel; SP—Available in Spanish

Note: Check the appropriateness of the vocabulary before making any selection for students to read independently.

Selection	Correlated Literature
Unit 2: The World of Animals (continued)	
"The Domestication of Animals" (Lessons 41–42) "The Cat That Walked by Himself" (Lessons 43–44)	• Arnold, Caroline *Cats: In from the Wild*—NF • Neville, Emily Cheney *It's Like This, Cat*—F • Patterson, Francine *Koko's Kitten*—NF • Ryder, Joanne *Without Words: Poems*—PO • Selden, George *The Cricket in Times Square*—F • Zeaman, John *From Pests to Pets: How Small Mammals Became Our Friends (Before They Were Pets)*—NF
"Journey to Dawson" (Lessons 45–46) "Buck" (Lessons 47–50)	• Cleary, Beverly *Ribsy*—F* • George, Jean Craighead *Julie of the Wolves*—F, SP • Gipson, Fred *Old Yeller*—F • Kimmel, Elizabeth Cody *Balto and the Great Race*—F • London, Jack *Call of the Wild*—F • Morey, Walt *Kavik the Wolf Dog*—F • Mowat, Farley *The Dog Who Wouldn't Be*—F

F—Fiction; FO—Folktales/Fables; NF—Nonfiction; PI—Picture Book; PL—Play; PO—Poetry; *Supplementary Novel; SP—Available in Spanish

Bibliography of Correlated Trade Literature

Note: Check the appropriateness of the vocabulary before making any selection for students to read independently.

Selection	Correlated Literature
Unit 2: The World of Animals (continued)	
	• Rawls, Wilson ***Where the Red Fern Grows***—F • Roe, Joann ***Alaska Cat***—F
"Trees" "In Time of Silver Rain" (Lesson 51)	• Asch, Frank ***Sawgrass Poems: A View of the Everglades***—PO • Fletcher, Ralph ***Ordinary Things: Poems from a Walk in Early Spring***—PO • Frost, Robert ***A Swinger of Birches: Poems of Robert Frost for Young People***—PO • Giovanni, Nikki ***The Sun Is So Quiet: Poems***—PO • Hughes, Langston ***The Dream Keeper and Other Poems***—PO • Levy, Constance ***A Crack in the Clouds: and Other Poems***—PO

F—Fiction; FO—Folktales/Fables; NF—Nonfiction; PI—Picture Book; PL—Play; PO—Poetry; *Supplementary Novel; SP—Available in Spanish

Bibliography of Correlated Trade Literature

Note: Check the appropriateness of the vocabulary before making any selection for students to read independently.

Unit 2: The World of Animals (continued)

Selection	Correlated Literature
Unit 2: The World of Animals (continued)	
"Amazing Animal Journeys" (Lessons 52–53) "Adventure on the Rocky Ridge" (Lessons 54–58)	• Cleaver, Vera and Bill **Where the Lilies Bloom**—F, SP • Houston, James **Frozen Fire**—F • O'Dell, Scott **Island of the Blue Dolphins**—F*, SP • Paulsen, Gary **Brian's Return**—F • Speare, Elizabeth George **The Sign of the Beaver**—F • Sperry, Armstrong **Call it Courage**—F, SP • Tunnell, Michael O. and George W. Chilcoat **The Children of Topaz: The Story of a Japanese-American Internment Camp Based on a Classroom Diary**—NF
"Animals in Danger" (Lessons 59–60)	• Facklam, Margery **And Then There Was One: The Mysteries of Extinction**—NF • George, Jean Craighead **There's an Owl in the Shower**—F • Pratt, Kristin Joy **Un paseo por el bosque lluvioso/A Walk in the Rainforest**—NF, SP

(Editorial Note: In Spanish, only the first word in a book title is capped.)

F—Fiction; FO—Folktales/Fables; NF—Nonfiction; PI—Picture Book; PL—Play; PO—Poetry; *Supplementary Novel; SP—Available in Spanish

Bibliography of Correlated Trade Literature

Note: Check the appropriateness of the vocabulary before making any selection for students to read independently.

Selection	Correlated Literature
Unit 3: Helping Others	
"Jackie Robinson" (Lesson 61–66)	• Cohen, Barbara ***Thank You, Jackie Robinson***—F • Gutman, Dan ***Jackie and Me***—F • Hopkins, Lee Bennett ***Extra Innings: Baseball Poems***—PO • Konigsburg, E. L. ***About the B'Nai Bagels***—F • Lord, Bette Bao ***In the Year of the Boar and Jackie Robinson***—F
"The Golden Touch" (Lessons 67–70) "Greek Gods and Goddesses" (Lesson 71) "The Miraculous Pitcher" (Lessons 72–75)	• Galloway, Priscilla ***Daedalus and the Minotaur***—FO • Lourie, Peter ***Lost Treasure of the Inca***—NF • Rubalcaba, Jill ***A Place in the Sun***—F • Tanaka, Shelley ***The Buried City of Pompeii: What It Was Like When Vesuvius Exploded (I Was There)***—NF

F—Fiction; FO—Folktales/Fables; NF—Nonfiction; PI—Picture Book; PL—Play; PO—Poetry; *Supplementary Novel; SP—Available in Spanish

Bibliography of Correlated Trade Literature

Note: Check the appropriateness of the vocabulary before making any selection for students to read independently.

Selection	Correlated Literature
Unit 3: Helping Others (continued)	
"Beauty and the Beast" (Lessons 76–80)	• Alderson, Brian ***The Arabian Nights***—FO • Krishnaswami, Uma ***The Broken Tusk: Stories of the Hindu God Ganesha***—FO • McKinley, Robin ***Beauty: A Retelling of the Story of Beauty and the Beast***—FO • Mutz, Martha ***El hombrecito de pan jengibre/The Gingerbread Man: A Bilingual Folktale Play for Children***—PL, SP • Osborne, Mary Pope ***American Tall Tales***—FO • Perrault, Charles ***Cinderella***—FO • Wu, Cheng-En and R. L. Gao ***Adventures of Monkey King***—FO
"The Spider and the Fly" (Lessons 81–82)	• Dakos, Kalli ***Mrs. Cole on an Onion Roll: and Other School Poems***—PO • Lear, Edward ***The Complete Nonsense of Edward Lear***—PO • Lewis, J. Patrick ***Boshblobberbosh: Runcible Poems for Edward Lear***—PO, NF • Silverstein, Shel ***A Light in the Attic***—PO

F—Fiction; FO—Folktales/Fables; NF—Nonfiction; PI—Picture Book; PL—Play; PO—Poetry; *Supplementary Novel; SP—Available in Spanish

Bibliography of Correlated Trade Literature

Note: Check the appropriateness of the vocabulary before making any selection for students to read independently.

Selection	Correlated Literature
Unit 3: Helping Others (continued)	
"Jane Addams" (Lessons 83–90)	• Adler, C. S. ***Willie, the Frog Prince***—F • Arnold, Caroline ***Children of the Settlement Houses***—NF • Collins, David R. ***Farmworker's Friend: The Story of Cesar Chavez***—NF • Fitzpatrick, Marie-Louise ***The Long March: The Choctaw's Gift to Irish Famine Relief***—NF • Mathis, Sharon Bell ***The Hundred Penny Box***—F • Voigt, Cynthia ***Dicey's Song***—F

F—Fiction; FO—Folktales/Fables; NF—Nonfiction; PI—Picture Book; PL—Play; PO—Poetry; *Supplementary Novel; SP—Available in Spanish

Bibliography of Correlated Trade Literature

Note: Check the appropriateness of the vocabulary before making any selection for students to read independently.

Selection	Correlated Literature
Unit 4: Living in History	
"England in the 1500s" (Lessons 91–94) "Mark Twain" (Lesson 95) *The Prince and the Pauper* (Lessons 95–115)	• Defoe, Daniel **Robinson Crusoe**—F • Grahame, Kenneth **The Wind in the Willows**—F • Gray, Elizabeth Janet **Adam of the Road**—F • Hodges, Margaret **Saint George and the Dragon**—F • Lewis, C. S. **The Lion, the Witch, and the Wardrobe**—F • Wise, William **Nell of Branford Hall**—F

F—Fiction; FO—Folktales/Fables; NF—Nonfiction; PI—Picture Book; PL—Play; PO—Poetry; *Supplementary Novel; SP—Available in Spanish

Additional Reading

Four novels are recommended for independent reading after the students have completed lesson 120. The novels, listed in order of difficulty, are:

- *Ribsy,* by Beverly Cleary
- *Jennifer, Hecate, Macbeth, William McKinley, and Me, Elizabeth,* by E.L.Konigsburg
- *Island of the Blue Dolphins,* by Scott O'Dell
- *The Trumpet of the Swan,* by E.B. White.

The word lists and questions for each novel appear on pages 190 to 199 of the *Literature Anthology.* Each novel is divided into four sections. A word list and set of questions is available for you and your students to use with each section. Use the word list to introduce and discuss vocabulary important to each section of the novel. You can use the questions as writing assignments, or they can be the basis for group discussions.

Procedures for introducing the novels:

Obtain several copies of each novel. All the novels are widely available through school and public libraries. You can also order the novels from a book store, a book club, or the Internet.

Either assign the novels to individual students or have the students select one of the novels. If you assign the novels, keep in mind that *Ribsy* is the easiest, and *The Trumpet of the Swan* is the most difficult.

Assemble the students who are to read the same novel. Have these students find the word list and questions for that novel in the *Literature Anthology.* Read the word lists for section 1 aloud as the students follow along. Then have the students read the same word list. Discuss any words the students do not understand.

Structure the reading of the first two or three pages of the novel. These pages typically contain vocabulary and sentence forms that may be new to students. Call on individual students to read several sentences in turn. Have them discuss any words and sentences they do not understand or that you think might be a problem.

Have students read the rest of section 1 to themselves. A good procedure is to have students put a paper clip on the last page of section 1 so they know to stop there. After students finish reading section 1, have them write responses to the questions for section 1 or discuss them as a group. You can evaluate their answers using the answer keys that appear on the following pages.

Follow a similar procedure for each of the remaining sections of the novel. However, students do not have to read the first pages of any of the remaining section aloud.

After students complete section 4 of the novel and the questions for that section, have them complete the writing assignment. Answer Key

Answer Key

Ribsy

SECTION 1

1. *Idea:* He had fleas.
2. *Response:* Left.
3. *Idea:* She wanted to keep the car clean.
4. *Idea:* Chased after the car.
5. *Ideas:* She felt sorry for him; she didn't want him to get hurt.
6. *Idea:* Took off his collar.
7. *Response:* A shopping center.
8. *Idea:* So Ribsy would have air.
9. *Idea:* He wanted to chase the little dog.
10. *Idea:* He pushed the button.
11. *Idea:* His sense of smell.
12. *Idea:* It smelled new.
13. *Ideas:* They can't tell colors apart; they can only see black and white.
14. *Ideas:* He couldn't find Henry; the people were taking him away.

SECTION 2

1. *Idea:* To get rid of his fleas.
2. *Idea:* Bubble bath/violets.
3. *Idea:* He couldn't find a way outside.
4. *Idea:* To rinse off the bubble bath.
5. *Idea:* If he could smell nothing but violets, he wouldn't know when danger was near.
6. *Ideas:* By running fast; by rolling around in the ditch.
7. *Ideas:* Put an ad in the paper.
8. *Idea:* Shake hands with his left paw.
9. *Response:* Coffee.
10. *Idea:* She was lonely.
11. *Idea:* Henry's ad.
12. *Ideas:* Mrs. Frawley fed him too much; Mrs. Frawley treated him like a person, instead of a dog.
13. *Idea:* To show it to the other ladies.
14. *Ideas:* He wanted to be treated like a dog again; he wanted to find Henry.

SECTION 3

1. *Idea:* Three girls.
2. *Idea:* He stole somebody's lunch.
3. *Response:* Mrs. Sonchek's.
4. *Idea:* Stood up with the rest of the class.
5. *Idea:* He wasn't making any trouble.
6. *Idea:* Chased the squirrel.
7. *Idea:* By throwing a coat over it.
8. *Idea:* He made too much trouble.
9. *Idea:* A football stadium.
10. *Idea:* The smell of hot dogs.
11. *Idea:* By pretending to be asleep.
12. *Idea:* People offered him so much.
13. *Idea:* He tripped the quarterback from the other team.
14. *Idea:* He wanted to be famous.

SECTION 4

1. *Idea:* Practicing the piano.
2. *Ideas:* No, because Mrs. Saylor was always complaining about how much things cost; No, because Joe looked for money at the football game.
3. *Idea:* Joe was a lot like Henry and did the same sorts of things.
4. *Idea:* Started practicing the piano.
5. *Idea:* He saw Ribsy's picture in the paper.
6. *Idea:* He wanted to keep Ribsy.
7. *Ideas:* A reward; ten dollars.
8. *Idea:* He could hear Henry, but he couldn't see him.
9. *Idea:* He wanted to find Henry.
10. *Response:* An apartment building.
11. *Response:* A tennis ball.
12. *Response:* An elevator.
13. *Response:* On the fire escape.
14. *Ideas:* His paws slipped between the bars.
15. *Idea:* He climbed a ladder up to the fire escape and dropped Ribsy to the ground.

Answer Key

Jennifer, Hecate, Macbeth, William McKinley, and Me, Elizabeth

SECTION 1

1. *Idea:* It was Halloween.
2. *Ideas:* It was older; it was the real thing.
3. *Response:* A witch.
4. *Idea:* Because she seemed so perfect.
5. *Idea:* Because Cynthia was mean.
6. *Idea:* Took off her tutu.
7. *Idea:* She couldn't see anything, but she didn't trip or fall.
8. *Idea:* She never said "please" or "thank you."
9. *Idea:* So they would give her more candy.
10. *Response:* Apprentice.
11. *Idea:* So Elizabeth could start becoming a witch.
12. *Response:* A raw egg.
13. *Ideas:* No, because there are no witches; Yes, because she does things that only a witch could do.

SECTION 2

1. *Idea:* Because Jennifer read so many books.
2. *Idea:* She wanted to be a witch.
3. *Ideas:* They couldn't pick which one they would turn into; they might be caged or killed.
4. *Idea:* A flying ointment.
5. *Idea:* She didn't like it.
6. *Idea:* The teacher probably thought she was so perfect.
7. *Idea:* Because she was the smallest student in the class.
8. *Idea:* Because Elizabeth smelled like onions.
9. *Idea:* In her mother's car.
10. *Idea:* Use it for the flying ointment.
11. *Idea:* She thought Cynthia was a creep.

SECTION 3

1. *Idea:* Because Christmas is so good, and witches are so evil.
2. *Idea:* Because you can't buy watermelons at that time of year.
3. *Idea:* Jennifer had given up watermelons.
4. *Idea:* Health foods.
5. *Idea:* Each one repeated what the other had said.
6. *Idea:* It almost worked.
7. *Response:* journeyman.
8. *Ideas:* Never lie on a pillow; never cut her hair; never eat after 7:30 P.M.; never use the telephone; never wear shoes in the house on Sundays; never use red ink; never light a match; never touch pins; never dance at a wedding; never get into bed without walking around it 3 times; never walk on the same side of the street as a hospital; never sing before breakfast; never cry before supper.
9. *Idea:* It was against the taboos.
10. *Idea:* So she wouldn't have to dance.
11. *Idea:* She knew who gave each present.
12. *Idea:* She remembered who had brought each present.
13. *Ideas:* Cynthia had stuck out her tongue; she wanted to get back at Cynthia.

SECTION 4

1. *Response:* Hilary Ezra.
2. *Idea:* One girl wanted to name him Hilary, and the other wanted to name him Ezra, so they named him both things.
3. *Idea:* To make trouble brew.
4. *Idea:* To make the flying ointment.
5. *Ideas:* Beware of the toad; the toad will cause you pain.
6. *Idea:* Elizabeth was filled with pain when she thought the toad was going to die.
7. *Idea:* She didn't want the toad to die.

Answer Key

8. *Idea:* No, she let Elizabeth save the toad.
9. *Idea:* Her father had a greenhouse.
10. *Idea:* They became good friends.

Island of the Blue Dolphins

SECTION 1

1. *Response:* A dolphin.
2. *Idea:* To hunt the otters.
3. *Idea:* To share the pelts equally.
4. *Ideas:* Yes, because then they might have helped him; no, because they couldn't be trusted.
5. *Idea:* They wouldn't have to share pelts.
6. *Idea:* A chest full of beads.
7. *Idea:* The men began to fight.
8. *Idea:* Kimki had told them.
9. *Idea:* Rescue the people.
10. *Idea:* She wanted to be with Ramo.
11. *Response:* The wild dogs.
12. *Response:* A canoe.
13. *Idea:* The wild dogs killed him.
14. *Ideas:* Wild dogs; starvation.

SECTION 2

1. *Idea:* Because the laws of her tribe forbade women from making weapons.
2. *Idea:* Weapons.
3. *Idea:* She realized they were worthless.
4. *Ideas:* She was lonely; winter was coming; life was hard.
5. *Ideas:* The mainland; the place where the white men lived.
6. *Idea:* Her canoe was leaking.
7. *Response:* The dolphins.
8. *Response:* Whale ribs.
9. *Response:* A rock.
10. *Idea:* She wanted to use it for a spearhead.
11. *Idea:* One of the sea elephants was killed in a fight.
12. *Idea:* While she was watching the sea elephants fight.
13. *Response:* A cave.
14. *Idea:* They killed her brother.

SECTION 3

1. *Ideas:* He was the biggest; he was the most powerful.
2. *Idea:* She shot him in the chest with an arrow.
3. *Idea:* She took good care of him.
4. *Ideas:* Karana fed Rontu; Rontu kept Karana company; Rontu helped her hunt.
5. *Ideas:* She could use it to escape from the Aleuts; she could use it for fishing.
6. *Idea:* In the sea cave.
7. *Idea:* Killing the devilfish.
8. *Ideas:* To show he was still the leader; to show they should leave him alone.
9. *Idea:* She clipped their wings.
10. *Ideas:* Squid, octopus.
11. *Ideas:* Yes, because it was so good to eat; No, because it was too dangerous.
12. *Idea:* Because the Aleuts came.
13. *Idea:* So the Aleuts would think that nobody lived there.

SECTION 4

1. *Idea:* Frightened.
2. *Ideas:* Yes, because he was an Aleut dog and was friendly to her; No, because he might have been friendly to anybody.
3. *Idea:* She was afraid that Tutok would bring the other Aleuts there.
4. *Idea:* Tutok left her a present.
5. *Idea:* She was happy that the hunters left, but she was sad to lose Tutok.
6. *Ideas:* Dogs, birds, otter.
7. *Idea:* They were her friends.
8. *Idea:* They thought hunters were coming.
9. *Idea:* She put a sleeping drug in his water and then captured him while he was asleep.
10. *Ideas:* The ground shook; rocks fell.
11. *Idea:* The earthquake ruined her old one.
12. *Idea:* With her hands.
13. *Idea:* She was proud of it.

Answer Key

The Trumpet of the Swan

SECTION 1

1. *Response:* Canada.
2. *Ideas:* Wild, no people, forests, beautiful.
3. *Idea:* There were no roads in the area.
4. *Response:* Spring.
5. *Ideas:* **a.** big, complicated. **b.** long, boring. **c.** short, to the point.
6. *Idea:* He scared away the fox.
7. *Idea:* To hatch her eggs.
8. *Idea:* He couldn't talk.
9. *Idea:* Something to help make noise.
10. *Idea:* "Stupid;" "unable to make noise."
11. *Ideas:* Because he wasn't a good listener himself; because all he did was talk.
12. *Idea:* It was too cold in the winter.
13. *Response:* A diary.
14. *Idea:* That he was very curious.

SECTION 2

1. *Idea:* So he could communicate with the other swans.
2. *Idea:* In Sam's school.
3. *Idea:* Wrote on his slate.
4. *Idea:* They couldn't read.
5. *Idea:* He was in love with her.
6. *Idea:* He couldn't say anything.
7. *Idea:* So he could make noise.
8. *Idea:* He stole it.
9. *Idea:* To pay for the trumpet.
10. *Idea:* He had so much stuff around his neck.
11. *Idea:* By being a bugler at Sam's camp.
12. *Idea:* The last bugle call of the day.
13. *Ideas:* It was on a lake in the middle of a forest; it had a big log cabin and tents.
14. *Idea:* The boys made fun of his name.
15. *Idea:* Started canoeing across the lake.
16. *Idea:* He saved Applegate's life.
17. *Idea:* He wore stuff around his neck.

SECTION 3

1. *Idea:* Cut the webbing on his right foot.
2. *Idea:* He swam in front of the Swan Boat, playing his trumpet.
3. *Idea:* Louis was good for business.
4. *Idea:* The Ritz didn't allow birds.
5. *Idea:* It was like a lake.
6. *Response:* Watercress sandwiches.
7. *Idea:* It was cheaper than the Ritz.
8. *Idea:* The Swan Boat didn't run in winter.
9. *Response:* Philadelphia.
10. *Idea:* Playing in a nightclub.
11. *Idea:* They clipped their wings.
12. *Idea:* So that they wouldn't clip his wings.
13. *Idea:* A storm blew her there.
14. *Ideas:* The song he wrote; "Oh, Ever in the Greening Spring".
15. *Idea:* She fell in love with him.
16. *Idea:* It's so wonderful that you forget about everything else.

SECTION 4

1. *Idea:* Clip her wings.
2. *Idea:* Louis attacked them.
3. *Idea:* They would go free, but they'd have to give one of their children to the zoo.
4. *Idea:* He loved animals so much.
5. *Idea:* Birds don't have to spend money, but people do.
6. *Idea:* All the money he had earned.
7. *Idea:* Give the money to the storekeeper.
8. *Idea:* Shot him.
9. *Idea:* Because he was responsible for Louis's father.
10. *Idea:* Gave it to the Audubon Society.
11. *Ideas:* Camp Kookooskoos; Boston; Philadelphia.
12. *Idea:* On the lake in Canada.
13. *Idea:* Wrote in his diary and asked himself a question.

ACKNOWLEDGMENTS

Grateful acknowledgment is given to the following publishers and copyright owners for permissions granted to reprint selections from their publications. All possible care has been taken to trace ownership and secure permission for each selection included. In case of any errors or omissions, the Publisher will be pleased to make suitable acknowledgments in future editions.

Arizona Quarterly
"The Circuit" Reprinted from Arizona Quarterly Volume 29 (1973) by permission of the Regents of the University of Arizona.

Harcourt
"The No-Guitar Blues" from BASEBALL IN APRIL copyright © 1990 by Gary Soto, reprinted by permission of Harcourt, Inc.

Farrar, Straus and Giroux
"Thank You M'am" from SHORT STORIES by Langston Hughes. Copyright © 1996 by Ramona Bass and Arnold Ramersad. Introduction copyright © 1996 by Arnold Rampersad. Compilation and editorial contribution copyright © 1996 by Akiba Sullivan Harper. Reprinted by permission of Hill and Wang, a division of Farrar, Strauss and Giroux, LLC.

Penguin Australia
"Without a Shirt" from UNREAL!: Eight Surprising Stories by Paul Jennings reprinted by permission of Penguin Books Australia Ltd.

Random House
"Like Jake and Me" Text copyright © 1987 by Mavis Jukes. Illustration copyright © 1987 by Lloyd Bloom. Reprinted by arrangement with Random House Children's Books, a division of Random House, Inc.

"Raymond's Run", copyright © 1971 by Toni Cade Bambara, from GORILLA, MY LOVE by Toni Cade Bambara. Used by permission of Random House, Inc.

Simon & Schuster
"The Bracelet" Reprinted with the permission of Atheneum Books for Young Readers, an imprint of Simon & Schuster Children's Publishing Division from THE SCRIBNER ANTHOLOGY FOR YOUNG PEOPLE edited by Anne Diven. Copyright © 1976 Yoshiko Uchida.

P9-CQX-428

Quick Guide

PONDS & FOUNTAINS

CREATIVE HOMEOWNER PRESS®

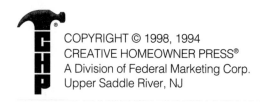

COPYRIGHT © 1998, 1994
CREATIVE HOMEOWNER PRESS®
A Division of Federal Marketing Corp.
Upper Saddle River, NJ

This book may not be reproduced, either in part or in its entirety, in any form, by any means, without written permission from the publisher, with the exception of brief excerpts for purposes of radio, television, or published review. Although all possible measures have been taken to ensure the accuracy of the material presented, neither the author nor the publisher is liable in case of misinterpretation of directions, misapplication, or typographical error. All rights, including the right of translation, are reserved.

Quick Guide is a registered trademark of Creative Homeowner Press®

Manufactured in the United States of America

Editorial Director: Timothy O. Bakke
Art Director: Annie Jeon

Author: Jim Barrett
Editors: Laura Tringali, David Schiff
Copyeditor: Marilyn Gilbert
Illustrator: Norman Nuding
Cover Illustrations: Brian Demeduk
Technical Consultants:
   Wayne Arter, Cal Pump
   John Hetzel, Henri Studio Inc.
   James A. Lawrie, Waterford Gardens
   Paul Martin, Beckett Corp.
   Lynn Nissom, Lilies of the Valley Water Gardens
   Charles B. Thomas and Virginia Crumb,
     Lilypons Water Gardens
   William C. Uber, Van Ness Water Gardens

Current Printing (last digit)
10 9 8 7

Quick Guide: Ponds & Fountains
LC: 93-073997
ISBN: 1-880029-29-4

CREATIVE HOMEOWNER PRESS®
A Division of Federal Marketing Corp.
24 Park Way
Upper Saddle River, NJ 07458

Visit our Web Site at: **www.creativehomeowner.com**

C O N T E N T S

S A F E T Y   F I R S T

Though all the designs and methods in this book have been reviewed for safety, it is not possible to overstate the importance of using the safest construction methods possible. What follows are reminders; some do's and don'ts of basic carpentry. They are not substitutes for your own common sense.

■ Always use caution, care, and good judgment when following the procedures described in this book.

■ Always be sure that the electrical setup is safe; be sure that no circuit is overloaded and that all power tools and electrical outlets are properly grounded. Do not use power tools in wet locations.

■ Always read container labels on paints, solvents, and other products; provide ventilation, and observe all other warnings.

■ Always read the manufacturer's instructions for using a tool, especially the warnings.

■ Always use hold-downs and push sticks whenever possible when working on a table saw. Avoid working short pieces if you can.

■ Always remove the key from any drill chuck (portable or press) before starting the drill.

■ Always pay deliberate attention to how a tool works so that you can avoid being injured.

■ Always know the limitations of your tools. Do not try to force them to do what they were not designed to do.

■ Always make sure that any adjustment is locked before proceeding. For example, always check the rip fence on a table saw or the bevel adjustment on a portable saw before starting to work.

■ Always clamp small pieces firmly to a bench or other work surface when using a power tool on them.

■ Always wear the appropriate rubber or work gloves when handling chemicals, moving or stacking lumber, or doing heavy construction.

■ Always wear a disposable face mask when you create dust by sawing or sanding. Use a special filtering respirator when working with toxic substances and solvents.

■ Always wear eye protection, especially when using power tools or striking metal on metal or concrete; a chip can fly off, for example, when chiseling concrete.

■ Always be aware that there is seldom enough time for your body's reflexes to save you from injury from a power tool in a dangerous situation; everything happens too fast. Be alert!

■ Always keep your hands away from the business ends of blades, cutters, and bits.

■ Always hold a circular saw firmly, usually with both hands so that you know where they are.

■ Always use a drill with an auxiliary handle to control the torque when large-size bits are used.

■ Always check your local building codes when planning new construction. The codes are intended to protect public safety and should be observed to the letter.

■ Never work with power tools when you are tired or under the influence of alcohol or drugs.

■ Never cut tiny pieces of wood or pipe using a power saw. Cut small pieces off larger pieces.

■ Never change a saw blade or a drill or router bit unless the power cord is unplugged. Do not depend on the switch being off; you might accidentally hit it.

■ Never work in insufficient lighting.

■ Never work while wearing loose clothing, hanging hair, open cuffs, or jewelry.

■ Never work with dull tools. Have them sharpened, or learn how to sharpen them yourself.

■ Never use a power tool on a workpiece—large or small—that is not firmly supported.

■ Never saw a workpiece that spans a large distance between horses without close support on each side of the cut; the piece can bend, closing on and jamming the blade, causing saw kickback.

■ Never support a workpiece from underneath with your leg or other part of your body when sawing.

■ Never carry sharp or pointed tools, such as utility knives, awls, or chisels, in your pocket. If you want to carry such tools, use a special-purpose tool belt with leather pockets and holders.

PLANNING YOUR POND

Whether it's a small, quiet reflecting pool tucked in a far corner of the yard or an elaborate waterscape complete with gurgling fountain, water lilies, and fish, a well-designed ornamental pond will provide hours of pleasure and relaxation for the entire family. This chapter covers some basic planning considerations that will help ensure the success of your project.

Selecting a Site

Even if you've already chosen what you think is the perfect spot for your pond, consider one or two alternate sites. Before making a final decision, think about the following points: What is the purpose of the pond? Should it dress up a bleak corner of the yard, provide a quiet place for meditation, or complement a deck, patio, or other existing feature? How accessible should the pond be? Do you want to stroll to it over a rambling path, or simply step out to it through your back door? Should the pond be secluded, or visible from inside the house so that you can enjoy it year-round? How will the sun, shade, and wind patterns of your property affect the placement of the pond? How easy will it be to provide water and electricity to the pond site? Will the excavation interfere with existing underground pipes and cables?

Proximity to the House. A pond visible from the house—perhaps through a large picture window or sliding glass doors—will provide pleasure, even in cold or inclement weather. Add underwater or low garden lighting around the pond perimeter, and you'll create a dramatic evening view. By contrast, a pond isolated from the house, perhaps surrounded by tall shrubs or screens, can become a private retreat, a peaceful place where family members can escape from day-to-day routines. A pond or fountain near the front entrance of the house adds an attractive focal point to the landscape. It also gives visitors something to admire while waiting outside your door. If your property is large enough, you can tuck a small pond in a side yard, perhaps to be viewed from a kitchen or bedroom window. If your yard is very small, you may simply wish to locate the pond right in its center, and then work all other landscape features (such as walks, plantings, and seating) around it.

Sun, Shade, and Wind. The pond site will require plenty of sunlight if you plan to grow flowering water plants. During the summer months, water lilies, for example, require at

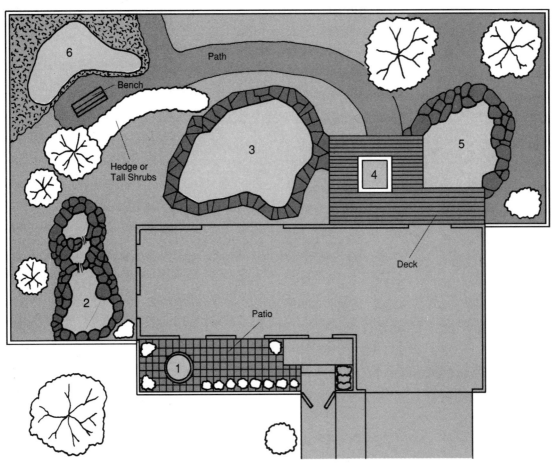

Selecting a Site. When selecting a site for your pond, decide how close you want it to the house and from which room or rooms you want to view it. A small formal pond or fountain (1) greets visitors at the front entry. A series of small ponds connected by short waterfalls (2) fits neatly into a narrow side yard. A large pond (3) is a dramatic focal point when viewed from a picture window. A pond incorporated into an attached deck or patio (4), or adjacent to it (5), can be easily viewed indoors or out. A pond in a far corner of the yard, away from the house (6), becomes a secluded retreat.

least six to eight hours of daily direct sunlight to bloom, although some varieties will bloom with as few as three or four hours of direct sun. The more direct sunlight the pond receives each day, the more choices of water plants you will have.

If you'll be adding fish to the pond, you'll have to balance the sun with some shade during the hottest part of the day. Shade can be provided from water lily or lotus pads, tall plants or shrubs around the pond border, a nearby fence or other structure, or a portable shade screen. You can make a simple, lightweight shade screen by building a wooden frame and covering it with a light-colored canvas, landscape fabric, or similar material. You can then position it to shade the pond during the hottest part of the day. Small ponds or tub gardens (100 gallons or less) also profit from some shade, since high water temperatures can promote excessive algae growth and increase water evaporation.

Even though some shade is desirable, you should avoid siting your pond under or next to large trees, because the falling leaves or needles will foul the water and accumulate on the bottom of the pond, clogging the pump/ filtration system. (If there is no other alternative, you can place netting or screen mounted on a wood frame over the pond to catch the leaves during the fall season.) You should also avoid proximity to "messy" trees that could drop excessive blossoms, fruit, or seed pods into the water.

Strong winds can wreak havoc on your pond by blowing leaves, dirt, and other debris into the water. These can increase water evaporation and ruin the effect of a fountain's delicate spray pattern. So, try to site your pond in an area sheltered from strong winds—for example, next to a tall fence or garden wall, the house, or other structure. If these sites don't fit into your plans, you can plant tall, fast-growing evergreen trees or shrubs on the upwind side of the

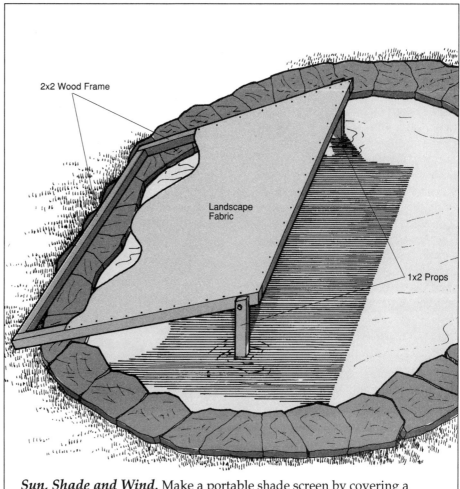

Sun, Shade and Wind. Make a portable shade screen by covering a wooden frame with landscape fabric or canvas.

pond to serve as a windbreak. Tall, dense evergreens, such as spruces and pines, make good windbreaks. Norway spruce and Australian pine are two good choices. So are tall, broad-leafed evergreen trees and tall shrubs, such as eucalyptus, holly, and oleander. If you live in a coastal environment, salt-tolerant species, such as Monterey cypress, Japanese black pine, and Atlas cedar, not only create a windbreak, but they also protect the pond from salt spray.

Trees and tall shrubs generally provide a better windbreak than solid walls or fences because they break the force of the wind over a greater area behind them (typically, for a distance equal to ten times the height of the tree). Wind tends to "wash over" solid barriers and continue at full force several feet behind them.

And don't forget that you should avoid placing the trees too close to the pond, or you'll have problems with falling leaves or needles. You can also erect freestanding lattice screens, perhaps covered with vines, to serve as a windbreak (as well as an attractive backdrop) on the windward side of the pond.

If you've lived in your house for more than a year or two, you probably have a good idea how sun, shade, and wind affect various spots in your yard at different times of the day and in different seasons. In the Northern Hemisphere, a southern exposure (shade screen on the north side of the pond) provides the greatest amount of sunlight year-round, with some late afternoon shade during the summer months. Conversely, a northern exposure (shade screen on the south side of the pond) provides the least amount of sunlight, with some late afternoon sun during the summer. An eastern exposure (shade screen on the west side of the pond) provides morning sun and afternoon shade. So, placing a shade screen on the northwest side of the pond will provide some shade to protect fish during the hottest summer afternoons, while allowing maximum solar gain to help keep water warmer during winter months in mild climates. If you're not sure how sun and shade affect your pond, erect a temporary shade screen, as described on page 7. Experiment with the location for a season or two before installing a permanent shade structure or plantings.

Existing Landscape Features

Determine which existing landscape features in your yard will complement the pond and which will detract from it. For example, siting the pond in one area of the yard may mean that you would have to remove (or prune) one or more large trees or shrubs to provide enough sunlight and to prevent excess leaves from polluting the water. You may have to reroute garden walkways or paths to provide better access to the pond.

View the pond site from several angles to see how it will be visually affected by what lies beyond it. If you've chosen an otherwise perfect location, you may find some eyesores that will need to be removed or disguised. Some unsightly elements, like an old board fence, a metal garden shed, or a bare house wall, can often be masked with plantings.

On the other hand, a pond stuck in the middle of a vast expanse of lawn may look artificial and barren. In this case, plan on how you can dress up the area surrounding the pond—perhaps by adding a rock garden or borders with flowering plants, or maybe a pond-side seating area with benches. Larger shrubs and trees can serve as a pleasant backdrop, either to add dimension to the pond or to screen unwanted views, like

property fences or a neighbor's house. Walks, bridges, ornamental statuary, and similar architectural elements can also be used to add interest to the site.

Remember that the pond must be in scale with the plantings and the architectural features of your property. Don't stuff a large pond into a small side yard. But also remember that a small pond would seem lost adjacent to a voluminous deck.

Soil and Topography

Flat Areas. The best location for a pond is on flat, level, well-drained ground. Even on flat ground, though, the material edging the perimeter of the pond should project at least 2 inches above the surrounding soil to prevent dirt, garden chemicals, and organic matter from polluting the water. In poorly drained clay soils (subject to large puddles of standing water after a heavy rain), grade the

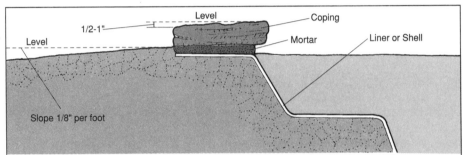

Flat Areas. Ponds are easiest to install on level ground. For good drainage, slope the soil away from pond at least 10 feet in all directions. Edging keeps soil and garden chemicals from washing into the pond.

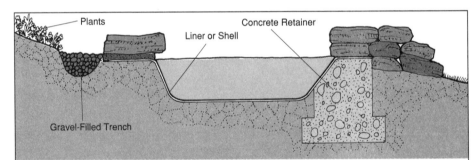

Hillsides. On a hillside, channel the water runoff with a gravel-filled trench on the uphill side of the pond. Ground covers and other plantings help control erosion. Poured concrete or a masonry block retainer supports a pond shell or liner on the downhill side.

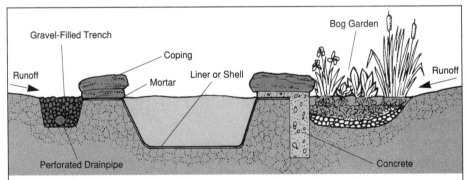

Low-Lying Areas. Avoid low-lying areas for pond sites. If you have no other choice, install a gravel-filled trench with a perforated drainpipe around the pond perimeter to direct surface runoff and subsurface water away from the site. Pipe leads to a dry well at the lower part of the property.

site so the ground slopes away from the pond edges at least 10 feet in all directions. A slope of 1/8-inch per foot will provide good drainage.

Hillsides. Hillside lots are a good opportunity to create beautiful ponds with one or more cascading waterfalls, especially if existing rock outcroppings or large boulders can be incorporated. However, hillside sites often present a greater challenge to the builder. Sometimes, extensive grading is required to provide a level area for the pond basin, and to direct runoff from uphill planting areas around the pond. A raised edging will help keep water from washing into the pond. A shallow, gravel-filled trench on the uphill side of the pond may be required to divert heavy runoff.

Low-Lying Areas. A pond usually looks most natural in a low-lying area; but if you place it there, you increase the chance of water runoff entering the pond from all sides. To direct runoff away from the pond edges, you'll need to raise the stone coping 3 to 6 inches above the surrounding soil. Around the perimeter of the pond, you could also install a gravel-filled trench leading to a dry well in a lower part of the yard. Or you can surround the pond with a bog garden. Above- ground ponds also work well in low-lying areas.

Utility Access

You'll need to run electricity to the site if your waterscape will include a pump and/or underwater or perimeter lighting. Some pumps simply plug into a three-prong electrical outlet; others must be "hard-wired" directly into the circuit and controlled by a switch. In either case, you should wire a switch into the circuit so that you can control the pump and lights from inside the house. (For plug-in devices, a switch controls the outlet.)

To get electricity to the pond, you'll need to run an underground electrical cable between the house and

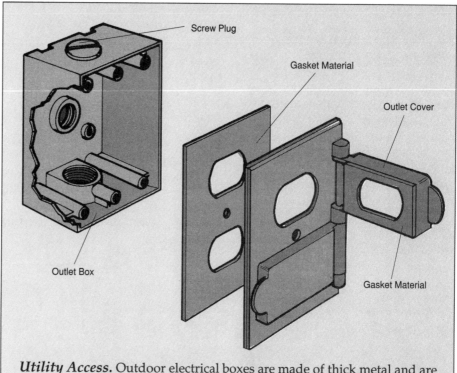

Utility Access. Outdoor electrical boxes are made of thick metal and are fitted with gaskets to protect wiring from the weather.

pond site to provide a convenient outlet in which to plug in the pump. This usually consists of nonmetallic shielded cable (Romex), run inside 1/2-inch (grey) PVC electrical conduit. But check local electrical codes. Although you may be able to tap into an existing circuit in the house, it is usually best to put the pump and pond lights on a separate circuit, with their own breaker at the main service panel. If you do tap into an existing branch circuit, make sure it has sufficient capacity to handle the additional load of the pump and any outdoor lighting you choose to install. Exterior electrical boxes, shielded cable, and PVC conduit are available at local hardware stores. If the pump and/or lights will be submerged, you probably will need to install a ground fault circuit interrupter (GFCI) or outlet in the electrical circuit. Again, check local codes.

Because ponds and fountains recirculate water, you needn't run a water line directly into the pond or fountain. Just make sure there is a nearby outdoor faucet so you can add water to the pond from a garden

hose as necessary. Small ponds, particularly, may require topping off every week or so during the hottest months of the year. To eliminate this chore, you can run 1/4-inch plastic tubing from a nearby water-supply line to the pond, then connect the tubing to a bobby-float valve to maintain a constant water level. (See the drawing, page 50.) These inexpensive setups are available through water-gardening catalog suppliers and nurseries that carry water-garden accessories. Simple ballcock valves, such as those used in toilet tanks, will also work, although these are larger than bobby floats and therefore harder to disguise.

Plan the most direct route possible between the house and pond for utility lines. However, avoid placing lines underneath cement patios, wood decks, or other permanent structures, because they will be harder to access should future repairs be necessary. Also, when siting the pond, make sure the site is not directly over any existing underground pipes, cables, sewer lines, or septic fields.

Pond Styles

The style of your pond is a matter of personal taste, although it will be more attractive if it complements the style of your house, garden, and other existing landscape features like decks and patios. For example, a naturalistic freeform pond with large, moss-covered boulders would look totally out of place in a formal garden with neatly pruned hedges and geometrically shaped planting beds. Conversely, a formal, geometric pond with an ornate fountain spray or classical Greek statue would probably look silly in a natural or informal garden behind a rustic home.

Ponds are generally classified as either informal (those that imitate nature) or formal (those that reflect a particular architectural style). However, this doesn't necessarily mean that you cannot mix natural and architectural elements to come up with a pleasing design. Japanese gardens are a good example of how informal and formal elements can be combined to reflect nature, yet give the viewer a sense of refinement and order.

Formal Ponds

Whether or not a pond is considered formal or informal depends largely on its shape and the edging materials used to define and cover the pond perimeter. Formal ponds and fountains generally conform to strict geometric shapes—circles, ovals, squares, rectangles, octagons, or hexagons. Many formal ponds are raised above the ground and contained by a low wall of concrete, brick, cut stone, or stucco. Often, they include a formal statuary fountain. Such ponds are intended to

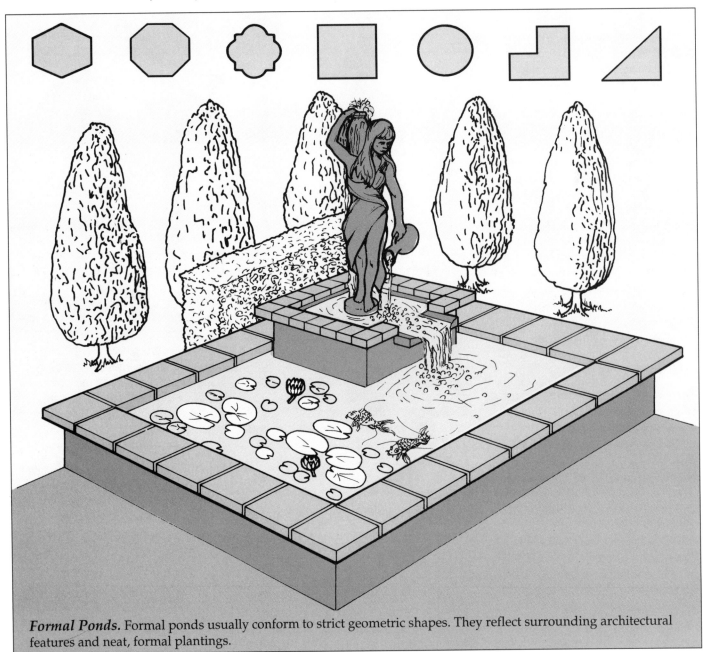

Formal Ponds. Formal ponds usually conform to strict geometric shapes. They reflect surrounding architectural features and neat, formal plantings.

look man-made and to complement the symmetry of the surrounding garden style and such architectural features on the property as a rectangular deck, a curving patio, or terraced planting areas. If your garden style is formal, with neatly shaped shrubs and hedges and symmetrical planting borders and walks, the pond should follow suit.

The site may also dictate the style. For example, a formal pond may be an extension of another architectural feature, such as a flagstone patio or raised-brick planting bed, or even a masonry wall. If, on the other hand, the pond is located some distance from the house or other structures, it could be formal

or informal, as long as the immediately surrounding plantings follow suit. Sunken formal ponds—also geometrical in shape——are often incorporated into patios, decks, masonry walks or formal planting borders. The material used for the surrounding patio, deck or walk features can also be used for the pond edging.

Informal Ponds

Informal ponds take a cue from the pools and streams found in nature. They usually have curvilinear shapes, and often they incorporate a short stream or small waterfall trickling over carefully placed natural rocks. They can also wrap around existing

landscape features, such as large boulders or a "peninsula" of tall plantings. Overhanging rocks and perimeter plantings are used to hide the pond edges above the waterline. Informal ponds usually look best in larger yards with informal or natural-looking gardens. But if yard space is limited, a bit of water splashing over a few large rocks into a small reflecting pool can be nearly as effective, suggesting a tiny mountain spring.

Informal or natural ponds must be designed carefully to blend into the surrounding landscape. Some of the most realistic-looking natural ponds incorporate locally quarried stones and native plants. Ferns and moss-covered granite boulders, for

Informal Ponds. Informal ponds simulate nature; they look best in a "wild" setting.

example, would be appropriate in a heavily wooded area, whereas clean, light-colored sandstone rocks with pockets of succulents, reeds, and clumps of bunch grass could suggest an oasis in a desert setting. To complete the natural effect, you can grow water lilies, water iris, lotus, and various bog plants in the pond itself. You should also plan access walks, pond-side sitting areas, and other nearby architectural features carefully, so as not to detract from the natural appearance of the pond.

Bog Gardens

Many ponds and water gardens incorporate marginal plants (see page 69). These plants require 2 or 3 inches of water over their roots at all times. Popular marginal plants include water iris, ornamental cattails, horsetail, parrot's feather, and various rush species. You can grow marginal plants in shallow areas of the pond by sinking earth-filled containers below the water surface.

Or you can create a separate bog garden or pockets of boggy soil by digging holes or trenches next to the pond, lining them with an EPDM pond liner and filling them with wet soil.

Pond-side bog gardens are separated from the pond by a barrier of compacted soil, mortared stones, or concrete between the bog area and the pond. They are fed by runoff from surrounding garden areas or by direct watering. The barrier prevents soil and garden chemicals from migrating into the pond water and polluting it. Although separate bog gardens are preferable when you want clear, clean pond water, you will need to monitor the soil more frequently so that it doesn't dry out.

In-pond bog gardens have permeable barriers of stacked edging materials, which allow water from the pond to seep into the bog area and keep it constantly moist. A layer of permeable landscape fabric can be used in the barrier to keep excess

soil from washing into the pond. Nutrients from the soil will migrate into the pond water, so the soil itself becomes part of the pond ecology. Because the soil nutrients also promote algae growth, the pond may take on a cloudy appearance, especially if it is small. So, if you want an in-pond bog garden, you must plan it so that runoff and chemicals from the surrounding garden don't enter the bog area.

Surrounds and Paths

The style of the walkways and paths around your waterscape should match the style of your pond. For informal ponds, create paths of loose aggregates such as gravel or bark chips; or place large, irregular stepping stones around the pond edge to provide access. If the pond is large enough, you might want to extend the stepping stones into or across the pond itself, or perhaps incorporate a wooden bridge. (See page 58.) Formal ponds may incorporate walks of brick, patio tiles, wood blocks, concrete, cut stone, or similar paving materials. You can extend the path around the perimeter of the pond to encourage strollers to view the pond from different vantage points.

Pond-side seating areas can be as simple as a wooden garden bench placed in a clearing, or as elaborate as a wood deck or masonry patio replete with lawn furniture. Such features should be in scale with the size of the pond and located to provide the best vantage point for viewing it. Don't let surrounding features overwhelm the pond itself.

Edgings

Pond edgings are typically wood or masonry materials that visually define the pond perimeter and keep surrounding soil from washing into the pond. Formal ponds may employ edgings of poured concrete, brick, concrete pavers, patio tiles, wood, or cut stone. Informal ponds generally have natural stone edgings. The edging material you choose should blend into or complement the sur-

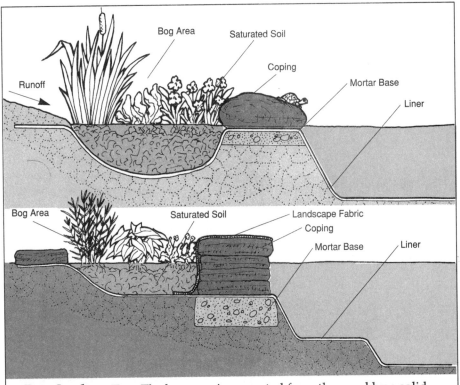

Bog Gardens. Top: The bog area is separated from the pond by a solid barrier of soil, concrete, or coping materials; water collects in the bog area from garden runoff. Bottom: The in-pond bog area is separated by stacked stones or other coping to keep soil in place; water from the pond seeps through the coping to keep bogs moist.

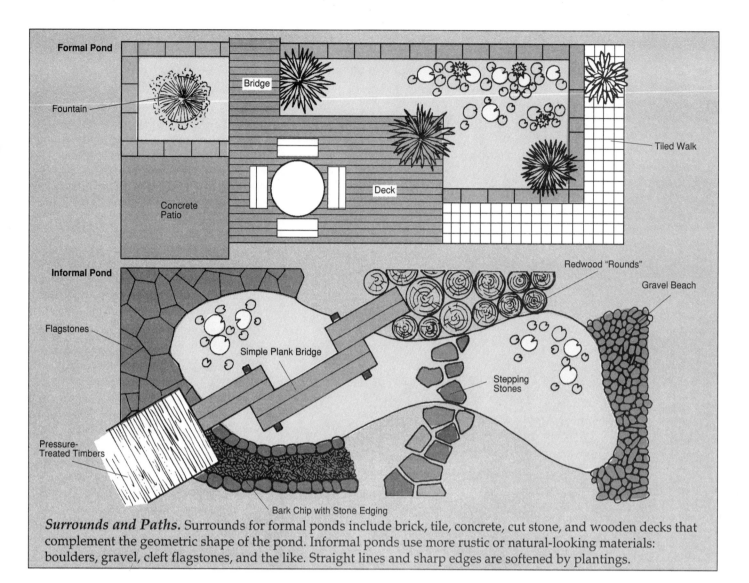

Formal Pond

Fountain

Bridge

Tiled Walk

Deck

Concrete Patio

Informal Pond

Redwood "Rounds"

Gravel Beach

Flagstones

Simple Plank Bridge

Stepping Stones

Pressure-Treated Timbers

Bark Chip with Stone Edging

Surrounds and Paths. Surrounds for formal ponds include brick, tile, concrete, cut stone, and wooden decks that complement the geometric shape of the pond. Informal ponds use more rustic or natural-looking materials: boulders, gravel, cleft flagstones, and the like. Straight lines and sharp edges are softened by plantings.

roundings. Allowing the edging to overhang the pond by a few inches will hide the pond structure.

At least one section of the edging should be wide and flat enough to allow easy access to the pond for maintenance purposes. An overhanging wooden deck, masonry patio, or flagstone walk bordering the pond could also serve this purpose. Although not absolutely necessary, it is best to mortar the edging stones or masonry units in place, to keep them from being dislodged and slipping into the pond. When installing edging materials, raise them slightly above the surrounding ground to direct runoff away from the pond, as shown.

If you use wood as a edging material, make sure it is pressure-treated with a nontoxic preservative and does not

come in direct contact with the pond water. Most pressure-treated wood sold at lumberyards is suitable; avoid woods treated with pentachlorophenol or creosote, which are toxic to fish and plants. If you use redwood,

allow it to season for at least a year (or until it turns grey), since fresh-cut redwood contains toxic tannins. Runoff from an overhanging redwood deck, for example, could leach these toxins from the wood into the pond.

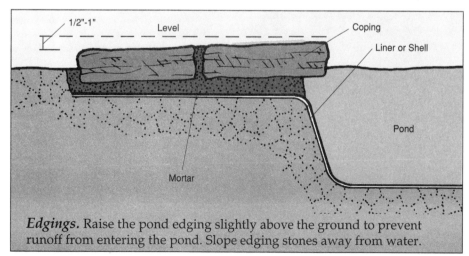

1/2"-1"   Level   Coping

Liner or Shell

Pond

Mortar

Edgings. Raise the pond edging slightly above the ground to prevent runoff from entering the pond. Slope edging stones away from water.

Lighting

There are several ways to illuminate a pond for night viewing. Underwater lights may immediately come to mind. But they are generally not as effective as a few well-positioned garden lights around the pond perimeter. In order for underwater lights to be effective, the pond water must be fairly clear and the lights positioned to avoid excessive glare. Also, when you place lights underwater, the pond surface loses its reflective quality, which can also be dramatic at night. However, when placed effectively, underwater lights can highlight specimen water lilies, waterfalls, and other features. Some fountain systems, in fact, come equipped with integral underwater lights.

You can also achieve a pleasing effect by directing hidden ground-level spotlights upward to illuminate surrounding trees or tall shrubs and reflect them on the pond surface. Similarly, placing lights at the pond edge to illuminate waterfalls or fountains will create a sparkling effect. Generally, a few well-placed spotlights or accent lights used to highlight specific areas or features in the garden will produce a more desirable effect than strong flood-lights that light up the entire yard.

Also consider using lighting for safety reasons, such as to illuminate walkways or steps leading to the pond. Low-level, ornamental down-lighting fixtures placed at intervals along the borders of a walk, or attached to step railings, provide enough illumination to define the walkways without lighting up the surrounding area.

Lighting. 1. Submerged lights can illuminate the entire pond, defining the waterline, or be directed upward at a fountain. 2. Spotlights at pond edges can be focused on specific areas or features in the pond, such as a specimen water lily or statuary fountain. 3. Uplighting trees, large shrubs, or other features near the pond can create dramatic reflections on the pond surface. 4. An overhead floodlight provides general illumination for a pond-side deck or patio; light should be pointed away from pond to avoid glare. 5. Paths leading to and surrounding the pond should be lighted for safety: Low-intensity downlights at knee level define a path without illuminating the surrounding area. 6. When possible, conceal fixtures from view.

Fixture Types

A variety of outdoor lighting fixtures is available for producing different effects. You can choose from two basic systems: standard 120-volt systems and low-voltage (12-volt) systems. Standard voltage systems run directly on household current; 12-volt systems require a transformer, which is connected to a 120-volt power source. In general, 12-volt systems are much safer and easier to install than standard systems, and the fixtures and bulbs are much less expensive (most use standard automotive-type bulbs). Many low-voltage systems are available as do-it-yourself kits, but the number of lights and various effects are limited. Bear in mind that low-voltage lights do not produce as much light as standard systems, and so they are not as effective in illuminating large areas. However, they are usually adequate for subtle lighting around ponds. No matter which system you choose, make sure the fixtures, bulbs, connectors, and junction boxes are designed for outdoor use. Because outdoor lighting will be exposed to the weather, the circuit should be protected by a GFCI (ground fault circuit interrupter). You should also check local codes for additional requirements.

Bulbs for outdoor lighting vary in color and intensity. For standard and low-voltage systems, standard tungsten bulbs are the cheapest and most readily available in a variety of wattages. The type most commonly used for outdoor lighting have thickened lenses and built-in reflectors (called PAR bulbs). They come in the form of spotlights, narrow floodlights, and broad floodlights in both high- and low-voltage versions. The more expensive high-intensity halogen bulbs are becoming popular for outdoor lighting, because they produce more light per watt than tungsten bulbs and have a longer life span. The incandescent light produced is a bright, clear white, yet still natural-looking.

Other high-intensity bulbs include mercury vapor (bluish-white), sodium (amber yellow), and metal halide (intense, harsh white). In general, these bulbs are not suitable for the subtle, natural lighting used around ponds, although they're clearly superior to tungsten bulbs for lighting up the whole backyard. Special bulbs and watertight housings are required for underwater lighting. Colored lenses are also available for underwater lights, as well as for general garden lighting, to create a fairyland effect. When planning to use colored lenses to highlight plants and trees, though, you should choose them carefully to avoid giving the foliage an unnatural appearance.

Fixture Placement

Place lighting fixtures to avoid excessive glare off the water surface. Also try to avoid placing lights where they will shine directly into the eyes of the viewer. Because many outdoor light fixtures are utilitarian and look out of place in a garden setting during the daytime, you should conceal these from view as much as possible. You can hide fixtures among thick plantings, beneath a deck overhang, behind a tree trunk, or within a tree canopy. Where such screening is not available, you can recess the fixtures in light wells below ground level. Special light-well fixtures are available. These consist of a bulb and reflector encased in a watertight housing, with a metal grille or clear Plexiglas cover. If you're recessing other types of fixtures below ground level, construct the well so it doesn't fill with water during heavy rains.

Wires and conduit can be buried underground, although junction boxes and transformers for low-voltage systems must be above-ground. In the daytime, fixtures with a black or dark green finish will be less obtrusive in the garden than those with a white or bright metallic finish.

Making a Site Plan

If you've selected a site for the pond and plan to leave the rest of the yard pretty much as it is, a site plan isn't necessary. However, sometimes the pond will be part of a larger landscaping project, which includes adding, removing, or relocating plantings and structures. In that case, it's a good idea to develop a site plan to help you (and others involved in the project) visualize how the pond fits into the overall scheme. The plan can also serve as a guide from which a landscape architect or designer can create finished drawings to submit to the building department, if these are required.

To make the site plan, you'll need to buy some grid paper for a base map (a scale of 1/4-inch equal to 1 foot is standard) and some tracing paper for overlays. If you have the original site survey map or site plan for your property, this could also serve as your base map. If you don't have the original map, use a 50-foot tape measure to help measure the size of the lot (or portion being landscaped), and to locate various existing features within it (house, decks, outbuildings, trees, shrubs, etc.). Here is how to proceed:

1 **Marking Property Lines.** On the grid paper, mark the property lines as shown. If only a portion of the property will be affected (the back yard, for instance), you needn't include the entire lot. Indicate north, south, east, and west; also mark the directions of prevailing summer and winter winds. Check with the building department to see how far the pond, or any other added structures, must be set back from lot lines; mark these as dotted lines on your plan.

2 **Locating Existing Structures.** Starting from a front corner of the house (marked X on the drawing), measure the dimensions of the house and transfer them to the plan. Again, if only one yard (front, side, or back) will be affected, you need only

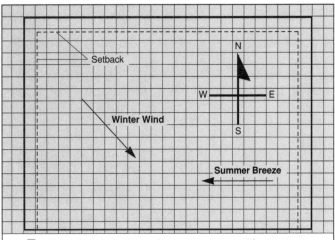

1 Start by drawing a base map on grid paper. Include property lines; north, south, east, and west arrows; property setbacks; and the direction of prevailing winds.

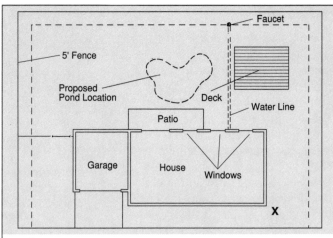

2 Measure the dimensions of the house and any other structures on the property; then transfer them to the plan.

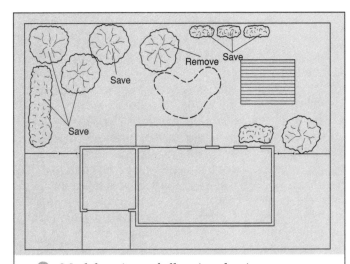

3 Mark locations of all major plantings; note which you want to save and which you want to remove.

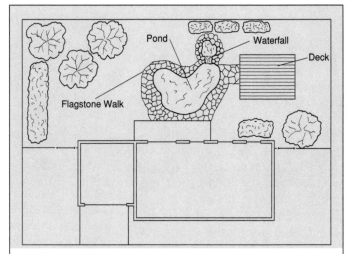

4 Attach a tracing paper overlay to the base plan and draw in any new features, including the pond and coping materials.

show the part of the house that faces it. Include the locations of exterior doors and windows on the wall facing the pond. Measure and mark the locations of other buildings and permanent structures, including patios, decks, fences, and paved walks. Also show any underground or overhead fixtures, such as utility lines and septic systems.

3 **Locating Plantings.** Mark the locations of trees, shrubs, and other major plantings; then specify which ones are to be kept and which ones will need to be removed or relocated. If applicable, make notations

on the shade cast by trees, tall shrubs, fences, or other structures near the pond site.

4 **Locating the Pond on Overlays.** On a tracing paper overlay, draw in the exact size and location of the proposed pond. Include coping materials, a waterfall (if one is used), and other features on the pond site, such as walks, planting areas and new plantings, and fountains. Also show the path of new utility lines to the pond.

Use as many overlay sheets as needed to come up with a suitable plan. Draw the final overlay neatly,

and then attach it to the base map. Make copies, if necessary, to show building officials or others involved in the project.

Note: If you're building a raised pond, or one on a sloping site that will be held in place with a retaining wall, you might also want to make one or more cross-sectional drawings. These drawings should include the pond depth, the type and thickness of materials used for the pond sides, the location of any underwater shelves for bog plants, and the location of any required plumbing (pipes, drain, pump, filter, etc.).

Choosing a Type of Pond

Even though some of the most beautiful ponds and pools occur in nature, you can't expect to simply dig a hole in the ground and have it hold water. Instead, you'll need to provide a watertight container, as well as a way to cover the pool edges and blend them into the landscape. Most ponds today are built of either flexible pool liners or preformed shells. Either can be used to create formal or informal ponds.

Flexible Pond Liners

Flexible pond liners can be used to create ponds of any shape and size. They offer reasonable cost with ease of installation. As detailed on page 24, you dig the hole for the pond, install the underlayment, lay the liner in the hole, fill the pond with water, cut the liner to size, and then weigh down the exposed edges of the liner with large rocks or other materials to keep it in place. These liners resemble the black polyethylene plastic sheeting sold in hardware stores, but they are much thicker and far more durable. The two most popular types sold today are made of either PVC (polyvinyl chloride) plastic or synthetic (butyl or EPDM) rubber. Both are formulated to be flexible, stretchable, and resistant to ultraviolet light. Rubber liners generally outlast the best of the PVC liners, but they're expensive. The PVC liners are avail-

able in thicknesses from 20 to 32 mil. Butyl or EPDM rubber liners are available in thicknesses from 30 to 45 mil. A thicker liner will be more expensive, but it will generally last longer. At the bottom end of the scale, a 20-mil PVC liner can be expected to last from five to seven years; a 32-mil PVC liner will last from ten to 15 years. A rubber liner will generally last from 20 to 30 years. The manufacturer's warranty is a good indicator of liner life. You should choose a thicker liner if you expect uninvited waders, either animal or human, in the pool. (Or apply a 1- to 2-inch layer of cement mortar over the liner to protect it.) If you will be raising fish, make sure you specify a fish-grade liner, because toxic chemicals can leach out of some liners.

Flexible pond liners come in stock sizes ranging from about 5 X 5 feet

to 30 X 50 feet. Some manufacturers offer custom sizes, which are priced by the square foot. By joining the edges of the sheets with a seam sealer (available from the liner dealer), you can make a pond of virtually any size. (Indeed, liners have been used to create lakes and reservoirs up to several acres.)

Because flexible liners are susceptible to punctures from rocks, gravel, broken tree roots, or other sharp objects in the pond excavation, installation instructions for plastic and rubber liners often recommend that you should place a layer of sand, carpet padding, or similar cushioning material in the excavation before laying the liner. The main problem with sand, however, is that it doesn't conform well to the steep sidewalls of the pond. Sand is also more expensive and heavy to transport, especially for larger pond excavations. Other

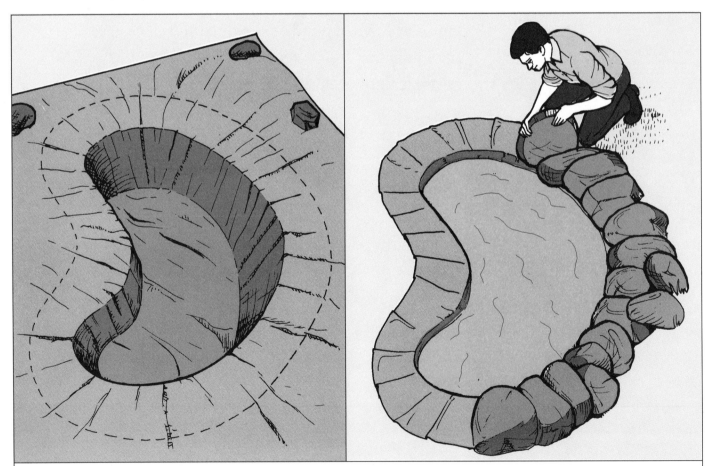

Flexible Pond Liners. Flexible pond liners fit ponds of any shape or size. Boulders or other masonry edging holds the liner in place and hides liner edges above the waterline.

recommended cushioning materials, such as carpet padding or old newspapers, tend to deteriorate over time, losing their cushioning effect. So, most sources that carry pond liners now also offer a tough, yet flexible, underlayment material specifically designed for use with pond liners. A recent product on the market is a thick, synthetic rubber liner with an integral underlayment material bonded to it, to provide a lifetime guarantee against puncture.

If you're digging the hole in soil that contains sharp stones or gravel, protruding tree roots, or soil subject to excessive shifting during winter months, you should install both sand and underlayment fabric. If the soil is stable, fine, and rock-free, however, the underlayment really isn't needed.

Both plastic and rubber liners are useful if you anticipate moving every few years or for other reasons you may have for building a temporary pond. Simply drain the pond and remove the liner. (See page 74 for information on draining ponds.) You can reuse the liner as long as it wasn't covered with cement mortar.

Premolded Pond Shells

Rigid or semi-rigid pond shells are easy to install yourself, as shown on page 34. These shells come in a variety of sizes, shapes, and depths. Although they're generally more expensive than flexible pond liners, they're also more durable and puncture-proof. Shells can last from five to 50 years, depending on their material, thickness, quality, and installation conditions. Generally, the thicker the shell, the longer it will last, and the more expensive it will be. The thickest shells (1/4-inch or more) can be installed aboveground with little support around the sides, provided the bottom rests on a firm base. As with most other products, you get what you pay for. The manufacturer's warranty is a good indicator of the durability of a premolded pond shell.

The first preformed pond shells appeared on the market in the mid-1950's, and were made of fiberglass-reinforced polyester (FRP). This is the same material used for fiberglass spas, boat hulls, auto bodies, and translucent roofing panels for patio overheads. Today, more shells are being made of molded plastics, such as ABS (acrylonitrile butadiene styrene) and various polyethylene formulations. The fiberglass shells are usually easier to repair than the plastic ones, but they tend to be more brittle. Whatever shell you buy, though, make sure it is resistant to ultraviolet radiation.

Most manufacturers offer between ten to 15 pond shell designs, in depths from 9 to 18 inches and with capacities from about 30 to 500 gallons. (If you want to raise water lilies, the shell should have a minimum depth of 18 inches.) Keep in mind that the shell will look larger when out of the ground than when installed.

Some shells have integrated premolded waterfall lips; separate premolded waterfall courses are also available. Many preformed shells have shelves or ledges around the edges below the water line for placing shallow-water plants in submersible containers. A few also have depressions around the perimeter for bog plants. You should carefully disguise the edges of the shell with rocks or other materials, so the pool will look natural.

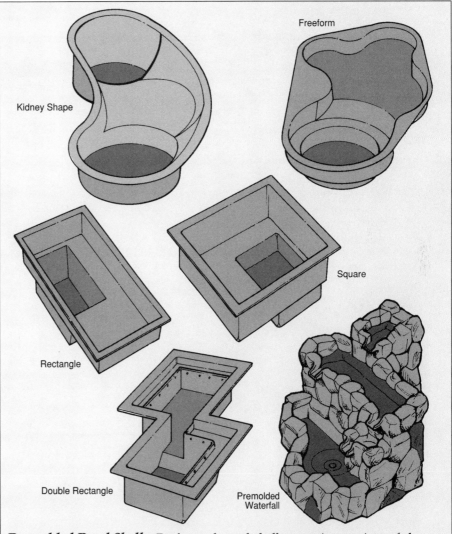

Premolded Pond Shells. Preformed pond shells come in a variety of shapes and sizes. They're the closest thing you can have to an "instant pond".

Concrete Ponds

Years ago, practically all garden ponds—formal and informal—were made of poured concrete, concrete block, or a combination of the two. With the advent of flexible pool liners and molded pond shells, however, few ponds today are constructed entirely of concrete.

Although a concrete pond can last a lifetime if it is properly installed, it will crack and leak almost immediately if it is not. Success in pouring a concrete pond—even a small one—requires experience with concrete. It is also a lot of back-breaking work. A larger pond, or one with straight or stepped sides,

will require extensive formwork. Once a crack opens up, there's usually no way to repair it. The only fix is to cover the concrete with a flexible pool liner. (See page 29.)

Concrete ponds are much more expensive to install than flexible liners or premolded shells, even if you do the work yourself. If you do decide to go with concrete, you should have the pond installed by a local masonry contractor familiar with this sort of construction in your particular climate. The following basic guidelines will help you discuss your plans intelligently with the contractor.

In cold climates, the concrete shell should be at least 6 inches thick and

adequately reinforced with 1/2-inch (No. 2) reinforcing bar or wire mesh to survive the effects of alternate freezing and thawing. (Check local codes for reinforcement requirements.) In milder climates, the shell can be 3 or 4 inches thick, depending on soil conditions.

Since new concrete can leach lime into the pond water, the lime must be neutralized by chemicals; or else you must paint the pond before adding fish and plants. Concrete can be painted with a rubber-based pool paint to create various efffects: earthtones for a natural look; white, blue, or turquoise for a more formal appearance; or dark colors for a "bottomless" look.

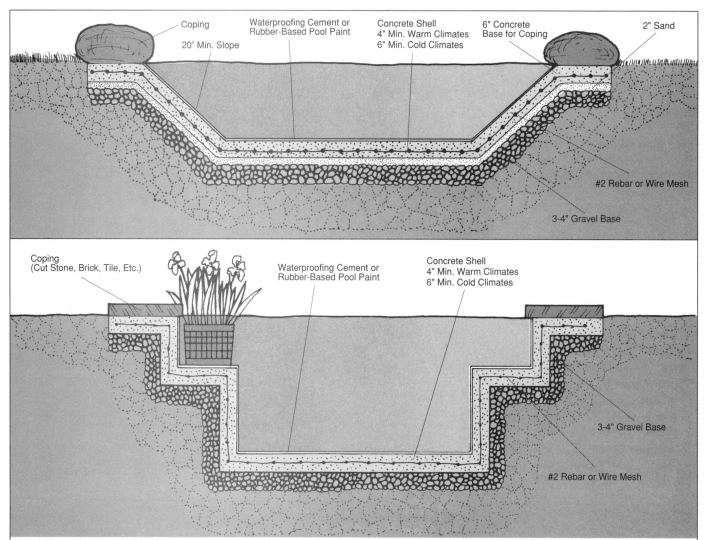

Concrete Ponds. The shell of a concrete pond must be adequately reinforced to prevent cracking. If the sides slope 20 degrees or more from the vertical, no forms are required (top). A formal concrete pond with straight sides requires extensive formwork that is best left to a professional installer (bottom).

Other Options

Pond Kits. Some manufacturers offer complete pond kits. These include a rigid shell or flexible liner with a matched pump, filter, and—in some cases—a fountainhead or self-contained waterfall, planting containers, and pond-treatment chemicals for the initial startup. If you find a design you like, the kits are much easier to install successfully than separate components, because everything is guaranteed to work together. Such kits are usually limited to smaller ponds, however.

Tub Gardens. If you want to have a small-scale water garden without the trouble of building a pond, you can raise a few water plants and small fish in large containers. Tub gardens make wonderful accents for decks, patios, porches, and planting beds. Prefabricated water-garden containers are available up to 36 inches in diameter; half-barrels also make good containers when lined with a flexible plastic or rubber liner, as do large terra-cotta or plastic pots, or any other large, rustproof, watertight vessel. Many people have even made successful water gardens in old clawfoot bathtubs! You could also use a large wooden planter box; just install a plastic or rubber liner, and fill it with water.

Pond Depth & Capacity

The most successful garden ponds are between 18 and 24 inches deep. Very small ponds (5 to 10 square feet) can be as shallow as 12 inches; very large ponds (500 square feet or more) can be up to 36 inches deep. The 18- to 24-inch depth is considered optimum for growing water lilies and other aquatic plants; this is sufficient, too, for raising most types of fish and other aquatic life. Also, except in the coldest climates, a depth of 24 inches is sufficient to prevent the pond from freezing all the way to the bottom, and killing fish or damaging the pond shell as a result. If you live in an area with extremely harsh winters, contact the local pond builders in your area for recommended depths.

If you're installing a Japanese koi pond, you may need to provide an area at least 3 feet deep where fish can escape heat in the summer and frozen water in the winter. (See page 71.) Small, shallow ponds (less than 18 inches deep) heat up and cool off more quickly than large, deep ones. These extreme temperature changes can stress fish. Shallow ponds are also more subject to excess algae growth during hot weather. In extremely cold climates, they may freeze all the way to the bottom, killing plants and fish. However, some plants (especially bog plants) may require water more shallow than the recommended depth. In such cases, you can create a shelf around the pond perimeter to raise water plants. Or, you can put the plants in containers and elevate them off the pond bottom with bricks or stones as discussed on page 68. (For more information on stocking the pond with plants and fish, see page 67.)

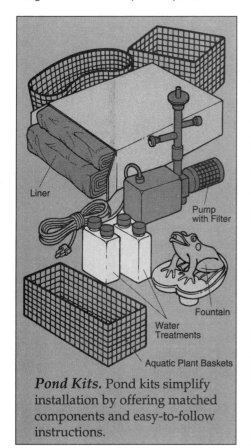

Pond Kits. Pond kits simplify installation by offering matched components and easy-to-follow instructions.

Tub Gardens. Old bathtubs, plastic or terra-cotta pots, and wooden planter boxes are just some of the imaginative ways you can create a container water garden.

Pond Capacity

The pond capacity (in gallons of water) becomes important when you size the pump and filter and when you determine correct dosages of plant fertilizers, fish medications, algaecides, and other chemical treatments. The most accurate way to determine pond capacity is to attach a flow meter to the faucet or water-supply line, and then to simply record the number of gallons needed to fill the pond. A less accurate, but easier and less expensive method, is as follows: Turn on the garden hose at a steady flow rate, and time how long it takes to fill a 5-gallon bucket (say, 10 seconds). Then time how many minutes it takes to fill the pond at the same flow rate (say, 20 minutes). Now figure out the flow rate of the hose in gallons per minute (5 gallons @ 10 seconds x 6 = 30 gallons per minute). Next, multiply the gallons per minute by the number of minutes it took to fill the pond (30 gallons x 20 minutes = 600 gallons).

If it isn't practical to fill the pond with water, you can calculate capacity using one of the following formulas, assuming the pond sides are straight (or steeply sloped) and the bottom is flat (not bowl-shaped).

Rectilinear ponds. If the pond is roughly square or rectangular, measure its average depth, width, and length; then multiply the three figures to determine cubic feet (D x W x L = cubic feet). Multiply the cubic feet by 7.5 to get capacity in gallons.

Circular ponds. To calculate the capacity of circular ponds, use this formula: diameterxdiameter (diameter squared) x depth x 5.9 = gallons.

Oval ponds. To calculate the capacity of oval ponds, use this formula: depth x width x length x 6.7 = gallons.

Freeform ponds. It is tough to accurately calculate the volume of an irregularly shaped pond. The best way is to determine the average width and length, and then use the equation for oval ponds above.

The Pond Bottom

No matter what material your pond will be made of, or what surface shape it takes, steep sloping sides are preferable to a shallow bowl shape. Not only will a pond made this way hold more water, but it will also look better. In very large ponds, you may want to include shallow areas for raising plants or viewing fish. In all cases, the pond bottom should not be perfectly flat. Slope it slightly toward a sump hole to trap dirt and debris, and also to facilitate cleaning. In some ponds, the sump contains a drain or submersible pump to improve water circulation.

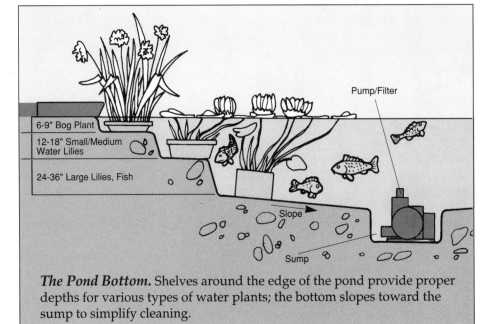

6-9" Bog Plant

12-18" Small/Medium Water Lilies

24-36" Large Lilies, Fish

Pump/Filter

Slope

Sump

The Pond Bottom. Shelves around the edge of the pond provide proper depths for various types of water plants; the bottom slopes toward the sump to simplify cleaning.

Local Codes & Pond Safety

Any body of water, no matter how shallow, poses a hazard for infants and small children. Many communities have zoning ordinances that require a wall or fence around ponds over a certain size or depth (usually 18 inches deep), to keep neighborhood children from straying into the pond area. If you have infants or toddlers in the family, consider encircling the pond area with a temporary wire fence and locking gate. Or you might want to postpone pond construction altogether, until the children are old enough to learn water-safety rules. Remember, too, it is your responsibility to make sure that neighborhood children don't have access to your pond— whether this means a fence around the pond or your entire yard.

Your local building department may have additional codes and requirements for the size and design of the pond itself; in some cases, a building permit and inspection may be required. If you're running electricity to the pond for a pump and/or lighting, you may need a separate electrical permit. Many communities require that a licensed electrician must perform any electrical work involving water or outdoor wiring. We highly recommend this practice, even if local codes don't require it. Be sure to choose an electrician with experience in this type of work. For referrals, local swimming pool contractors are a good source.

INSTALLING A FLEXIBLE POND LINER

Most garden ponds are created with flexible PVC plastic or rubber pond liners. Why? Because the liners are inexpensive and easy to install, and they provide unlimited creative opportunities in pond size and shape. Ponds with flexible liners are also easy to remove should your landscaping plans change in the future.

Sizing the Liner

Flexible pond liners come in a variety of stock sizes, with larger sizes available as special orders. Some garden suppliers carry large rolls of liner material in standard widths: You simply pull as much off the roll as required. Here's how to estimate the amount of liner you need.

1 **Outlining the Shape.** After clearing the site of plantings and other obstructions, outline the pond shape on the ground. For irregularly shaped ponds, use a rope or garden hose to mark the pond perimeter. For squares or rectangles, use batter boards, stakes, and string, and employ the "3-4-5" triangulation method to make sure all corners meet at an exact 90-degree angle. From each corner, measure along one string a distance of 3 feet; along the other string, measure a distance of 4 feet; then mark these locations on the strings with chalk or a piece of tape. Adjust the strings on the batter boards until the diagonal distance between the two points measures 5 feet.

For circular ponds, make a simple "compass" with a stake; sturdy twine or rope; and a sharpened stick, screwdriver, or other pointed object. Scribe the outline of the pond in the dirt, and mark it with flour, powdered gypsum, marking paint, or a garden hose.

2 **Measuring Pond Dimensions.** Measure the overall width and length of the pond; then determine the smallest rectangle that would enclose the pond area.

3 **Calculating the Liner.** To allow for pond depth, decide on the maximum depth of the pond (usually 24 inches), double it, and add this figure to the width and length of the rectangle. To allow for overlap, add an additional 24 inches to the width and length of the liner. This will provide

1 Outline the shape of the pond on the ground. For irregular shapes, use a garden hose or rope; for square or rectangular ponds, use batter boards and string; for round ponds, use a rope, stake, and pointed stick as a giant compass.

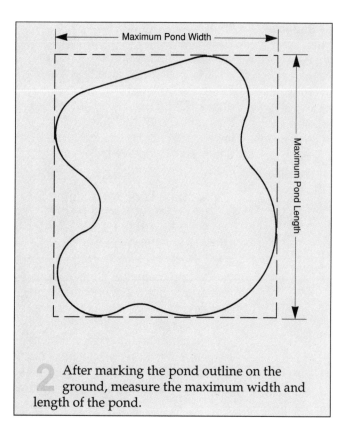

Maximum Pond Width

Maximum Pond Length

2 After marking the pond outline on the ground, measure the maximum width and length of the pond.

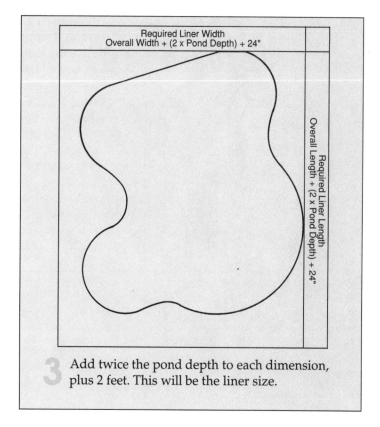

Required Liner Width
Overall Width + (2 x Pond Depth) + 24"

Required Liner Length
Overall Length + (2 x Pond Depth) + 24"

3 Add twice the pond depth to each dimension, plus 2 feet. This will be the liner size.

12 inches of overlap around the pond rim once the liner is installed.

Example: The pond is 24 inches deep and fits inside a 10x12-foot rectangle. To figure liner width, add 10 feet (the width), plus 4 feet (the depth, doubled), plus 2 feet (for overlap)—for a total of 16 feet. To figure the liner length, add 12 feet (the length), plus 4 feet (the depth, doubled), plus 2 feet—for a total of 18 feet. You would therefore need a 16x18-foot liner for a 10x12-foot pond. Note that for irregularly shaped ponds, you may need to trim excess liner material to provide an even overlap around the entire pond.

Installing the Liner

Installing a vinyl liner requires four basic steps: first, digging the hole; second, laying down the liner; third, filling the pond with water; and fourth, adding stones or other edging around the pond perimeter. The actual procedure, however, involves a few more steps than listed above. These are presented on the following pages. Depending on your particular requirements, you may be able to skip a few of these steps.

1 **Removing Sod.** If you've located the pond in a lawn area, use a flat shovel to remove patches or strips of sod within the pond area, and about 6 to 12 inches beyond the perimeter. Reestablish the pond outline, if necessary.

If the pond is in a lawn area, remove the sod within the pond area and about 6 to 12 inches beyond it.

2 If the pond will have shallow-water shelves, dig the pond to the depth of the shelves; tamp the shelf area with a tamper; then dig the deep area of the pond.

2 **Digging Shelves for Shallow-Water Plants.** This step is optional. If the pond will include shelves around the perimeter for bog plants, excavate for these. Typically, shallow-water shelves are about 12 to 16 inches wide and 9 to 12 inches below the top edge of the excavation. First, excavate the entire pond area to the depth of the shelf; then use a tamping tool to compact the soil firmly in the shelf area (hand and power tampers are available at tool rental shops). Use a straight board and 2-foot level to make sure the shelf is level around the entire perimeter of the pond. Then excavate the remainder of the pond down to the maximum depth, sloping the sides as described in step 3.

3 **Digging the Hole.** Start by digging around the shelf perimeter to the depth of the shovel blade (9 to 12 inches); then remove all dirt within the pond area, by layers, to the final depth. Check the depth frequently with a tape measure or yardstick and long board placed over the hole, as shown. The sides should slope inward at about a 20-degree angle from the vertical; in loose or sandy soil, the sides may have to conform to a shallower slope. Slope the bottom of the excavation about 1/2- to 1-inch per foot toward the center or toward one end; at the lowest point, dig a shallow (6- to 8-inch) sump hole to facilitate draining the pond.

4 **Cutting Ledge for Edging Material.** With a flat-blade shovel, cut a 12- to 15-inch-wide ledge around the pond rim to provide a flat, level surface on which to install the edging materials. Cut the ledge to a depth that will accommodate the combined thickness of the edging and any underlayment materials. (If you're mortaring the stones in place, be sure to include the thickness of a mortar bed—about 2 to 3 inches.) As shown, the edging should extend at least 1 inch above the surrounding terrain to prevent runoff from entering the pond. Also keep in mind that edging looks best if it overhangs the pond edges by a few inches.

3 Dig the hole to the proper depth. As you dig, check the depth with a long, straight board and tape measure.

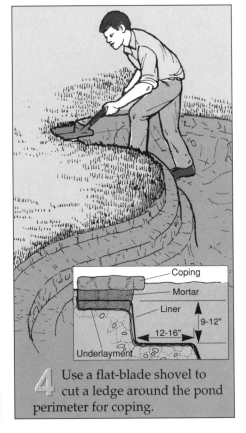

4 Use a flat-blade shovel to cut a ledge around the pond perimeter for coping.

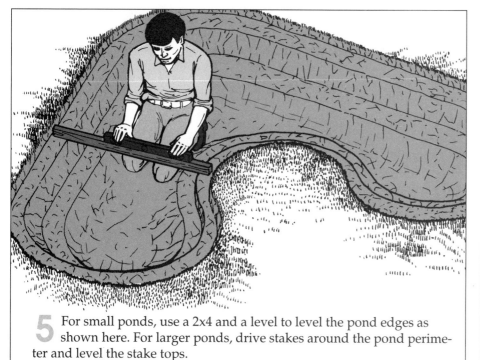

5 For small ponds, use a 2x4 and a level to level the pond edges as shown here. For larger ponds, drive stakes around the pond perimeter and level the stake tops.

6 Pack sand into the excavation to cushion the liner. Underlayment may also be used.

5 Checking Edges for Level. Once the pond is filled with water, the water level will quickly reveal any high or low spots around the pond rim. For small ponds, place a long, straight 2x4 across the pond excavation, with each end resting on the edging ledge. Place a level on top of the board; then move the board to various points across the length and width of the pond while checking the level. If necessary, cut down high spots on the ledge (or build up low ones) until the entire pond rim is level.

To check a large pond, drive short stakes or pegs 3 to 4 feet apart around the rim of the pond; then level the tops of the stakes with a long spirit level, or a short level placed on top of a straight board. Measure how much each stake protrudes from the ground. If the same length of each stake protrudes, you know the perimeter is level.

6 Preparing the Hole. Carefully inspect the excavation for any sharp stones or projecting roots, and remove them. Place carpet padding or a 2- to 3-inch cushion of damp sand in the bottom of the

excavation and on any shelves cut into the sides of the pond. Also pack damp sand into any voids in the sidewalls, such as where large rocks were removed. If the soil is very rocky or infested with roots, lay down a fabric underlayment material (see page 18) for additional protection.

7 Positioning the Liner. Pick a warm, sunny day to install the liner. To make it more flexible and easier to handle, warm up the liner for a few minutes by spreading it out on sun-warmed pavement. With a helper (or two), drape the liner loosely into the excavation, with an even overlap on all sides; then

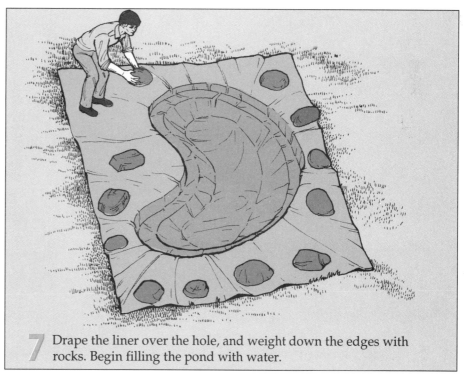

7 Drape the liner over the hole, and weight down the edges with rocks. Begin filling the pond with water.

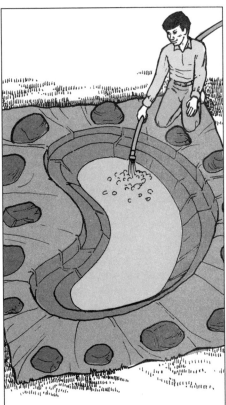

weight down the edges with a few smooth, flat stones or bricks. Avoid dragging the liner across the ground, since this may cause a puncture. Once the liner is in place, start filling the pond with water.

8 Fitting the Liner. As the pond fills with water, adjust the liner to conform to the sides of the pond; smooth out as many creases and wrinkles as possible. Large creases at tight corners can be stretched out and pleated to make them less noticeable. As the pond fills, periodically ease off the stone weights to avoid overstretching the liner.

9 Trimming Excess Lining. When the pond is full, trim off excess lining with a heavy pair of scissors or a utility knife. Leave enough liner around the pond rim to extend underneath, and a few inches behind, the first course of edging stones. To keep the liner in place while adding edging, push 20d nails through the liner into the ground every foot or so around the pond rim.

10 Adding Edging Materials. If you're using natural stones (boulders or flagstone, for example), make several trial arrangements until you find one that looks most natural. Although large, flat stones or masonry units can be placed directly over the liner, you must position them carefully so they won't slip into the pond. It's usually better to set the stones in a 2- to 3-inch-thick mortar bed (reinforced with chicken wire or metal lath). You can buy mortar premixed, or make your own mix. Typically, a mix consists of 1 part cement, 1/4 part hydrated lime, and 3 parts sand by volume. If you expect frequent foot traffic on the edging, pour a 4-inch-thick base of reinforced concrete under the stones. Allow the mortar to cure (about one week); next, scrub the edging with distilled vinegar to neutralize the lime in the mortar. Then drain the pond, rinse the liner, and refill the pond with fresh water. (See page 74 for information on draining ponds.)

8 As the pond fills, stretch the liner to remove any wrinkles; fold excess liner into neat pleats. Ease off the stones as the water pulls the liner into the hole.

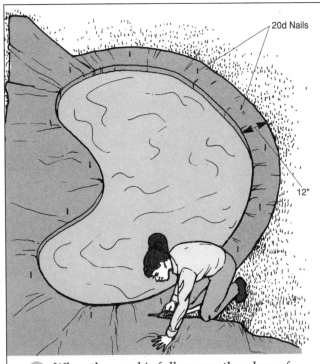

20d Nails

12"

9 When the pond is full, secure the edges of the liner with large nails. Use scissors to cut off excess liner. Save cut pieces for future repairs.

10 Place coping stones around the edge of the pond. To prevent stones from moving, mortar them in place.

Liner Over Concrete. In certain situations, concrete can be combined with a flexible plastic or rubber pond liner to provide the best of both materials. For example, you can pour a concrete retainer around the sidewalls of the pond to provide additional support for liners—especially in loose or crumbly soil, where the walls tend to break down because of soil slippage behind the liner. A concrete retainer allows you to have steeper walls and to place large or heavy pots on the shallow-water shelves. Because the liner acts as a watertight barrier, the concrete itself needn't be waterproof. Furthermore, minor cracks in the concrete shell won't result in leaks. You can also use liners in conjunction with a thick, concrete perimeter footing or collar. This will support heavy rocks around the pond perimeter, or it will serve as a base for a brick or stone patio or walk around the pond.

When you excavate for the pond, allow extra space for building wooden forms (if required) for the concrete retainers and footings. If you're not experienced here, you should hire a masonry contractor to do the work. For more information on mixing and pouring concrete, refer to "Quick Guide: Patios & Walks."

Cement Over Liner. A thin layer of a plastic cement mixture (1 part plastic cement to 4 parts sand) placed over the liner will protect it from the damaging effects of ultraviolet rays, as well as punctures caused by waders in the pond. Plastic cement has latex additives that make it highly resistant to cracking. (Most lumber yards and masonry suppliers carry this product.) If you want, you can add coloring agents to the cement and/or produce various surface textures by brooming or troweling. After installing the flexible liner (see page 25), you should cover it

with a chicken-wire reinforcement; then you hand-pack a 1-inch layer of cement over the entire surface of the pond (wear heavy gloves for this procedure). Start packing cement at the base of the sidewall, building up to the top in 6-foot-long sections. After the sidewalls are covered, do the pond bottom. Brush or trowel the surface smooth; then allow the cement to harden (about 10 to 12 hours, or overnight). Once the cement has hardened, fill the pond with water. Add 1 gallon of distilled white vinegar per 100 gallons of water, and allow this mixture to stand one week. (The vinegar serves to neutralize the lime leaching from the cement.) Drain the pond; rinse it thoroughly; then refill the pond with fresh water. (See page 74 for infomation on draining a pond.) Test the water for pH (see page 63) before adding fish or plants. If the water is too alkaline, repeat the vinegar treatment.

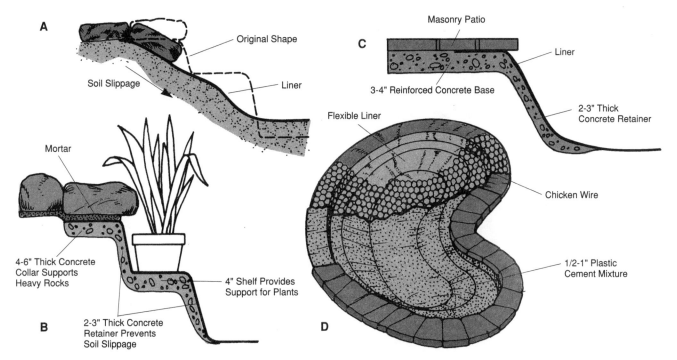

A. In loose or sandy soil, slippage causes walls to break down. B. A concrete retainer prevents soil slippage and provides support for heavy coping and plant shelves. C. A concrete base provides support for a pond-side masonry patio or walk. D. A thin (1-inch) layer of plastic cement protects flexible liner from UV rays and punctures.

Building a Raised Pond with a Flexible Liner

Flexible liners also adapt well to raised-pond enclosures. The supporting sidewalls can be wood, mortared bricks, concrete blocks, or any other material that provides firm support for the liner. You can build masonry enclosures on a simple concrete perimeter footing. (Check local codes for the footing depths.) Or you can install a wooden frame directly on the ground. In both cases, the pond bottom needs to be nothing

more than 1 or 2 inches of compacted damp sand or finely sifted soil to protect the liner from punctures. If you make a wooden frame, use pressure-treated wood or redwood to prevent rot. Avoid boards with rough, splintery surfaces, which could puncture the liner.

The raised pond shown here is a 6x8-foot wooden box, approximately 20 inches tall. It will provide a water depth of about 16 inches. Each side is made of two 2x10 boards. By changing the width and

number of boards used to make the sides, you can change the pond depth, although for practical purposes the depth shouldn't exceed 24 inches. Also, the length and width should not exceed about 8 feet, or the boards may bow outward from the weight of the water.

1 Making the Sides. Cut the four 1x4 middle battens to 17 inches long. Place two 2x10x 8-foot side pieces together as shown. Center a batten across the side pieces, with the bottom of the batten flush to the bottom of one of the boards. Attach the batten with 2-inch galvanized deck screws. Repeat for all four sides.

2 Joining the Sides. Select a level site for your pond, and join the sides in place. Join the sides with four 3½-inch galvanized deck screws in each corner. Lap the long sides over the ends of the short sides. Be sure the corners are flush at the top, and drive the screws below the surface of the wood. Set a carpenter's level on top of a long

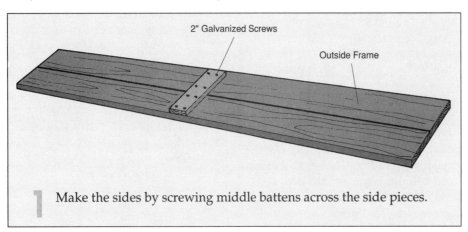

1 Make the sides by screwing middle battens across the side pieces.

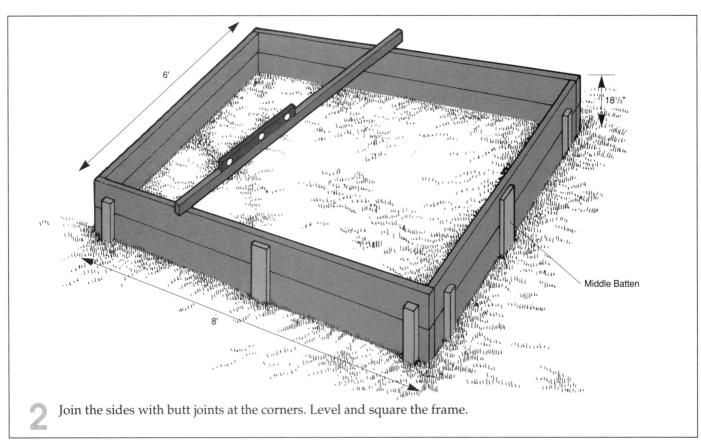

2 Join the sides with butt joints at the corners. Level and square the frame.

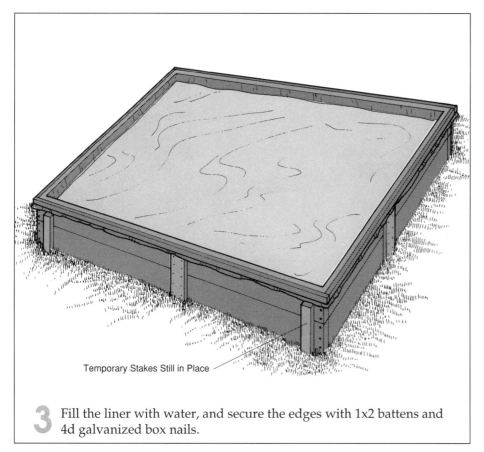

Temporary Stakes Still in Place

3 Fill the liner with water, and secure the edges with 1x2 battens and 4d galvanized box nails.

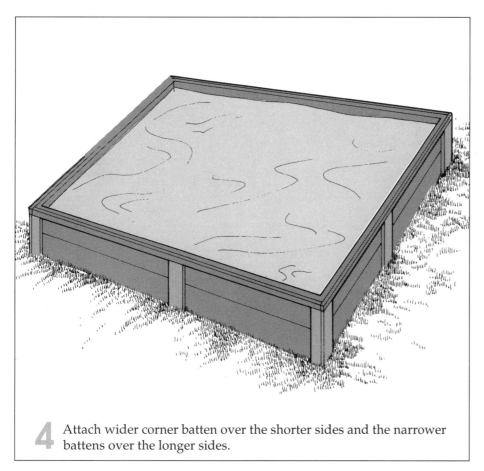

4 Attach wider corner batten over the shorter sides and the narrower battens over the longer sides.

straight board, and use it to check for level across the frame. Measure across the diagonals of the frame. If the measurements of both diagonals are the same, the frame is square. After the frame is square and level, drive stakes into the ground at each outside corner; then temporarily screw the stakes to the frame to hold it in position. With medium-grit sandpaper or a rasp, lightly round over any sharp edges on the pond rim.

3 **Installing the Liner.** Carefully check the ground within the frame for any sharp rocks, projecting roots, or other sharp objects, and remove these. Backfill inside the frame with 1 to 2 inches of sand or finely sifted soil. (You may use a liner underlayment material in lieu of sand; see page 18.) Loosely drape the liner into the box, keeping an even overlap on all sides. Then slowly fill the pond with water, lightly stretching and folding the wrinkles into neat creases as the water level rises. Take care not to overstretch the liner. When the water level is about 6 inches below the top edge of the box, shut off the water. Wrap the liner edge over the top of the pond, and secure the edges with 1x2 battens and 4d galvanized box nails, as shown. Trim the liner along the bottom of the 1x2 battens with a utility knife.

4 **Attaching the Corner Battens.** Each corner has a 1x4 batten (actually 3½ inches wide) that laps over the edge of a 1x2¾-inch batten. This way, the width of the corner looks the same on both sides. Work on one corner at a time. Remove the temporary stake and attach the corner battens with 2-inch galvanized decking screws. Attach the wider battens over the shorter sides and the narrower battens over the longer sides. This will stagger the butt joints at the corner, making the corners stronger.

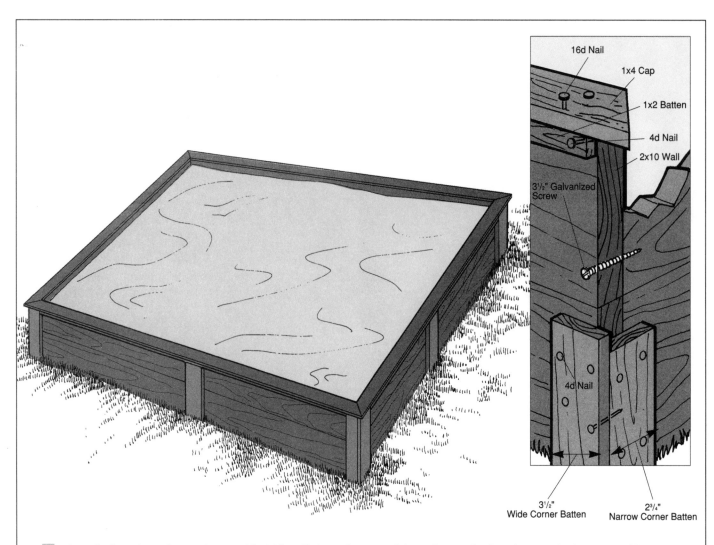

Labels in illustration:
16d Nail
1x4 Cap
1x2 Batten
4d Nail
2x10 Wall
3½" Galvanized Screw
4d Nail
3½" Wide Corner Batten
2¾" Narrow Corner Batten

5 Attach the mitered top pieces with 16d nails into the top of the sides and 4d nails into the horizontal battens.

5 **Cutting and Attaching Cap Pieces.** Cut the cap pieces to the lengths in the Materials List, with a 45-degree miter at each end. Nail the cap pieces into the top side pieces with 16d galvanized common nails, and into the horizontal battens with 4d nails galvanized finishing nails.

Materials List

Qty.	Part	Lumber
4	Long Walls	2x10x8'
4	Short Walls	2x10x69"
4	Middle Battens	1x4x17"
2	Long Battens	1x2x8'
2	Short Battens	1x2x73½"
4	Wide Corner Battens	1x4x17"
4	Narrow Corner Battens	1x2¾x17"
2	Long Cap Pieces	1x4x8'2"
2	Short Cap Pieces	1x4x74"

INSTALLING A PREFORMED SHELL

Rigid, preformed pond shells made of molded plastic or fiberglass are available in a variety of shapes and sizes. This chapter describes the basic installation steps; use these in conjunction with the instructions that come with the shell.

Basic Requirements

The ground in which you install the pond must be firm, stable, and free of rocks, projecting roots, and other sharp objects. Also, the shell must be fully supported by firm, well-packed earth in the excavation. Because a shell full of water can weigh up to several tons, any voids or bumps underneath may cause the shell to crack or buckle. In extremely loose or sandy soil, ground water can cause erosion around the shell, creating voids that will weaken it. Similarly, frost heaving in cold climates can deform or buckle the shell. If you anticipate either of these conditions, make the excavation about 6 to 8 inches deeper and wider than the shell. Next, backfill the hole with 3 to 4 inches of smooth pea gravel, topped with 2 inches of finely sifted soil; then tamp firmly. If you plan to place a statuary fountain, boulders, or other heavy objects in the pond, you may want to pour a concrete slab in the bottom of the excavation to support the additional weight before you install the shell.

Shell Installation

1 Marking the Shell Outline. Place the preformed shell upright in the desired location. Use plumbed stakes or a plumb bob to transfer the shape of the pond rim to the ground, and mark the outline with a rope or garden hose. Use stakes (spaced about 12 inches apart) to keep the hose or rope in place.

2 Digging the Hole. Excavate the hole to conform to the shape of the pond shell, allowing an extra 2 inches around the pond perimeter and 2 to 3 inches in the bottom of the hole. If the shell has shallow-water shelves, cut ledges at the appropriate locations to support them. The thinner shells, in particular, must be fully supported at all points. Remove any rocks or other sharp objects; then line the bottom of the hole with 2 to 3 inches of damp sand or finely sifted soil. (For thinner shells, you may also want to use an underlayment fabric; see page 18.) Flatten the bottom of the hole with a short board or screed, and then firmly tamp the soil to provide a stable base for the shell. Make sure the bottom of the excavation is perfectly level in all directions. You can do this with a 4-foot spirit level, or a shorter level placed on a 2x4 laid on the sand base.

3 Setting the Shell. With a helper, set the pond shell into the excavation, and check the height of the rim. It should be about 1 inch above the surrounding ground to prevent runoff from entering the pond. Add or remove soil from the bottom of the hole as necessary to achieve the desired height.

4 Leveling the Shell. Place a long, straight 2x4 across the shell rim in several places, and

1 Set the shell in position. Use leveled stakes and a garden hose to transfer the pond shape to the ground, as shown.

2 Dig a hole slightly larger than the shell; then backfill with damp sand. Use a short board to level the bottom of the excavation.

3 With a helper, lift the shell and lower it into the excavation.

4 Place a long 2x4 and level across the top of the shell in several locations to level it. Add more sand to support the bottom of the shell, if necessary.

check with a level. If the shell isn't level, pull it out of the hole and re-level the excavation as necessary. Just make sure the pond is perfectly level before you fill it with water. Even a few inches of water in the pond bottom will make the shell virtually impossible to move.

5 **Backfilling Around the Pond.**
After the shell is leveled, slowly fill it with water. As the water level rises, backfill the hole around the shell with sifted dirt or damp sand, tamping it gently with a shovel handle or the end of a 2x4. Make sure you fill all voids, especially around any shallow-water shelves. Check the rim for level frequently as you go. Do not allow the water level inside the pond to rise above the backfilled earth outside the rim, or else the shell will tend to bulge outward. In other words, try to equalize the pressure exerted on both sides of the shell as you backfill around it.

5 Slowly fill the shell with water, backfilling around the pond edges as the water level rises. Check frequently with a level.

6 **Adding Coping.** When the shell is filled with water, you can conceal the exposed rim with rocks, masonry materials, or overhanging plants. If you are using flagstones or flat pavers, allow them to overhang the pond edges by 1 to 2 inches. Don't allow the full weight of the edging to rest on the pond rim, because its weight may deform or damage the pond walls. Instead, embed the edging in a 3- to 4-inch-thick bed of mortar, raised slightly above the lip of the shell. After the mortar cures (in about one week), scrub the coping with distilled vinegar to neutralize the lime in the mortar. Then drain the pond, rinse it, and refill it with fresh water. (See page 74 for information on draining a pond.)

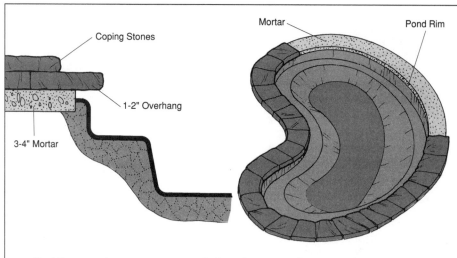

6 Place coping stones around the edges, overhanging them slightly to hide the shell rim. For a more permanent installation, mortar the stones in place.

Building a Raised Pond with a Preformed Shell

Some of the thickest shells can be installed freestanding, with only a thin, decorative skirt of wood, brick, or masonry block to support the rim. Thinner shells will require additional support—usually earth or concrete backfill—between the wall and the pond shell. Check with the shell manufacturer or dealer for the recommended application for the shell you've chosen. Follow the same backfilling procedure as for in-ground ponds (page 35). The drawings show details for a partially raised pond and a fully raised pond. For a partially raised pond, sink the lower part of the shell up to the shelf level. Then build

the wall from ground level up to the lip of the pond, backfilling behind the wall as you go (if required). If you are using brick, stone, or concrete blocks, you'll need to pour a footing to support the wall, as shown. Make the footing at least twice the width of the wall and a minimum of 4 inches deep. (In cold climates, deeper footings may be required; check local codes.) Build the wall up to the pond lip; then you can use mortar edging or cap stones over the lip to hide it, as shown.

Fully raised shells require a firm foundation. You can't install them on loose or shifting soil because this settling of the soil beneath will crack or buckle the shell. To play it safe, install the pond on a reinforced

concrete slab. Make the slab large enough to support both the shell and the outside supporting wall. The slab should be a minimum of 4 inches thick, with thickened edges (typically 6 inches thick) to support the wall. In cold climates, you may need to add a perimeter footing that extends below the frost line. Reinforce the slab with 1/2-inch reinforcement bars (rebar), spaced on a 12-inch grid; or use wire-reinforcing mesh. Check local codes for recommendations. In addition to the outside wall, install a second interior wall of bricks or concrete blocks to support the shallow-water shelves. Try to sandwich carpet padding or liner underlayment material between the shell and supporting masonry surfaces.

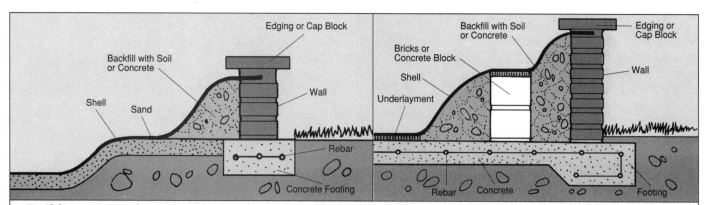

Building a Raised Pond with a Preformed Shell. The aboveground portion of a partially raised pond uses a brick skirt to conceal the shell (left). A fully raised pond requires firm support around the edges and underneath the shelf. Backfill voids with tamped soil or concrete (right).

STREAMS & WATERFALLS

Not only are streams and waterfalls attractive features in a pond, but they also aerate the water, providing additional oxygen for fish and other pond life. This chapter presents various design options and step-by-step directions for installing a simple series of cascading falls and pools.

Planning Pointers

Waterfalls can imitate the streams and cascades found in nature, or they can be formal in design. Natural-looking watercourses use rocks of various sizes: from large boulders to create a cascading effect, to smaller stones and pebbles placed in the watercourse itself. For formal ponds, you can incorporate timbers, poured concrete slabs, precast concrete basins, masonry blocks or bricks, or even ceramic tiles. In both formal and informal ponds, waterfalls usually consist of a series of small pools or catch basins linked by low cascades. If space is limited, you can install a single raised basin above the pond, connected by a single fall; or you can have the falls gush spring-like from a fissure in a rock wall or ledge above the pond. If space permits, you could include a meandering stream between the falls.

Building a successful watercourse is largely a matter of trial and error. To create the effect you want, you'll have to experiment with different sizes and shapes of rocks, as well as their placement in and around the watercourse. Before starting, try to have a good idea of the effect you want to create. Look at as many photographs of waterfalls as you can find. Take hikes along local streams, noting the size, shape, and texture of the rocks, and how the water moves over and around them. Study public and private man-made streams and waterfalls in your area. If possible, ask landscape architects and designers to show you their work. When observing man-made water features, find out the type and size of pump used to produce the effect.

Design your waterfall so all water drops directly into the pool or catch basin beneath it; large amounts of water will be lost if water is allowed to splash outside catch basins or the pond. Keeping the falls low and the watercourse relatively short will minimize water loss through evaporation. Smaller, deep basins are preferable to larger, shallow ones, too, for keeping evaporation to a minimum. Also, you must build the watercourse carefully to avoid leaks between rocks along the bank and behind the falls.

Sizing the Waterfall

You should keep the waterfall in scale with the pond. A small trickle in a large pond won't be very dramatic, and it will be relatively ineffective in recirculating and oxygenating the water. On the other hand, a large cascade gushing into a small pond will disrupt a large portion of the water surface, stirring up sediment and making it nearly impossible to raise fish, water lilies, and other aquatic plants that prefer still water. If you want both a large, cascading fall and aquatic plants, you should design the pond so that plants can be placed away from the wave action and splashing.

Choosing a Pump

Recirculated water from the pond supplies the running water in a waterfall or fountain. This is accomplished by a small electric pump. A variety of pumps made specifically for ponds are available from water-garden suppliers and local swimming-pool dealers. When choosing a pump, the first step is to select a size that will provide enough flow to operate the waterfall or other water feature in your pond. Beyond sizing, you must decide whether or not you want a submersible (in-pond) pump or one located outside the pond. Other considerations are the overall pump quality and durability. Let's start with sizing.

Sizing the Pump

In general, a pump that recirculates one half of the pond's total water volume per hour will provide the minimum flow required to produce a pleasing proportion of moving water for the size of the pond. For example, if the pond holds 1,000 gallons of water, you should select a pump that will deliver at least 500 gallons per hour (gph) at the top of the falls. For a larger, bolder cascade, select a pump that will turn over the total gallonage of the pond in one hour.

Planning Pointers. The most effective waterfalls consist of a series of small pools connected by short cascades.

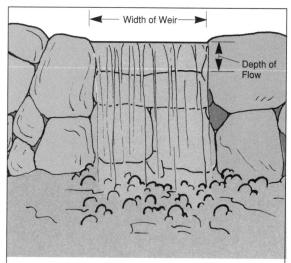

Sizing the Pump. For a heavy (1-inch) depth of flow over the weir, allow 150 gallons per hour for each inch of width; for a light (1/4-inch) depth of flow, allow 50 gallons per hour for each inch of width.

Pump Performance. Pump performance is determined by the amount of water the pump can deliver at various heights above water level. Pump makers provide this information in their performance data. For best performance, locate the pump near the base of falls.

Another way to determine the pump size is to directly calculate the amount of water required for cascades of various sizes. First measure the width of the spillway over which the water will flow (called the weir). Then decide how deep you want the water where it flows over the weir. For a light sheet of water (1/4-inch deep), allow 50 gallons per hour for each inch of weir. For a heavy flow (1 inch deep), allow 150 gallons per hour for each inch of weir. For example, if the falls will be 6 inches wide, you'll need a pump that can deliver 300 gph for a 1/4-inch-deep flow. It will deliver 900 gph for a 1-inch-deep flow.

Pump Performance. When shopping for a pump, check the performance charts that come with the product. Most pumps are rated in gallons per hour at a height of 1 foot above the water surface. The charts also list the amount of water delivered at various heights above the pump. This height is referred to as "head" or "lift." The higher you place the discharge for the waterfall above the pond, the lower the pump output. For example, a pump that delivers 300 gallons at a 1-foot head may deliver only 120 gallons at a 4-foot head.

In their performance charts, the manufacturers also provide a maximum

head figure, which is the theoretical maximum height to which the pump can lift water. In practice, the amount of water delivered near or at the maximum head will be reduced to a trickle. Also, the actual maximum head might be lower than the theoretical maximum, depending on how the pump is installed. Some pumps are designed with a low flow and high maximum head, whereas others of the same size are designed with a high flow but a low maximum head. For best pump performance, keep the total height of the falls well below the maximum head height. A total height of 2 to 3 feet above the pond surface should be enough for a visually

pleasing waterfall (or series of falls) while optimizing pump performance.

Positioning the Pump. Placing the recirculating pump or pump inlet close to the falls will increase the pump efficiency, because less tubing or pipe will be required between the pump and the head of the falls. As a rule of thumb, every 10 feet of horizontal pipe or tubing is equal to 1 foot of vertical rise in reducing the performance of the pump. A filter added to the system will also restrict flow. If you want to incorporate a fountain in addition to the waterfall, add the gallons per hour required to operate the fountain to your overall figure. Consult your pump supplier for details.

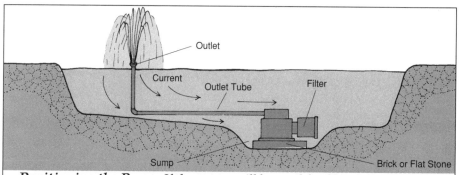

Positioning the Pump. If the pump will be used for filtration only, place the pump/filter at the deepest part of the pond. Or, in a sump, run the outlet tube to the opposite side of the pond for increased water circulation. Raise the pump/filter a few inches off the pond bottom to prevent frequent clogging of the filter.

If the pump will be used for filtration only (no waterfall or fountain included), arrange the system so that the pump intake is at one end of the pond and the discharge is at the other. This will produce a slight current across the bottom of the pond, which will aid in recirculating the water to remove sediment and other water impurities. Usually, you place the pump intake at the deepest part of the pond, and then you design the pond so that a slight current moves the sediment to this point. If you're using a submersible pump, raise it 2 or 3 inches off the pond bottom by setting it on a few bricks or flat stones to prevent silt and other sediment from clogging the pump intake. Most pumps have built-in strainers to prevent leaves and other heavy debris from clogging the pump.

Buy a pump slightly larger than you think you'll need. You can always restrict the flow, if necessary. Some pumps have valves to adjust the flow, or you can restrict the flow by installing a separate valve on the outlet side of the pump or by using a special restriction clamp that attaches to the outlet tubing. (Never restrict the flow on the inlet side of the pump; also, do not restrict the flow on the outlet or discharge side by more than 25 percent.) A typical flow-control valve is shown on page 54. Before buying the pump, find out if the dealer will allow you to exchange it for a larger size if it turns out to be too small to operate the waterfall to your satisfaction.

Other Pump Considerations

After you've determined what size pump you need, you still have several other decisions to make about the type of pump you want.

Submersible or External? First, decide whether you want to use a submersible pump or an external (recirculating) pump. For most garden ponds, submersible pumps are a better way to go because they run cooler and quieter than external

pumps, and they are generally less expensive. In most cases, they're also more economical to install and operate because less plumbing is required. Reasonably priced models range from 180 gph to 1,200 gph; high-capacity models are at 3,400 gph. Most submersible pumps can be used in conjunction with mechanical or biological filters to produce clear water. These filters are discussed on page 65. The pumps themselves come with strainers or prefilters on the pump inlet to keep leaves and other debris from clogging the pump impeller. The only time you need to remove the pump from the pond is to clean the attached filter or strainer. Some submersible pumps come with flow-regulator valves; others don't.

Usually, external pumps, like those used for swimming pools, are practical only for very large waterfalls and fountains, or in situations where a submersible pump would be unsightly or impractical, such as in a pond that doubles as a wading pool. With capacities ranging from 2,400 gph to over 8,000 gph, and a maximum head of up to 80 feet, external pumps are overkill for most backyard ponds. If you're installing a swimming pool, though, you might consider plumbing the pump and filtration system to also operate a pond and waterfall. If a submersible pump doesn't work with your pond design, you can buy a pump designed to operate either in open air or submersed. Compact in size, they're a good compromise in situations where a submersed pump would be unsightly or prone to damage and typical external pump would be too big for the pond. For external operation, these pumps usually have to be placed in a dry sump below the water level of the pond. Capacities are similar to submersible pumps above.

Determining Quality. When selecting a pump, buy the best you can afford. The least expensive (and least durable) pumps have plastic

housings and components. Their output is limited to about 300 gph or less, and they have a relatively short life span. They are suitable for occasional operation of relatively small water features, and they are designed for submersible use only.

Most pumps used for ponds have cast-aluminum housings with a corrosion-resistant epoxy finish. They are more durable and impact-resistant than plastic pumps, they are moderately priced, and they come in a wide range of capacities. However, aluminum-housed pumps are designed for freshwater use only, since aluminum will quickly corrode in saltwater, chlorinated water, or water frequently treated with pond chemicals. Also, if you add fish to the pond, the water will be slightly acidic. This condition will eventually erode the aluminum housing and components of the pump. So, aluminum-housed pumps are not recommended for such situations.

The most durable (and most expensive) pumps use a combination of brass, bronze, and stainless-steel components and housings. These pumps will withstand a variety of water conditions, including salty and chlorinated water. They're rated for continuous operation and will outlast the other pumps mentioned. Usually, they come in larger sizes only (800 gph or higher). If you expect the pond to be a permanent feature in your yard, these pumps are well worth the extra initial cost. When selecting a pump, also consider energy efficiency. Compare the pump's amp rating (or wattage, if it is given) to the output in gallons per hour. If two pumps have the same output, the one with the lower amp rating will usually be more energy-efficient. If you plan to add a biological or mechanical filter to the system, find out if it can be fitted to the pump you've chosen. With some pumps, your choices of filters will be limited; other pumps are more versatile. For more on choosing and installing pond filters, see page 65.

When selecting a pump, make sure the cord is long enough to reach the proposed or existing electrical outlet. Many pumps come with a 6-foot cord, which won't work if local codes require the electrical outlet to be 6 or more feet away from the pond edge. However, you can usually order longer cords from the pump manufacturer as an option. Use only cords and plugs specifically designed for use with the pump. Do not use extension cords to increase the cord length. For more on wiring pumps, see page 9.

Waterfall Types

Waterfalls look best and are less prone to water loss when large, overhanging rocks are used for the lip of the falls. Use smooth, flat flagstones to produce a wide, thin curtain of water; or direct the water through a narrow gap between large boulders to produce a gushing effect. Creating a hollow space behind the falls will amplify and echo the sound of falling water. To avoid losing a lot of water, you can use rocks or masonry materials to build up the pond walls behind the lip and on both sides of the falls to direct any splashes back into the pond. The lips of formal waterfalls can be brick, tile, flagstone, or timbers. Some designs incorporate a clear sheet of acrylic plastic to create a wide, nearly transparent curtain of water. The plastic itself is all but invisible when the falls are in operation. The drawings show several options for natural and formal waterfalls.

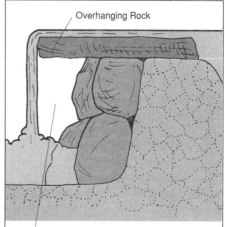

Waterfall Types. Flat, overhanging rock allows water to fall curtain-like, directly into the pond. Hollow space behind the falls echoes the sound of splashing water.

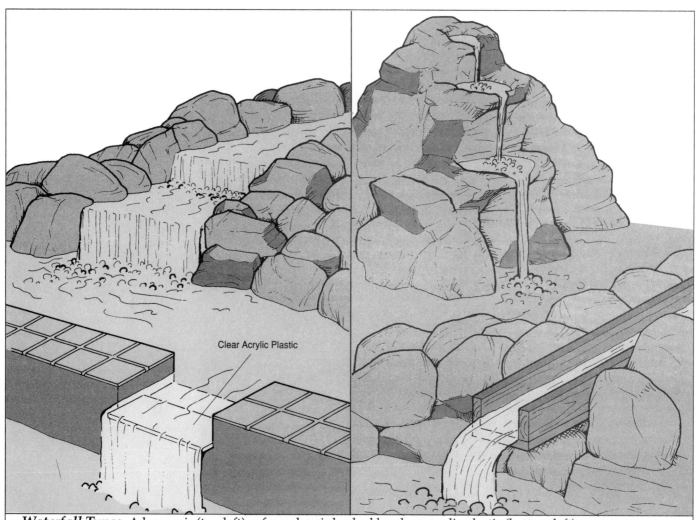

Waterfall Types. A low weir (top left), a formal weir backed by clear acrylic plastic (bottom left), a narrow cascade (top right), and a wooden flume (bottom right) are just a few of the many possibilities for waterfalls.

Streams

We've all admired swift-flowing streams and rivulets in nature. But contrary to what you might think, the stream bed is not steeply sloped to produce this effect. Natural mountain streams usually arrange themselves into a series of short, fairly flat sections, separated by low falls or cascades. So, when building a stream between a series of falls, be sure to make the bed as level as possible along its length, so that it will retain some water when the pump is turned off. Alternating between wet and dry conditions can crack mortar or concrete, or shorten the life of the plastic or fiberglass liner materials. A stream with some water at all times will also look more realistic. A drop of 1 to 2 inches per 10 feet is all that is needed to make the stream flow downhill. Also make sure that the stream bed or catch basin is level across its width, and that the banks are roughly of equal height; otherwise, the watercourse will look lopsided.

Controlling Water Speed & Direction

To increase the speed of the current, bring the stream banks closer together; for a more leisurely current, move the banks farther apart. A deep, wide, slow-moving stream is preferable to a fast, narrow one if you want to grow shallow-water bog plants along the edges. However, you should avoid large areas of slow-moving shallow water, because they will soon become clogged with thick mats of algae. In either case, a meandering course will look more realistic than a straight channel. Vary the size of the rocks along the banks and the distance between the banks. Placing large rocks inside the watercourse will create rapids, and placing smaller stones and pebbles produce a rippling effect. Both of these make the stream look and sound more natural.

When placing rocks for the stream and waterfall, do not mortar the top layer of rocks in place until you have installed the pump and run water down the course. With the water running, experiment with the placement of stones of different sizes and shapes in the stream bed and along the banks. Producing the exact effect you want may take a bit of trial and error, so take your time. In some cases, you may need to build up the banks of the stream or basin behind the falls to prevent water from splashing outside the watercourse or overflowing the banks.

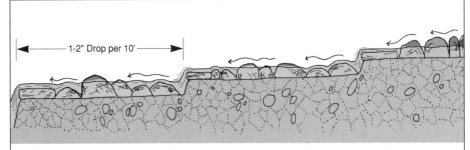

Streams. Dig the stream bed in a series of short, level sections between low waterfalls. Each section should hold some water when the pump is turned off.

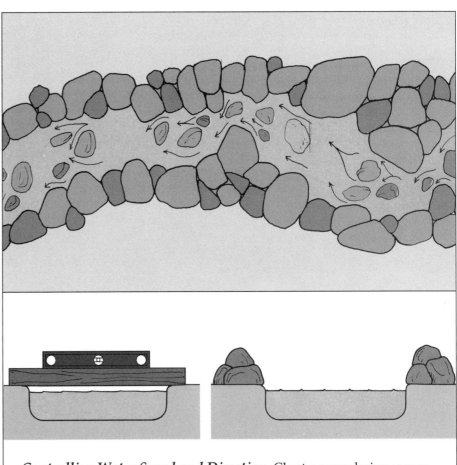

Controlling Water Speed and Direction. Chart a meandering course for the stream. Placing rocks in the stream bed will increase the current speed and make the stream look more natural (top). When digging the stream bed, make sure it is level across its width. Build up the banks with rocks to prevent splashing and overflow (bottom).

Lining the Watercourse

As with ponds, the stream beds and catch basins for waterfalls must be lined to prevent water loss. The same materials used to line ponds are also used to line the watercourse. The easiest to use and most versatile material is a flexible EPDM liner, although preformed rigid shells of plastic or fiberglass are also available. Don't line a watercourse with concrete or plastic cement, though, because the alternating wet and dry cycles will cause cracks. However, either cement or mortar is often used in conjunction with a flexible liner or preformed shell to hold large rocks in place along the watercourse and at the waterfall lip.

Flexible Liners

In waterfall construction, a flexible liner serves as a waterproof barrier under rocks, pebbles, and other decorative materials and directs any seepage back into the main pond. Flexible liners adapt well to both formal and informal waterfall designs.

Ideally, you should use one large piece of liner for both the waterfall and the main pond, to provide a continuous, seamless barrier. In practice, though, it is not always easy to align a square or rectangular sheet of liner material with the selected waterfall site without creating large amounts of waste material. More often, you'll have to figure the amount of material required by the pond and the waterfall separately. Usually, it is less expensive to order one large sheet, and then cut one or more strips from it to line the watercourse, rather than to order separate sheets for the watercourse and pond. You then glue or tape the sheets together where they overlap. (Special seam tapes and vinyl seam adhesives are available from the liner dealer for this purpose.) For more on sizing liners, see page 25. If the watercourse will be approximately the same width along its entire length, one long strip can be used. If the watercourse consists of pools and cascades of different lengths

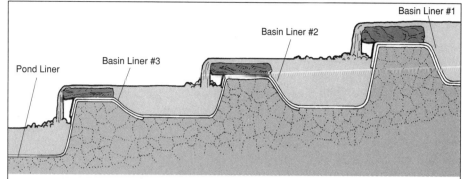

Flexible Liners. Flexible liner material can also be used for the watercourse. A continuous liner for the pond and waterfall is best, although pieces can be overlapped as shown here.

and widths, two or more separate pieces may be required. Allow sufficient overlap (at least 12 inches) at joints to prevent seepage due to capillary action.

Preformed Watercourses

Most companies that make rigid, preformed fiberglass or plastic ponds also offer preformed waterfall runs or courses made of the same material. These are installed much like a preformed rigid pond shell. (See page 34.) Informal preformed watercourses are shaped (and sometimes colored) to simulate natural rock, although most look fake unless the edges are disguised with overhanging stones or other materials.

Preformed watercourses have one main advantage over flexible liners: The design has been worked out in advance. Formal preformed waterfalls are usually smaller versions of square or rectangular preformed ponds, with a built-in lip or spillway. The units are arranged in overlapping tiers to produce a symmetrical series of falls into the main pond. Fiberglass and plastic

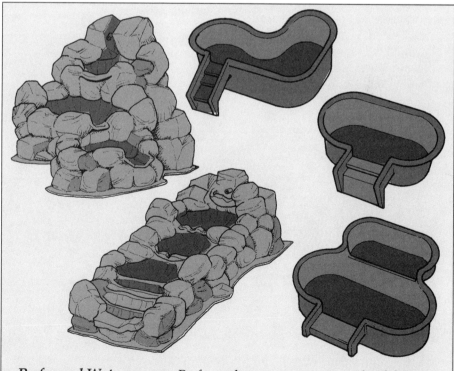

Preformed Watercourses. Preformed watercourses are made of the same rigid plastic or fiberglass material as preformed ponds.

water runs are lightweight and inexpensive; but, as with preformed ponds, the sizes and designs are limited. The premolded units consist of one or more small basins with built-in cascades and a lower lip that empties into the pond. You can combine two or more short watercourses in a series to produce a longer watercourse, each run emptying into the one below it. However, often you're still limited to the combinations recommended by the manufacturer, because each watercourse is designed to match the output of a particular-size pump: specifically from 200 to 500 gph for small units, and up to 1,300 gph for larger ones. If the pump is too small, the flow will be insufficient to achieve the desired effect; if the pump is too large, water will splash outside the watercourse or overflow the banks. (If you do oversize the pump, you can always divert some of the flow to operate another water feature or to run directly back into the pond.) Your supplier can help you choose a preformed watercourse to match the pump requirements of your pond. Preformed watercourses made of cement or reconstituted stone are also available. Although these are more substantial and natural-looking than plastic or fiberglass units, they are much heavier. As a result, the practical size of these units is limited to only a few square feet.

Installing a Preformed Watercourse

Preformed watercourses are installed much like the preformed pond shells discussed on page 34. The main difference is that you'll be recessing the watercourses into a slope or berm (mound) above the pond. Here is how to proceed.

1 Grading the Site. If you're working with a natural slope above the pond, all you need to do is excavate a pocket in which you place the watercourse. On flat ground, you'll have to build up a firm soil base to support the shell at the appropriate height above the pond. Use the soil from the pond excavation. The sides of the berm should slope gently away from the watercourse in all directions, with enough space to add rocks, plants, or other landscape materials to disguise the edges of the watercourse. Firmly tamp the built-up soil to provide support for the unit. Next, set the preformed watercourse in position on top of the mound; and mark its outline on the ground with flour, powdered gypsum, or a series of short stakes.

2 Digging the Hole. If you are installing more than one unit, start with the bottom one. Dig a hole to match the size and shape of the watercourse. If you're using a pre-

cast stone or concrete unit, tamp the soil firmly to prevent settling; then add a few shovel loads of wet cement in the bottom of the excavation to anchor the unit in place. Fiberglass and plastic units require firm support on the sides and bottom, or else they will deform when filled with water. Add or remove soil as necessary to conform to the shape of the shell. Also, before installing a watercourse, determine where the pump outlet tubing or pipe will go, and bury it in place a few inches beneath the soil. Some manufacturers suggest that you run the pipe or tubing in the same excavation, underneath the watercourse. Check the instructions that come with the unit.

3 Placing the Watercourse. Position the watercourse in the excavation so that the lip or spillway overlaps the pond edge. Check to make sure the basin or basins of the watercourse are level in all directions with a 4-foot level. If the level isn't long enough place a straight 2x4 across the rim and put the level on the 2x4. Backfill around the edges with sand or sifted soil, packing it firmly into the excavation and checking the level frequently. Build the backfilled soil to a height of 1 to 2 inches below the outside edge of the shell (flange), or as recommended by the manufacturer. Run the unburied length of pump outlet tubing

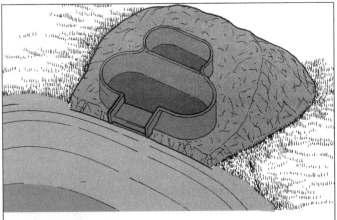

1 Build up a soil berm and set the unit in position. Mark the outline of a watercourse on the ground.

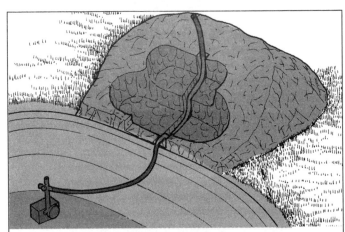

2 Excavate a hole to recess the unit into the side of the berm, or hill, above the pond. Run the pump outlet hose to the head of the watercourse.

into the top basin; secure it in place outside the watercourse with rocks, or as specified in the instructions.

4 **Testing the Watercourse.** Fill the watercourse with water, and check the water level around the rim to make sure the unit has remained level during the backfilling. If you haven't already done so, install the pump, attach the outlet tubing to it, and fill the main pond with water. Then pump water down the course. The water should flow evenly over the lip and any built-in cascades at a level of about 1 inch below the rim. (You should adjust the pump flow rate, if necessary.)

5 **Placing Additional Units.** If you will be installing additional sections of watercourse, follow steps 1

through 3 to install each successive one above the first. After installing and leveling each one, test it by running water down the course (step 4) and make any needed adjustments to the height and position of the unit. Make sure each unit is firmly positioned before installing the one above.

When all of the units are in place, connect the pump outlet pipe or tube to the top of the watercourse. Some units have built-in pipe or hose fittings for this purpose. With others, you can attach a short piece of plastic tubing to the outlet pipe; run the tubing over the rim at the top of the course; and disguise it with rocks or plants. Run the watercourse continuously for 48 hours; then recheck it for any settling, and readjust, if necessary.

6 **Landscaping.** Depending on the design of the unit, you may be able to use rocks or overhanging plants to disguise the edges of the watercourse and help blend it into the surrounding landscape. When setting large rocks or boulders around the rim, be careful that their weight does not crush or buckle the shell. For additional support, set the rocks or edging stones in a ribbon of concrete or cement mortar placed along the banks of the watercourse. If necessary, build up the edging above the surrounding ground level, and mortar between them to prevent soil from washing into the watercourse. Additional stones and ground-cover plants placed on the mound or surrounding slope will help prevent soil erosion.

3 Place the watercourse in the excavation and check that it is level. Backfill to hold the unit in place. Route the outlet tube into the top basin.

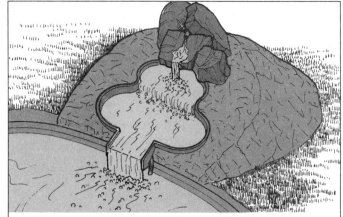

4 Turn on the pump and run water down the unit to make sure it works properly. Re-level the unit if necessary.

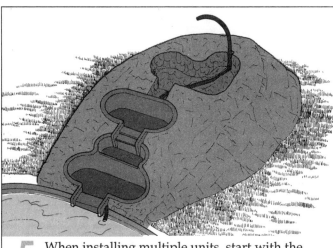

5 When installing multiple units, start with the bottom one; follow steps 1 to 4 to install each.

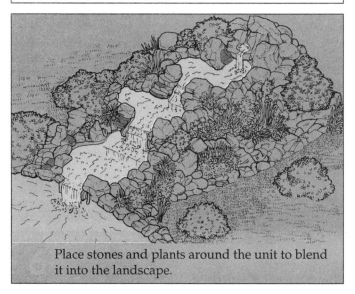

Place stones and plants around the unit to blend it into the landscape.

Installing a Lined Watercourse

If you're using a flexible plastic or rubber liner for your pond, excavate for the watercourse and install its liner at the same time. You can also add a lined watercourse to an existing pond of any material. Follow the instructions on page 24 for installing a vinyl-liner pond, along with the steps below for building the watercourse. When sizing the liner, allow enough extra material in the main pond to extend up and over the first waterfall lip and into the first catch basin.

1 **Grading the Site.** On flat ground, build up a berm of compacted soil next to the pond at the waterfall location. Make the berm large enough to accommodate the watercourse, with additional space around the perimeter to accommodate rocks and other landscaping materials. Where possible, slope the sides gently away from the proposed excavation to prevent runoff from washing dirt into the watercourse. Avoid steeply-sloped mounds, because they will be more prone to soil erosion. On sloping sites, cut level terraces into the hillside in which to dig the catch basins. Allow enough level space around each proposed hole to add rocks or other edging materials. For short lengths of stream, use a similar cut-and-fill procedure to provide a level course for the stream bed. On the ground, mark the location of the catch basins and connecting streams or cascades with stakes, flour, nontoxic spray paint, or a similar marking device.

2 **Excavating Catch Basins.** When you dig holes for the catch basins, remember that the finished watercourse will look smaller than the excavated holes once the rocks or other edging materials are in place. Because the catch basins are essentially mini-versions of the main pond, follow the same procedures outlined in steps 1 through 7 on pages 25-28 to dig and level

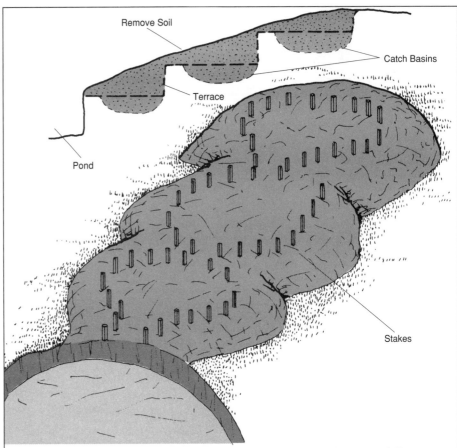

1 On a hillside site, cut level terraces into the hill at the waterfall location for catch basins. On flat sites, build up a soil berm and mark the basin locations with stakes.

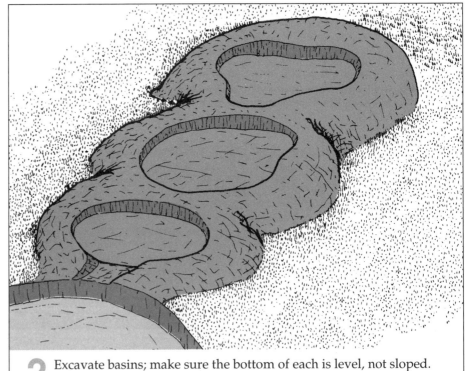

2 Excavate basins; make sure the bottom of each is level, not sloped.

the basins. If the catch basin is large enough, you may want to cut a shallow ledge around the perimeter of the basin in which to set partially submerged boulders or other edging materials.

3 Excavating a Stream Bed.
Use a series of leveled strings as guides to dig the stream to the appropriate depth. The bottom of the stream bed should be level, or at a very slight slope toward the pond, so that some water will remain in the stream when the pump is turned off. Streams look most natural if they are made in a series of short, level sections connected by low waterfalls. Use stakes and string or a level placed on top of a 2x4 to level the stream bed across its width.

4 Supporting the Waterfall Lip.
Allow a minimum of 12 inches of compacted soil between each catch basin to provide a stable base for the waterfall lip. For a firmer base in loose or sandy soil, use masonry blocks, poured concrete, or rubble to separate the catch basins and to provide support for waterfall lip materials.

5 Positioning the Liners. Start
by fitting the liner for the main pond, allowing enough overlap at the waterfall end to extend up and over the first waterfall lip. If you're using a single liner for the pond and watercourse, drape the liner over the entire excavation. Slowly fill the pond with water to hold the liner in place, and allow it to settle into its final position. To protect the liner, place a piece of liner underlayment under the liner where it overlaps the waterfall lip. Cut and fit the next piece of liner in the lowest catch basin, providing sufficient overlap with the main pond liner. Overlap the liners for additional catch basins in the same manner. For additional protection against leaks, join each liner with a special seam adhesive or seam tape (available from the liner dealer).

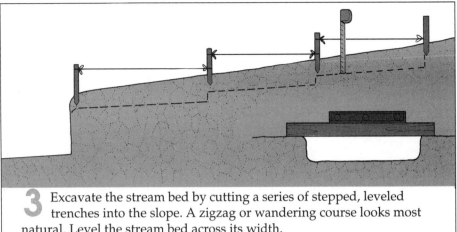

3 Excavate the stream bed by cutting a series of stepped, leveled trenches into the slope. A zigzag or wandering course looks most natural. Level the stream bed across its width.

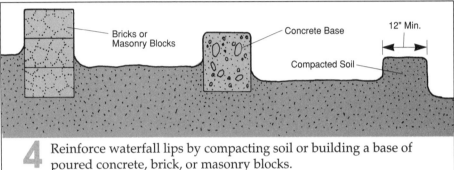

4 Reinforce waterfall lips by compacting soil or building a base of poured concrete, brick, or masonry blocks.

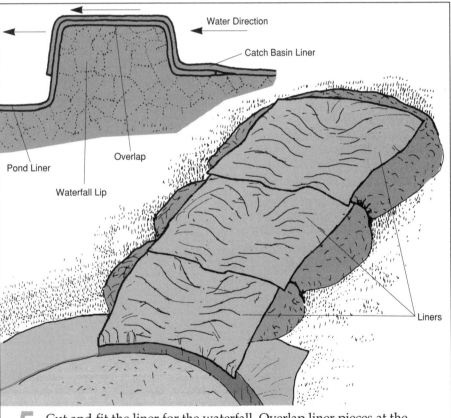

5 Cut and fit the liner for the waterfall. Overlap liner pieces at the waterfall lips, as shown. Adhesive or seam tape can be used to join pieces at overlaps.

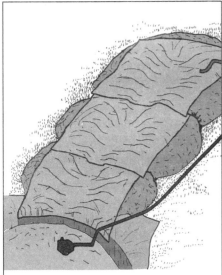

6 Install the pump and run outlet tubing or pipe alongside the watercourse to its top basin.

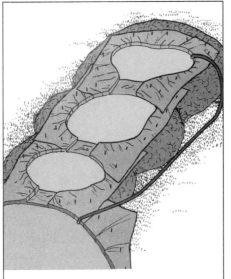

7 Fill catch basins with water, and use 20d nails or long spikes to hold the liner in position.

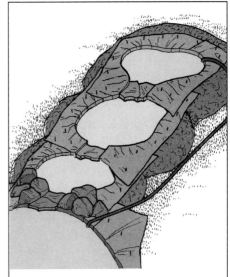

8 Position flat rocks or masonry units for waterfall lips. Build up large stones on either side of the lip to form channels.

6 **Installing the Pump.** Run the pipe or tubing alongside the watercourse from the point where it exits the pond to the top catch basin or head of the falls. (For more on installing pumps, see page 49.)

7 **Checking for Level.** After placing each liner, fill the catch basin(s) with water, as you did for the pond, to settle the liner in place. Check for leaks, and note the water level around the rim of each basin. If you note any high or low spots, remove or add soil beneath the liner, as necessary, to level the basin. To keep the liner in place while adding edging, push 20d nails through the liner into the ground every foot or so around the edges, above the waterline.

8 **Finishing the Waterfalls.** Start by positioning the overhanging rocks or other edging materials across the waterfall lip and on either side of it. For a more natural effect, you can also place stones behind the waterfall beneath the lip, to hide the liner. The top surface of the stones, or weir, should be just slightly below the water level of the stream or basin above, so that water will flow from one basin to the next without

overflowing the banks. Turn on the pump and notice how water flows over each weir; adjust the height and angle of the stones, if necessary, to provide a pleasing cascade. When you're satisfied with the results, place remaining stones around the perimeter of each basin or along the stream banks to hide the liner edges. Mortaring the rocks in place will prevent them from slipping into the watercourse. Additional stones may be placed in the watercourse to alter the flow pattern, although you should avoid using gravel in the stream bed because it will soon become clogged with algae and silt.

9 **Landscaping.** If you're building a natural-looking watercourse, arrange additional rocks and boulders of various sizes in the vicinity of the waterfall. Provide planting pockets between the stones for low shrubs, annuals, ground covers, succulents, and the like.

Use a combination of large boulders, medium-size rocks, and small pebbles to avoid making the waterfall area look like a man-made pile of rocks.

9 Finish landscaping the waterfall by placing rocks to hide liner edges. Turn on the pump, and run water down the falls to see how they work. Rocks placed in stream and basins will alter the course of water down the falls. Experiment with sizes and placement of rocks in falls to achieve a desired effect.

Installing the Pump

Follow the pump manufacturer's instructions for plumbing and wiring the pump. When you order the pump, also order all the required fittings, valves, and pipe needed to operate the waterfall. At the same time, order any other water features you may wish to include, such as a separate filter or fountain. As mentioned, you should order an electrical cord long enough to reach from the pump location to the electrical outlet. (For more on plumbing filters in the system, see page 39)

Electrical Requirements

In many municipalities, a licensed electrician must do the wiring. In all cases, though, you should check local codes for outdoor electrical requirements before you start. Make sure all outlets, wiring, and connections are designed for outdoor use. Most small submersible pumps come with a waterproof cord, which you plug into a GFCI receptacle housed in a weatherproof outlet box. With some larger pumps (submersible and external), you wire the cord directly into the circuit, with the connection enclosed in a weatherproof junction box near the pond. The latter method requires a GFCI breaker wired into the circuit, either in the main panel or in a subpanel. In either case, it is a good idea to wire the circuit so you can control the pump by a switch located inside the house. If possible, locate the outlet or junction box in an inconspicuous and protected area, such as under a deck or against the side of a building. Unless the cable you're using is designed for underground use, encase it in PVC (grey) electrical conduit. In either case, bury the cable at least 18 inches deep so it won't be disturbed by spades, rototillers, or other gardening equipment. Again, check local codes for outdoor electrical requirements. (See Utility Access on page 9.)

Plumbing Requirements

Plumbing requirements will vary, depending on the pump model, length of the pipe run, and the number of water features the pump will operate. Some pumps are sold with a length of inexpensive clear plastic tubing, which is a larger-diameter version of the type used for aquarium pumps. Although such tubing is adequate for short runs, it has several drawbacks. First, the thin walls of the tubing are easily crushed or kinked, so you can't bury it underground or make it conform to sharp bends. If, on the other hand, the tubing is exposed to sunlight, algae will build up on the inner walls, restricting flow. Because exposure to sunlight will eventually make the tubing brittle, it must be replaced periodically.

One solution is to run a short piece of flexible tubing from the pump to the pond edge; then connect it to a rigid PVC pipe that runs to the top catch basin at the head of the falls. Or, you can use a higher-grade reinforced flexible tubing for the entire run, or a special black vinyl tubing sold by pump suppliers. Do not use garden hose, however.

When ordering tubing or pipe, the diameter must match or exceed the hose requirements for the pump. If you reduce the diameter, the pump flow will be restricted.

When you run the end of the outlet hose or pipe into the top of the watercourse, you may find that the water pressure produces a strong jet that causes water to splash outside the catch basin. If this happens, run the hose under a small pile of rocks in the catch basin; or fit a short section of larger perforated pipe or hose over the end of the outlet.

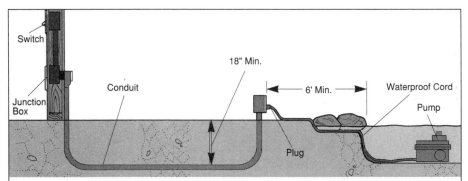

Electrical Requirements. Submersible pumps must be connected to a GFCI-protected circuit. Here, the circuit is wired so the pump can be operated from inside the house.

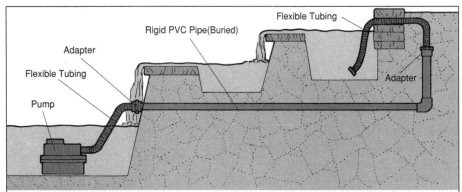

Plumbing Requirements. For long pipe runs, use rigid PVC pipe, buried in a trench alongside the waterfall. Connect the pump to the pipe with a short length of flexible tubing. This enables you to easily remove the pump from the pond for cleaning and maintenance. Secure all connections with hose clamps.

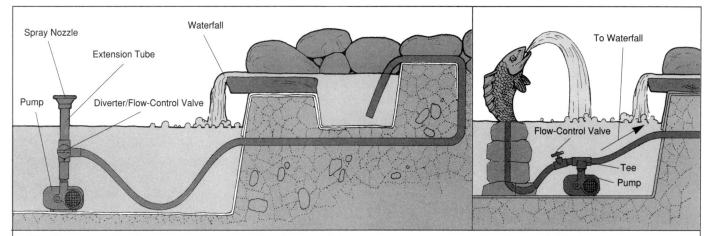

Fittings. Install a flow-control valve in the shorter of the two pipe runs to regulate flow to both features. As you restrict flow to one feature, the flow to the other feature increases (left). A diverter valve controls the flow to both the fountainhead and waterfall. Many spray fountain kits come with this feature (right).

Fittings. Pump suppliers offer a wide range of fittings and adaptors for their pumps to connect them to various water features. Your pump supplier can help you choose the appropriate fittings for your particular application. Most fittings for flexible plastic tubing are a barbed, push-fit type, whereas fittings and connections for rigid PVC pipe are either threaded or welded with PVC cement. When using push-type fittings, install hose clamps at all connections to prevent leaks. Some pumps require brass fittings on the pump discharge (volute), which may or may not include a flow-control valve. Depending on the pump design, you may need to install an adaptor fitting to convert to flexible tubing or rigid PVC pipe. Adding a tee fitting with a diverter valve enables you to operate two water features at once, such as a fountain and waterfall. You can accomplish the same result by installing an in-line flow-control valve in the shorter of the two pipe runs, as shown. Both types of fittings enable you to regulate the amount of water supplied to each feature. If you don't install a diverter or flow-control valve, the pumped water will take the path of least resistance (i.e., the shorter pipe run). The result will be either too little flow to operate one feature, or too much flow to operate the other, or both.

Keep in mind that the pump should have enough capacity to operate both features, pond and waterfall. When plumbing the waterfall, keep sharp bends and right-angle couplings to a minimum, as these tend to restrict flow. Use nontoxic plastic valves and fittings wherever possible; brass and other metal fittings can corrode and may be toxic to fish. Plastic ball valves have largely replaced old-fashioned metal gate valves in pond and swimming pool plumbing applications.

Float Valves. Another fixture you may find useful is a float valve used to top off the pool. Several different types are available. They work much like a ballcock valve in a toilet tank;

when the water level drops, the float lowers, opening a valve that allows more water to be fed into the pond through a pipe or tubing connected to a nearby faucet. The system is separate from the pump plumbing. A simple setup using a bobby-float valve (like the ones used for evaporative coolers) is shown. Here, the valve is clamped to a short steel rod mortared between stones just below the waterline. The valve is connected to the main water supply by means of 1/4-inch diameter copper or plastic tubing. When installing such a system, make sure there is no chance of pond water siphoning back into the water supply. As usual, check the local codes about installation.

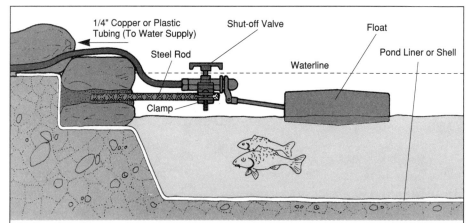

Float Valves. An inexpensive bobby-float valve attached to the pond edge will keep the water level constant. Similar devices are available at water-garden suppliers.

F O U N T A I N S

Whether you incorporate a fountain into your garden pond or install a fully self-contained unit, you've added the element of moving water into an otherwise static landscape. From simple to ornate, fountains please the ear as well as the eye, providing a striking focal point in the yard. This chapter shows some of the options and provides installation details.

Types of Fountains

There are two basic kinds of fountains: sprays (or fountain jets) and ornamental statuary.

Sprays

A fountain spray consists of a jet nozzle or ring attached to the outlet pipe of the pump above the pond's water level. It produces an attractive ornamental spray. When run from the pump to a level just beneath the water surface, a fountain spray made from a length of vertical pipe will provide a natural-looking geyser effect. For a larger, more dramatic geyser, you should use a geyser jet fitting like the one shown. Because they introduce air bubbles into the spray, geyser jets are excellent for aerating the water, although they must be sized and placed carefully to avoid stirring up silt and sediment in the pond and producing cloudy water as a result. To be visually effective, geysers usually require large-capacity pumps. The drawing shows several popular fountain-spray patterns.

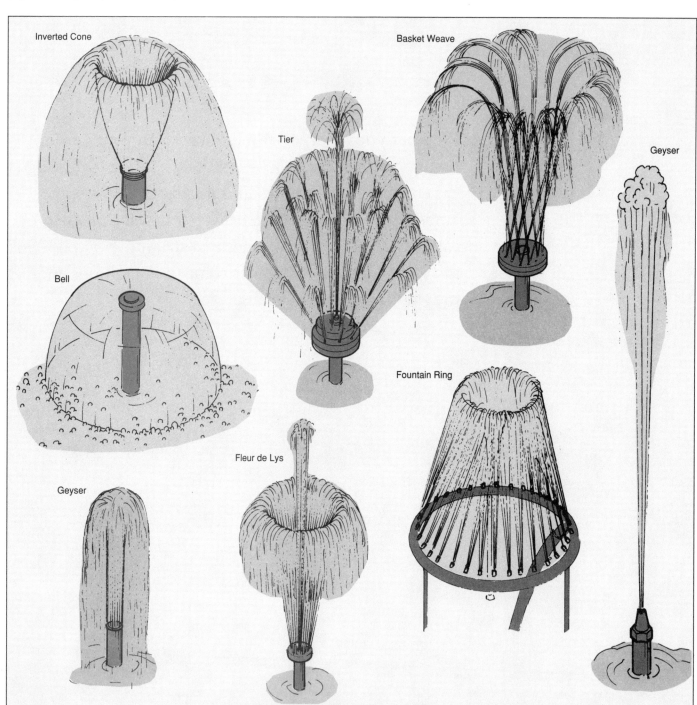

Inverted Cone

Basket Weave

Tier

Geyser

Bell

Geyser

Fleur de Lys

Fountain Ring

Sprays. Fountain Jets come in a wide variety of ornamental spray patterns. Shown here are some of the classics. Choose a pattern that fits the size, design, and mood of your pond.

Most jet nozzles are made of molded plastic and come with all the fittings required for installation. These include the correct-size pump and usually a flow-control valve that enables you to adjust the height of the spray. Higher-quality nozzles can be disassembled to make cleaning the jet holes easier; lesser-quality nozzles are more difficult to clean. Brass nozzles are generally used for larger water displays, but they're more expensive than plastic. Keep in mind that nozzles with small holes clog easily and will require frequent cleaning.

If you choose a spray-type fountain, place it in a sheltered area so that wind gusts don't disrupt the spray pattern or blow the water outside the fountain receptacle. Nozzles that produce delicate sprays or thin films of water (such as water-bell jets) need to be installed in a virtually wind-free location.

Statuary fountains

Statuary fountains run the gamut of designs from classical Greek figures and wall-mounted gargoyles to modern art forms and whimsical spouting frogs or fish. Most statuary fountains sold at garden and patio suppliers are precast concrete or cement. They come with a variety of colors and surface finishes to simulate other materials, such as stone, alabaster, or bronze. Some suppliers also carry modern sculpture fountains made of copper, brass, or bronze. Although on-site selections are usually limited, most suppliers can order what you want through catalogs. In times past, fountain statuary was often made of lead. If you find one of these relics, be warned that lead is toxic to fish and other aquatic life.

You can buy statuary fountain ornaments separately to put in the pond or next to it. Or you can buy these ornaments as complete, self-contained units with precast reservoir bowls and integrated pre-plumbed pump/filter systems. Precast pool pedestals of various heights are available for mounting statues or water jets in the pond. Fountain options are too numerous to describe in this book. Make sure, though, that you choose one that fits the style and size of your pond or garden. A large fountain can visually overwhelm a small pond and disrupt the water surface, making it difficult to raise water plants or to view fish beneath the surface. Also, if the spray is too large for the size of the pond, excessive water evaporation will be a problem.

Statuary fountains. Whether traditional or contemporary, ornamental statues lend a formal touch to the garden. Thumb through catalogs at your local patio supply or statuary dealer.

Installing a Fountain Spray

The way to install a spray nozzle depends largely on the pump you've chosen and the fittings available for it. Because so many variations exist, we cannot provide specific instructions for every situation. The easiest route is to buy a fountain spray kit, which includes your choice of spray nozzle, all required fittings, and a matched pump. Fittings are either press-fit or threaded, and they can be assembled in just a few minutes.

The outlet for most submersible pumps designed for fountains is located on the top of the pump. With this arrangement, the vertical rigid PVC discharge pipe can be attached directly to the outlet. (On some units, an adaptor fitting may be required.) You cut the pipe to extend the required distance above the water level (typically 4 to 6 inches); then you attach the spray nozzle, as shown. If the pump has a side discharge, you'll need to install an elbow fitting. If you're also operating another water feature, such as a waterfall or second fountain, install a diverter control valve in the pipe, as shown. To prevent the nozzles from clogging, attach a special pre-filter or filter screen to the pump inlet (this is available from the pump supplier). Or, you can buy units that combine the pump and filter in a single housing. The filter should be easily accessible for routine cleaning.

To install the fountain, attach the fittings and spray nozzle according to the manufacturer's instructions. Place the pump on a flat, level section of the pond bottom. Make sure the pump and discharge pipe are firmly supported so the pipe remains perfectly vertical after it is installed. If the unit has a tendency to tip or move out of position, place a few bricks around and on top of the pump to hold it in place. To provide the appropriate electrical connection for the pump, follow the guidelines on page 49.

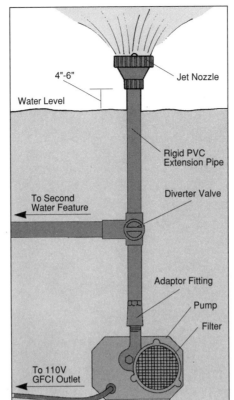

Installing a Fountain Spray.
Jet nozzles can be attached directly to the pump outlet via extension pipes. Place the nozzle 4 to 6 inches above the water surface. You can plumb in a diverter valve to operate a second water feature (another fountain, waterfall, pond filter, etc.).

Underground Geyser

This simple water feature gives the illusion of a natural spring or geyser, welling up from the earth and returning to it. It is a good alternative if you don't want the hassle of maintaining a pond. As shown on the drawing, you create a lined, stone-filled "reservoir" in which you place the fountain assembly. The reservoir should hold about the same amount of water as the gallon capacity of the pump you've chosen. For a natural appearance, use a foaming geyser jet like the one shown. You could also use small bell sprays and single jets. Just make sure the spray does not extend past the edges of the reservoir. After installing the liner, place the assembly in the bottom of the reservoir. Then fit a large, inverted plastic plant basket (used for water plants) over the pump to keep gravel or rocks away from the pump inlet. Cut a small hole in the bottom of the basket, and slip it over the extension pipe; then install the jet nozzle. Next, fill the reservoir with clean, smooth creek stones, pebbles, or decorative rock about 2 to 4 inches in diameter. Weight down the edges of the liner with larger stones, or simply extend the rock fill as far beyond the edge of the reservoir as you want.

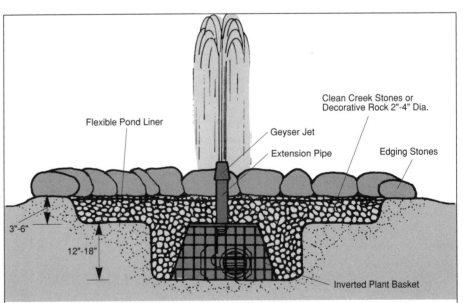

Underground geyser. Underground geysers fit well into small yard spaces; they make excellent water features if you don't want the hassle of maintaining a pond.

Installing a Statuary Fountain

Most statuary fountains come with a set of basic installation instructions. Use these in combination with the guidelines below to install the unit you've chosen.

A Self-Contained Fountain

In this type of fountain, a small submersible pump is typically housed in the statue pedestal, which sits in the reservoir bowl. The pump cord runs down an overflow tube inside the pedestal, through the bowl and hollow base. Most self-contained fountains have some way to access the pump for cleaning and maintenance. You should follow manufacturer's directions for assembly.

In-Pond Statuary

You can also place fountain statuary or ornaments inside the pond itself. The drawing below shows the basic setup. The statue itself has a supply pipe projecting from its base, which you connect to the pump with flexible tubing, as shown. You can mount the statue on a hollow in-pond pedestal, or build your own pedestal with mortared bricks, stones, or other masonry units. Some statuary fountains can be quite heavy, so you'll need to provide a firm base on the pond bottom.

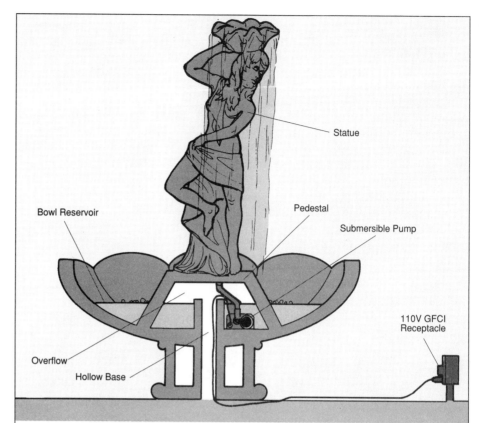

A Self-Containted Fountain. Self-contained fountains include pump and all fittings required to operate. A miniature submersible pump is hidden inside the hollow statue pedestal in the bowl reservoir.

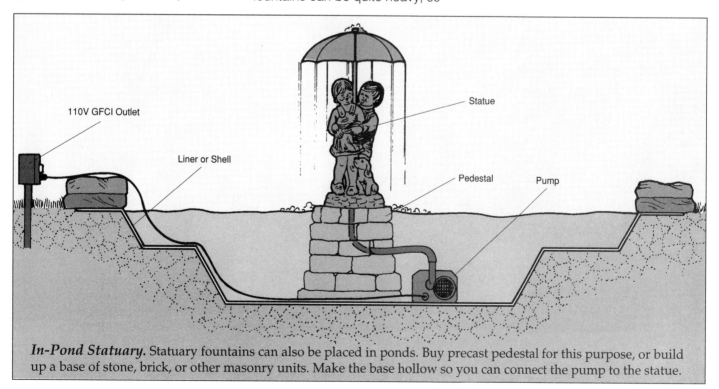

In-Pond Statuary. Statuary fountains can also be placed in ponds. Buy precast pedestal for this purpose, or build up a base of stone, brick, or other masonry units. Make the base hollow so you can connect the pump to the statue.

Installing the Fountain

1 Making A Footing. For heavy statues (over 100 pounds), provide a suitable footing underneath the pond shell or liner. This usually consists of a 4-inch-thick concrete subbase, a few inches wider and longer than the statue base, or pedestal. If you don't provide such a footing, the weight of the statue may tear the flexible pond liner or crack the rigid pond shell. Install the footing before you place the shell or liner. For lighter statues, all you need do is compact the soil firmly under the statue location before placing the shell or liner.

2 Installing the Pedestal. If you've purchased a statue pedestal, place it in the pond on top of the footing area. Otherwise, build up a pedestal with mortared bricks or stones. If you are using a flexible liner, cut a small piece of liner underlayment to place between the base of the pedestal and liner. Leave an opening near the bottom of the pedestal to run flexible tubing from the pump to the statue. To facilitate cleaning and maintenance, locate the pump outside the pedestal.

3 Installing the Pump. Situate the pump next to the pedestal. Run flexible tubing from the pump up through the pedestal, allowing enough extra tubing at the top to connect to the statue or ornament.

4 Installing the Statue. With a helper, move the statue in position on top of the pedestal. Tilt the statue slightly to make the connection between the pump outlet tubing and the pipe projecting from the statue base. (An adaptor fitting may be required.) Secure the connection with a hose clamp, and then rest the statue in its final position. It is not a good idea to mortar or otherwise affix the statue to the pedestal, in case you need to replace the outlet tubing at a later date.

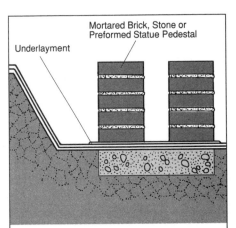

1 When installing a flexible liner, provide a concrete footing underneath to support the weight of the statue.

2 Build up the pedestal. Allow an opening near the pedestal base to run the pump outlet tubing. Underlayment protects the liner under the base.

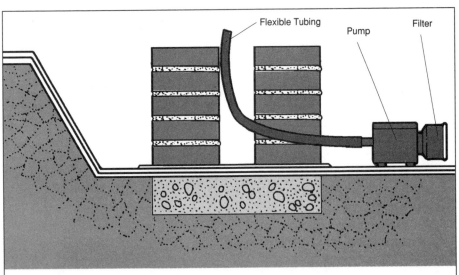

3 Install the pump and filter; run flexible outlet tubing up through the base, allowing some extra at the top to facilitate the connection to the statue.

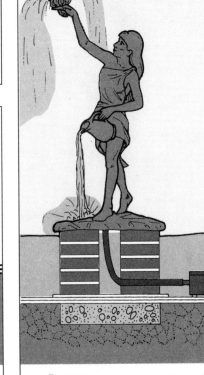

4 With a helper, position the statue on the pedestal and connect outlet tubing to the fitting on the statue base.

BRIDGES & STEPPING STONES

Bridges and stepping stones not only provide a way to cross a pond or stream, but they also enable you to enjoy the pond from a different viewpoint. Plan these features when designing the pond rather than incorporating them as add-ons later.

Wooden Bridges

A wooden bridge across a stream or a portion of a large pond provides architectural interest, as well as a shortcut from one side to the other. Bridges can be simple to ornate, depending on the style you've chosen for your pond and the various features around it. So, when designing a bridge, take the surrounding landscape into account. Also decide where the bridge will originate and end, and how

it will affect the location of paths and other landscape features in the yard. Size the bridge so that it is in proportion with the pond or stream. For a very narrow stream or small pond, a couple of wide planks laid from one bank to the other may suffice. Increase the width and height of the bridge accordingly for a larger body of water. Make the bridge wide enough to cross safely, yet in proportion with the pond and surrounding landscape. Bridges more than 12 to 18 inches

above the water should have handrails, both for safety and appearance. Bridges with spans longer than 8 feet will usually require vertical support posts set into the pond at midspan or every 6 to 8 feet. Be sure to provide a sturdy foundation for the support posts when you install the pond. The drawings show several simple bridge designs. Use pressure-treated or decay-resistant lumber, as well as rust-resistant hardware and fasteners, for all bridge members.

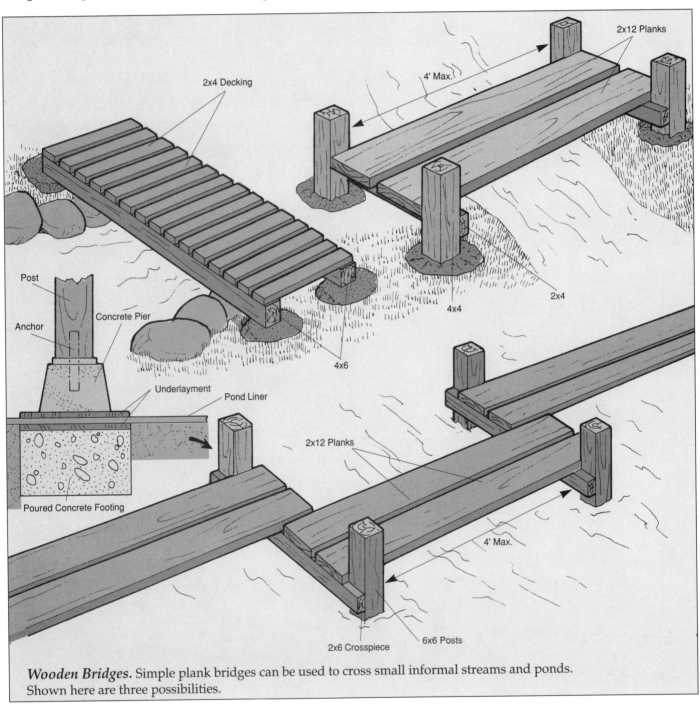

Wooden Bridges. Simple plank bridges can be used to cross small informal streams and ponds. Shown here are three possibilities.

A simple footbridge across your pond can be built with 2x8s for support beams, 2x4s for decking and handrails, 4x4s for the posts, and 3/8-inch diameter anchor bolts to hold the structure in place. The following describes a 4-foot-wide bridge to span a 4-foot depression.

1. Positioning the Posts. Pairs of 4x4 posts set 4-foot apart on center, and 7 feet apart on center on opposite sides of the depression. To be sure the post hole locations are square, lay the 2x8 supports across the depression as visually parallel and square as possible, and as close as possible to their final position.

On one side of the depression lay a 4-foot long 2x4 across the ends of the ties so that the 2x4 overhangs by 4 inches on each side. Using the outside edges of the beams as guides, stake the locations of the posts. Repeat on the other side. Remove beams and dig post holes to at least 18 inches deep.

2. Installing the Posts. Set the 4x4 posts in a bed of gravel. Pour concrete an inch or so above grade at the support post. Slope the concrete away from the post for good drainage. The posts should reach above the planned top level of the 2x8 beams. You can trim the posts after the 2x8s are in place.

When the concrete sets, you are ready to lay the beams.

3. Installing Beams. Set the 2x8s against the support posts with the posts outside the beams; the 2x8s will extend beyond the posts by 4 inches. Check the beams for level with a carpenter's level. Make minor adjustments by placing stones under the beams to level them. When the 2x8s are level in the position relative to the posts, nail them to the posts with 20d nails. Trim the posts off flush with the top of the beams.

4. Securing Beams and Decking. With the 2x8s secured to the posts, drill two 3/8-inch holes through the posts and the beams where the posts meet the beams. Secure the beams to the posts with 3/8x6-inch diameter bolts.

Nail the 2x4 decking across the top of the beams, 2-inch side up.

The 2x4s should overlap the ties 8 inches on each side. Keep the decking square by starting at either end of the beams with the first 2x4 flush with the end edges of the beams. Space the 2x4s 1 inch apart; use a spacer scrap to keep the distance equal. Toenail 2x4s to ties with 20d nails. The decking will be even more secure if you tie it all together by nailing 1x4 spacers between each 2x4 as you lay the 2x4 deck members. The 1x4s should be as long as the 2x4s.

5. Installing Handrails. If the codes permit, you may wish to omit the handrail. For a handrail, extend the 4x4 supports above the top of the ties by 3 feet or to the height specified by the local code. Attach a 2x4 or 2x6 handrail, 2-inch side up. Handrails should be bolted with a minimum of two 3/8-inch diameter bolts at each post.

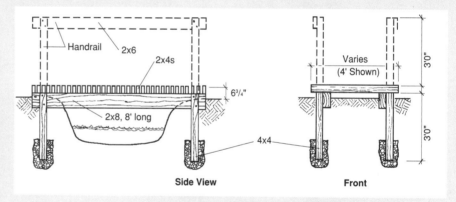

Side View   Front

Arched Bridge

If you would like a footbridge with a slight arch, use two 2x8s. Cut the tops of the 2x8s in an arc that drops from the full width at the center down to 4 inches at the ends. Handrails can be arched in the same manner. To lay out a smooth curve, tack nails into the board about every foot and bend a 1/4-inch thick piece of wood against the nails. Make the cut with a saber saw or band saw. Another option is to use curve-sawed boards, available at some lumber companies.

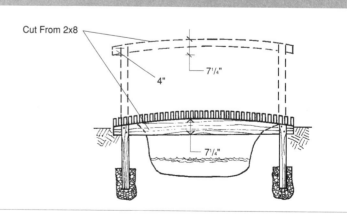

Stepping Stones

Stepping stones are a convenient way to cross a pond or stream, but are not as visually obtrusive as a bridge. They can either lead all the way across the pond, or simply a few feet out into it for observing or feeding fish. For formal ponds, you can use square or rectangular cast-concrete stepping stones or slabs, large quarry tiles, cut stone, or similar geometric masonry units. These are usually supported by piers of mortared bricks or concrete blocks. For informal ponds, you might use irregularly shaped flat rocks or flagstone, placed in a random pattern. If the pond is shallow enough, you may be able to use large rocks or stone slabs set directly in the pond. Otherwise, build up a layer of mortared flat rocks, or construct piers of poured concrete, brick, or block to support the stones.

If you've installed a flexible liner or preformed shell, you'll need to provide a suitable footing to support the stones and piers (if they are used). Protect the liner or shell by sandwiching it between layers of pond liner underlayment, as shown. Stepping stones usually look best if staggered in a zigzag or random pattern across the pond, rather than in a straight line. Place the stones close enough together so that people can walk without hopping, and make sure the stones are large enough to provide a stable footing. The surface of the stones should be high enough above the water so that they stay dry. Avoid placing the stones near a waterfall or fountain. Keep in mind that algae or moss will grow on wet surfaces, and make the stones slippery.

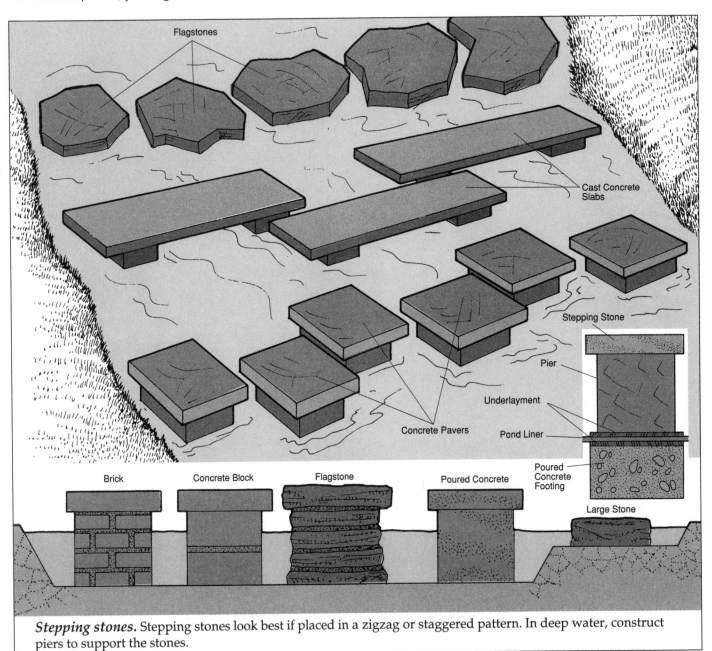

Stepping stones. Stepping stones look best if placed in a zigzag or staggered pattern. In deep water, construct piers to support the stones.

WATER QUALITY

Keeping pond water clear and healthy for fish and plants is one of the greatest challenges in water gardening. But even if you're able to achieve crystal-clear water, it may contain invisible chemical and mineral pollutants that can adversely affect the life within. To keep your water pure, you'll have to provide both biological balance and adequate filtration. This chapter gives the basic guidelines you'll need in order to do both.

Balancing the Water

The term "biological balance" simply means establishing a healthy ecological balance between plants, fish, and other aquatic life in the pond. Various factors affect ponds, including the size and depth, the amount of sunlight or shade, water temperature, water movement, pollutants in the water, and the kind and number of plants and fish. Depending on how these factors affect your pond, it may take anywhere from several weeks to several months to achieve this balance. Once the pond water is balanced, it will remain relatively clear provided you don't add fish, plants, or other pond life. Of course, if you do add any of these, you will need to take other measures to keep the water clear. Usually, you can do this just as you would with a swimming pool, by incorporating a mechanical or biological filter, using chemicals periodically, and routine cleaning.

How It Works

Think of your pond as a small, self-contained ecosystem. When you introduce aquatic plants, they draw nutrients (nitrates and phosphates) directly from the water and also the soil—if the plants are potted. These nutrients, combined with sunlight, cause the plants to grow and release oxygen into the water in a process known as photosynthesis. When fish are introduced, they consume the oxygen produced by the plants. To some measure, the fish rely on the plants as a source of food, and so keep excessive growth of the plants in check. In turn, the fish provide nutrients (carbon dioxide through breathing and nitrogen from fish wastes) to promote plant growth. Surface plants such as water lilies also benefit fish by providing shade during the hot summer months and controlling the water temperature. Plants give fish a place to hide from other fish, cats, raccoons, birds, and other predators. For their part, fish help control populations of plant-eating insects. Scavengers such as snails and tadpoles also help balance the pond by consuming excess fish food, algae, and organic debris. When the numbers of fish and plants in the pond are stabilized (not too many of one or the other), the pond is in biological balance.

The reason balanced ponds are relatively clear is because the plants and fish in tandem help control the algae growth that can turn the water cloudy.

Controlling Algae

When you first add water to your pond, it will be crystal clear. After a few days, however, the water will turn murky, taking on a greenish tinge. This is caused by microscopic single-celled free-floating algae. Unless you take measures to control these creatures, you'll end up with a thick pea soup of them.

It is normal for a pond to have excess algae growth until aquatic plants have established themselves. Submerged plants (oxygenating grasses) eventually starve out the algae by consuming available nutrients directly from the water. Surface plants like water lilies and

Balancing the Water. 1. Fish: Provide nutrients for plants (carbon dioxide, nitrogen); consume insect pests and some algae. 2. Submerged plants (oxygenating grasses): Provide the highest level of oxygen of all plants; consume nutrients to control algae growth; and provide a dietary supplement and spawning area for fish. 3. Scavengers (snails, tadpoles, polly-wogs): Consume algae, decaying plant matter, and fish waste; provide nutrients for plants. 4. Water lilies, floating plants: Provide oxygen and shade; leaves help prevent water evaporation; offer hiding places for larger fish to escape animal predators; consume nutrients to control algae growth. 5. Marginal bog plants: Provide oxygen; consume nutrients to control algae growth; provide hiding places for small fish and snails; taller species shade pond edges in early morning, late afternoon.

various floating plants also consume nutrients, and they cut off the sunlight needed for algae to grow. The addition of fish and snails, and the eventual unplanned introduction of algae-eating insects like water fleas, also help to control algae, but to a lesser degree than plants.

You can always expect to have some algae in the pond, even after it is balanced. The slightly greenish tinge caused by floating algae is not harmful to fish or plants, and it helps conceal planters and the pump on the pond bottom. As the pond matures, most of the free-floating algae will eventually be replaced by various visible forms of hairy (filamentous), mossy, and slime algae growing on the sides and bottom of the pool, plants, rocks, and any other convenient surface. A small population of visible algae is actually beneficial, because it helps conceal the artifical-looking pond liner or shell. Like other plants, it also oxygenates the water. But when growth becomes excessive, it can choke out other plants and form unsightly mats of scum on the water surface. When such conditions exist, you'll need to physically remove the scum from the pond.

Adding a mechanical or biological filter to the system will help control both types of algae on a continuing basis, by trapping the algae cells and spores in the filtering medium. You can also use chemical algaecides for initial algae control after you first install the pond, and for periodic algae blooms afterwards. However, be careful in their use; some algaecides are toxic to fish, and most will affect the growth of other water plants. Consult your water-garden supplier or aquarium dealer for appropriate products and recommended dosages. Also, algaecides are just a temporary cure, killing existing algae in the pond. They do not guard against the growth of new algae, which is inevitable. If algae are a continuing problem, consult a pond specialist.

Starting the Process

To achieve an initial balance in a new pond, follow these procedures.

Testing the Water. When you first fill the pond with water, it may contain chemical and mineral pollutants that are toxic to fish and plants. The chemicals include chlorine, chlorine dioxide, chloramines, ammonia, and others present in tap water. Also included are various pollutants from pond-building materials, and poisonous chemicals that may have been washed or blown into the water from outside sources. Free chlorine in tap water usually dissipates after the water has stood for a few days. Other chemicals, such as a combination of chlorine and ammonia, take much longer to break down.

Before introducing plants or fish to the pond, test the water. After filling the pond, wait at least one week before testing. You can detect the presence of most toxic substances in water by testing for pH, ammonia, chloramines, nitrites, and water hardness. The pH is a measure of acidity or alkalinity. The scale ranges from 0 (highly acid) to 14 (highly alkaline), with 7 being neutral (indicating pure water). Healthy pond water ranges in pH from 6.5 to

8.5. Water-testing kits are available to test one or all of the conditions above. You can buy these kits at pet shops, garden suppliers, and pond dealers. Or you can order them from water-garden catalogs. The kit instructions usually tell you which water conditioners to use to correct the problem. Some pond dealers and pet shops also provide comprehensive water-testing services, and can advise you on proper treatment.

Correcting Water Conditions. A variety of water-conditioning treatments are available to balance the pH and remove toxic substances from ponds. But you should use them only if tests indicate that they are needed. Some fish and plant dealers recommend giving the pond a dose of a general-purpose water conditioner before adding fish or plants, just to be on the safe side. But if the water tests out all right, a conditioner isn't needed. If you do use one, follow the label directions. Even if you use a conditioner to achieve the initial water balance, you should still try to determine the source of pollution to prevent future problems.

In new ponds, lime leaching from concrete, cement, or mortar can cause severe alkaline conditions.

Testing the Water. Test water for pH and presence of chlorine, ammonia, and other toxic substances (see text). Simple test kits for monitoring water quality are available at pet shops and water-garden suppliers.

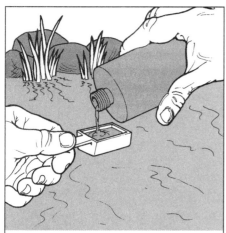

Correcting Water Conditions.
If necessary, add a water conditioner to remove chlorine and other harmful chemicals in the water. Follow label directions.

Removing Algae and Plant Debris. If algae is present, treat water with algaecide. Remove leaves and other debris from the pond with a leaf skimmer.

will maintain depends on various environmental factors, including the amount of available oxygen, sunlight, and nutrients. A pond with good water circulation and filtration will support a larger population of fish than a stagnant pond with no filtration. A shaded pond may be healthier for fish, but will limit the types of water plants you can grow. It will take time and experimentation to find out what will grow in the pond and what won't, and to achieve a balance between plant and animal life.

For starters, use the following formulas for stocking your pond:

■ Two bunches of submerged plants (oxygenating grasses) per square yard of pond surface area.

■ One inch of goldfish or 1/2 inch of koi per 3 to 5 gallons of water, or 15 inches of fish per square yard (9 square feet) of pond surface area at a depth of 18 to 24 inches (three 5-inch fish, for example). Remember that small fish will grow into big fish.

■ One medium to large water lily for each square yard of surface area, or enough water lilies, lotus, or floating plants to cover 50 to 70 percent of

You can correct the problem by treating the concrete or mortar with a vinegar solution or commercial concrete curing agent, as described on pages 20 and 29. Metal pipes, pool paints, wood stains and preservatives, pipe-joint glues, and various other chemicals associated with pond materials can also poison fish and plants. Allow these to dry thoroughly before filling the pond with water. If you've already filled the pond and suspect pollution from these sources, drain the pond; clean all the surfaces and components thoroughly; and refill the pond with fresh water. (See page 74 for information on draining a pond.) If you suspect high concentrations of chemicals in the water supply, call the water company to find out what chemicals have been used, and how to neutralize them.

Removing Algae and Plant Debris.
Even though it is not necessary to completely eliminate algae from the pond before introducing fish or plants, you can control any excess growth with the use of an algaecide. (See the precautions in Controlling Algae, on page 62.) If you have installed a filter, run it continuously for the first few days before introducing plants; clean mechanical filters daily. Also remove wind-blown leaves, blossoms, twigs, grass clippings, and

other debris from the pond daily with a leaf skimmer or pool net.

Introducing Fish and Plants. After filling the pond, wait several days to a week before introducing plants. Then, allow another two to three weeks for the plants to establish themselves (and to start the oxygenating process) before adding fish, snails, tadpoles, and other aquatic creatures. The size and number of plants and fish a pond

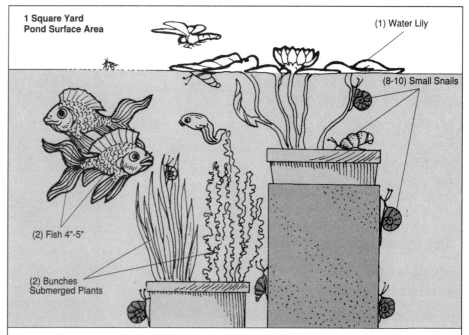

Introducing Fish and Plants. Add plants first; wait a few weeks for them to start the oxygenating cycle, and then add fish and snails. Use the ratio shown here for each square yard of pond surface area.

the pond surface during the summer months. Most water plants die back during the winter, and then re-establish themselves in spring. Once established, lilies and other water plants will occasionally need to be divided or pruned to prevent overcrowding.

◾ Eight to ten small snails or six to eight large snails per square yard of pond surface area.

Filtration

The primary purpose of a filter is to trap suspended matter in the pond, including fish wastes, decaying organic matter, floating algae, leftover fish food, and other minute particles that cause cloudy water. Some types of filters also remove ammonia and other toxic chemicals. Although filters aren't essential to maintaining a healthy, balanced pond, they can help the process and dramatically increase water clarity. If your aim is to have a small ornamental pond with a few fish and plants, and you don't mind slightly cloudy water from time to time, you may not need a filter. If, on the other hand, you want crystal-clear water or you will be raising large numbers of fish, a good filter will certainly help. Koi ponds, particularly, require clear, relatively pure water, both for viewing the fish and to maintain their health. There are two basic types of filters: mechanical and biological.

Mechanical Filters

A wide variety of mechanical filters are available for ponds. Some are plumbed into the pump inlet (suction filters); others are plumbed to the pump outlet (pressure filters). Some go inside the pond; others, outside the pond. Most small ponds (under 1,000 gallons) employ an in-pond cartridge-type filter. These use a corrugated polyester filter medium, which looks much like an automobile oil filter and works in the same manner. Other small filters use small screens, foam, or woven fiber pads or wraps as filter media. Some

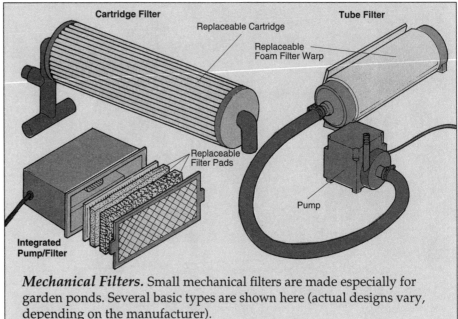

Mechanical Filters. Small mechanical filters are made especially for garden ponds. Several basic types are shown here (actual designs vary, depending on the manufacturer).

have provision for adding activated charcoal or a mineral called zeolite to remove ammonia and other chemical impurities from the water. None of these filter media has any particular advantage over another. The effectiveness of the filter depends more on the overall size of the filter (surface area of filter media in square feet and amount of water pumped through it in gph) than the type. Manufacturers generally provide performance specs for their filters, as for example, "for ponds up to 300 gallons."

For very large ponds (1,000 gallons or more), you can install a DE (diatomaceous earth) filter or a high-rate sand filter, like those used in swimming pools. These large filters must be placed outside the pond and require a large pump and extensive plumbing. Do not confuse mechanical filters with the filter screens and prefilters attached to pumps. The screens are meant to keep debris from clogging the pump impeller and fountain jets. (See page 40.)

To be effective, mechanical filters rely on a high flow rate. As a rule of thumb, you need a pump that can circulate the entire volume of pond water through the filter once every two hours (or as recommended by the manufacturer). Like pumps, filter

capacity is rated in gallons per hour. If you have installed a fountain or waterfall, you'll probably need a larger pump to provide sufficient circulation through the filter and still operate the fountain or waterfall. Your pump dealer can help you choose the right-size filter for your application. If your budget allows, select a filter that exceeds the minimum requirements for your pond. The larger the filter, the less often you'll have to clean it. The main drawback to mechanical filters is that they require frequent cleaning— at least once a week, and usually daily during the summer. Cleaning usually takes only a few minutes: You simply remove the filter pad, cartridge, or screen, and wash it off with a garden hose.

Biological Filters

These filters rely on beneficial bacteria (called nitrifiers) that feed on impurities in the water. The filter contains two or more layers of gravel or other media that harbor large concentrations of nitrifying bacteria naturally found in ponds. As water slowly flows through the media, the bacteria break down fish wastes and other organic matter. In the process, toxic ammonia created by fish waste and decaying organic matter are

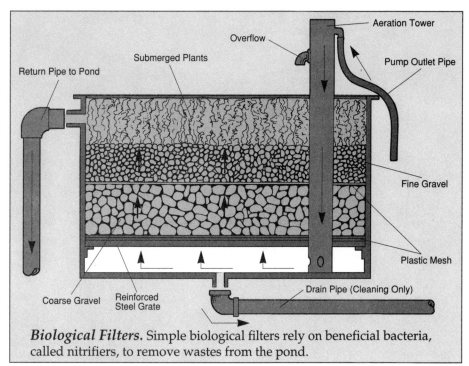

Biological Filters. Simple biological filters rely on beneficial bacteria, called nitrifiers, to remove wastes from the pond.

transformed into harmless nitrates, which return to the pond to nourish plants. Other specialized microorganisims feast on single-celled algae passing through the filter. A simple biological filter is shown in the drawing. More complex types may incorporate mechanical prefilters or compartments filled with activated charcoal, zeolites, or other media. As shown, dirty water is pumped from the pond through an aeration tower to the bottom of the filter, where it slowly percolates up through the gravel filter media (giving the bacteria a chance to eat their fill!). It exits near the top of the filter by gravity flow through a return pipe to the pond. The aeration tower, combined with oxygenating grasses planted in the top layer of gravel, provides oxygen to help support the bacteria culture, as well as aquatic life in the pond. The layers of gravel also serve as a crude mechanical filter to trap suspended particulate in the water, further clarifying it. To clean the filter, all you need do is open a drain valve at the bottom to remove accumulated silt and sediment and lightly rinse the filter media to dislodge trapped particles. (Don't use heavy sprays of chlorinated tapwater, as this tends to

dislodge or even kill the beneficial bacteria in the filter media.)

Unlike mechanical filters, biological filters do not require a high flow rate to operate efficiently. (The pump need only turn over the total water volume every four to six hours.) Also, they need only be cleaned once every one to two months. On the downside, most biological filters are large, unsightly tanks located outside the pond above water level. So, you'll have to figure out a way to disguise the filter in the landscape (such as behind a shed or underneath a raised deck). Several manufacturers have recently introduced small in-pond biological filters, but their capacity is limited to ponds of 300 gallons or less.

When shopping for any type of filter, biological or mechanical, ask the advice of an independent dealer who carries several brands. Many filter manufacturers overrate the filtering ability of their products.

Other Filtering Devices

In addition to mechanical and biological filters, you can add other filtering devices to the system. Ultraviolet (UV) water sterilizers are sometimes used in conjunction with a biological filter.

Plumbed into the inlet side of the filter, these units consist of an ultraviolet bulb encased in a transparent, waterproof sleeve, which in turn is placed inside a tube plumbed into the system. When microscopic organisms are exposed to concentrated ultraviolet light, the UV energy causes the cell content (protoplasm) of the microorganisms to explode. Algae, bacteria, viruses, and certain fish parasites can be killed in this manner. The light also encourages minute organic particles to clump together so they can be trapped in the filter. The UV units are expensive, and usually they aren't needed if you have a good biological filter.

Ozone Generators. These devices sterilize water by reducing organic chemicals to their major elements of carbon dioxide and water. The generators convert oxygen in the air into ozone, and they infuse it into the water. The ozone effectively breaks down chloramines, ammonia, nitrates and phosphates into harmless gasses that escape the pond. Like UV sterilizers, ozone promotes the bonding of minute toxic waste particles so they are more easily trapped by the filter. Used for many years to sterilize water in swimming pools and spas, ozone generators are becoming popular for use in koi ponds because they remove nitrates from the water that otherwise must be consumed by plants. They're a good investment if you want a crystal-clear fish pond, with few or no plants in it.

Natural Plant Filters. This is another option for ponds with few or no plants. The filter is nothing more than a small pond or large tub filled with a thick growing bed of water plants, such as water hawthorne, watercress, shellflower, or water hyacinth, placed between the filter outlet and the main pond. Because the plants consume nitrates and other nutrients produced by the biological filter, they reduce algae growth in the main pond. They can also be made an attractive part of the landscape.

PLANTS & FISH

Plants and fish not only serve to keep the pond water balanced, but they also add life and color. This chapter will help you choose the best kinds of plants, fish, and other aquatic life to enhance your water garden. You'll also find planting and stocking tips, plus information on plant and fish care, to ensure a healthy, beautiful pond environment.

Aquatic Plants

When we think of aquatic plants, water lilies immediately come to mind. Water-gardening catalogs and pond books certainly give water lilies a good percentage of their space, and no water garden is complete without at least one of them. Nevertheless, many other water plants are suitable for garden ponds. Some, like submerged plants (oxygenating grasses), serve strictly utilitarian purposes; others have fascinating leaves or showy flowers. Most water gardeners want a good mixture of plants in and around the pond to create visual interest.

Water Lilies

Varieties of the water lily number in the hundreds, if not the thousands. But they are classified in two major groups, hardy and tropical.

Hardy lilies are frost-tolerant perennial plants. In temperate and cold climates, they die back to the roots during the cold season and re-emerge in the spring. In warm climates (not subject to heavy frosts), they stay in leaf all year around, although some species do poorly in tropical and subtropical environments. Most hardy lilies are charac-

terized by blossoms that float on the water surface or rise slightly above it. Some varieties are fragrant; others have little or no fragrance.

Tropical lilies are frost-tender, which means they can be killed by repeated heavy frosts. Even though they can survive winters in tropical and subtropical zones (Southern Florida and Southern California, for example), they are treated as annual plants in most other parts of the country. To save them over the winter, you'll have to move the entire plant into a greenhouse. Tropicals are characterized by their strong fragrance and blossoms that stand well above the water level. If you want shades of blues and purples, you'll have to use tropicals, because hardy lilies don't come in these colors. Profuse bloomers, the tropicals produce four to five times as many blossoms as hardy lilies. They are also viviparous plants. This means they're capable of producing small plantlets on the leaf surface that can be removed and replanted. Tropicals can further be divided into day bloomers and night bloomers. The night bloomers open their blossoms at dusk, and they close in mid-morning to noon. You don't really need a flashlight to see them. With a few lights around the pond, you will be able to

enjoy their striking nocturnal displays on warm summer evenings.

Both hardies and tropicals include some shade-tolerant varieties, which require only three or four hours of direct sunlight a day. But even these will do much better with more sun. Most other varieties require at least five or six hours of direct sunlight a day.

Because there are so many varieties, with more being developed each year, a comprehensive species list is beyond the scope of this book. However, we've included a few of the more popular varieties in the chart on page 78. Water garden catalogs will be your best bet for selecting lilies.

Planting Tips. Usually, lilies are first available from water gardens at the beginning of the growing season (once the danger of frost has passed). Instead of a plant with leaves and flowers, you'll get a piece of rootstock (called a rhizome for hardy lilies, or a tuber for tropical lilies), with a few emerging growing tips. Order as early as possible so the lily will have a chance to get established over the summer months.

Plant water lilies in wide, shallow containers, or special water lily bas-

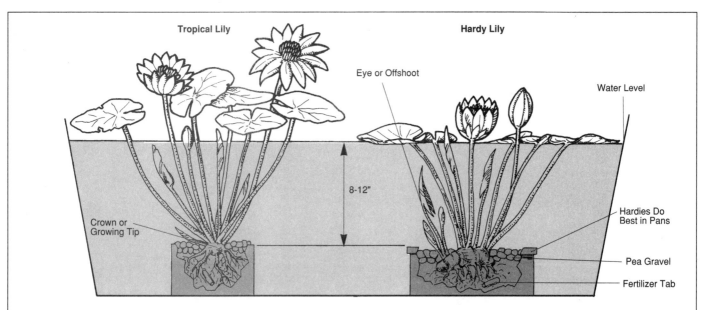

Water Lilies. Water lilies are by far the most popular pond plants. Hardy lilies grow as perennials in most climates; tropicals are treated as annuals in all but the warmest regions of the country.

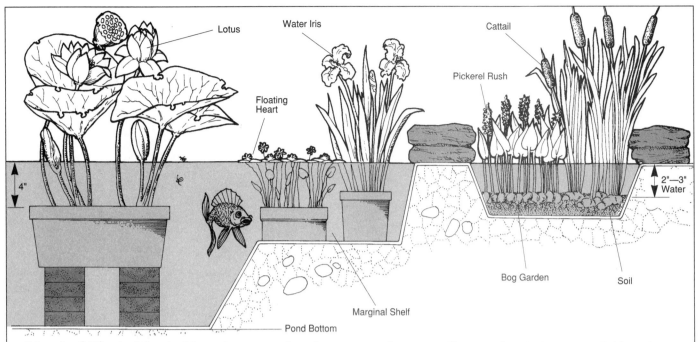

Marginal Plants. Marginal bog plants complete the water garden scene. Dozens of varieties are available; a few of the more popular species are shown here.

kets available from the water lily dealer. Allow plenty of room for growth. Add fertilizer tablets, if desired. Fill the container one-half full with heavy loam garden soil. If you are using plant baskets, line them with burlap to prevent soil from washing into the surrounding pond water. Avoid the use of organic mulches, peat moss, compost, commercial planting mixes, or ordinary garden fertilizers in your soil mix. Place the rootstock of hardy lilies horizontally, with the crown, or growing tips, near the edges of the container. For tropicals, place the rootstock vertically, in the center of the container. Fill the container with soil to a level just beneath the crown; then top it with a layer of pea gravel to hold the soil in place and to protect the roots from being uncovered or dislodged by larger fish. For tropicals, submerge the pot so that the crown or growing point on the lily is 6 to 12 inches below the water surface. With some hardies, the tips can be as much as 24 inches below the surface, although 6 to 18 inches is standard for most varieties. During the growing season, lightly spray the leaves with a garden hose every few days to dislodge aphids and other

harmful insects. (The plants and fish will thank you for this.) Special water-lily fertilizer tablets can be added each time you divide and repot the lilies, or once a year at the beginning of the growing season. For more specific growing instructions, refer to a water-gardening catalog.

Marginal Plants

A wide variety of shallow water plants is suitable for growing around the edges of the pond or in a separate bog garden. Marginal plants also do well in container gardens. Most marginal plants do best in rich soil topped with 2 to 3 inches of water, although some of the larger ones will grow in water up to 12 inches deep. Common marginal plants include lotus, floating heart, water iris, water hawthorne, cattail species, horsetail, sagittaria, pickerel rush, water clover, creeping jenny, taro, umbrella palm, water canna, and a wide variety of ornamental aquatic grasses. As with water lilies, there are tropical and hardy marginal plants. Consult a local nursery or water-garden supplier for plants that do well in your area.

Planting Tips. Planting techniques vary, depending on the species, and

there are many of them. The key is not to let the soil dry out! (Keep an eye on the water level, especially during the summer months.) Planting in pots will help confine the root system, and you can take frost-tender plants indoors for the winter. Put the pot in a larger, waterproof container, and fill it with water to keep the soil constantly wet. Select an indoor location that receives direct sunlight. To plant in the pond or bog garden, do the following:

First, gently hose off plants to remove any foreign matter, and keep the plant wet while planting. Fill the planting container (if one is used) with soil; then add a fertilizer tablet, as for water lilies on page 68. If the plant has a rhizome, trim and plant it horizontally with the growing tips just above the soil surface. Plants with tubers should be planted vertically. For all plants, tamp the soil firmly around the roots and cover them with 1/2-inch of washed pea gravel. Saturate the soil with water; then plant at the correct depth in the pond or bog garden. You can consult the plant dealer for more specific planting instructions and growing tips for the plants you've chosen.

Submerged Plants

As the name implies, submerged plants grow entirely underwater. Once you've planted them, you may not even be able to see them. Even so, they play an extremely important role in the pond ecology, as mentioned in the previous chapter. Also referred to as oxygenating grasses, they include some of the same species grown in aquariums, with the fernlike anacharis being the most common. Other submerged plants include cabomba (also called fanwort), with fan-shaped lacy leaves; myriophyllum, with fine, hairlike foliage (a favorite of spawning fish); and vallisneria (ribbon grass), with long, ribbonlike leaves.

Planting Tips. Plant in soil-filled pots to prevent excessive spreading. Add a thin layer of coarse gravel to keep soil in place and to help anchor the plant. (If the roots become dislodged, the plants will float to the surface.) Plants will grow in up to 30 inches of water, but they will do best if the topmost leaves are submerged to a depth of 6 to 12 inches beneath the water surface. Make sure the entire plant is well submerged. To keep fish from overgrazing the plants (fish are especially fond of anacharis), make a protective cover of lightweight plastic 1/2-inch mesh (bird netting). Wrap the mesh around the plant container, allowing 8 to 10 inches of material to extend above the container rim. Close the sides and top with twist ties to prevent fish from getting trapped inside. If you have enough fish in the pond, they'll keep the plants neatly pruned.

Floating Plants

These plants have buoyant leaves to keep them afloat, with roots dangling in the water beneath and requiring no soil. Floating plants such as water lettuce (also called shellflower), water fern, and duckweed are grown for their attractive or interesting foliage. This foliage provides shade for fish and helps control the algae growth. Some varieties, such as water poppy and water hyacinth, also produce showy flowers during the summer.

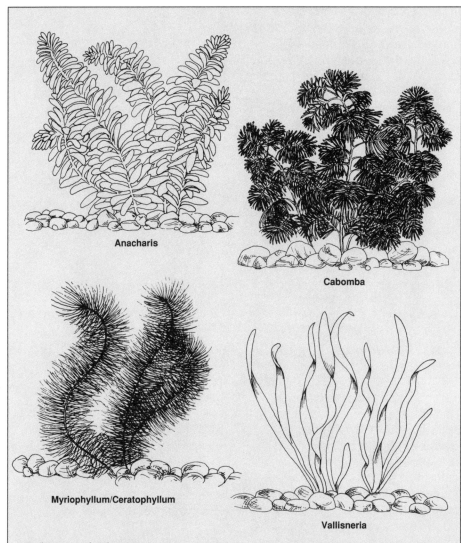

Anacharis

Cabomba

Myriophyllum/Ceratophyllum

Vallisneria

Submerged Plants. Submerged plants are essential to a balanced pond. Their main function is to oxygenate the water. They also provide food and hiding places for fish.

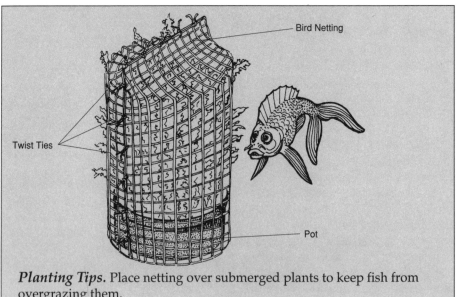

Bird Netting

Twist Ties

Pot

Planting Tips. Place netting over submerged plants to keep fish from overgrazing them.

Planting Tips. Like submerged plants, floating plants are sold by the bunch. Once you set them afloat in the pond, they require no particular care. These plants are considered hardy in warm climates; but they are treated as annuals in colder climates, where they're killed by winter frosts. The main drawback to floating plants is that they're highly invasive. During the summer months, they can quickly spread over the entire surface of a small pond, and occasionally they must be thinned out to keep their numbers in check. In warmer climates, they're considered a pest because they grow year-round, clogging natural waterways. For this reason, interstate shipments are forbidden in some of the southern states and in California.

Fish & Other Water Creatures

No water garden is complete without a few fish and water snails. Goldfish are the all-time favorites, although the Japanese koi is becoming increasingly popular as a playful water garden "pet." Other creatures, like tadpoles and salamanders, capture the interest of young and old alike. This section discusses these and other popular pond denizens.

Goldfish

Members of the carp family, goldfish are surprisingly hardy. They can withstand a wide range of climates and water conditions. Under favorable conditions, they breed readily in outdoor ponds. If you've ever visited a pet store (and who hasn't?), you know that in addition to common varieties (comets, moors, and fantails), you can also find fancier varieties. Stick with the common varieties in the beginning, since these usually tend to be hardier and can withstand a wider fluctuation in water temperature. Also, make sure the fish you choose are pond goldfish, which have been raised in outdoor conditions. For best results, choose healthy fish between 3 and 6 inches long. Avoid fish with

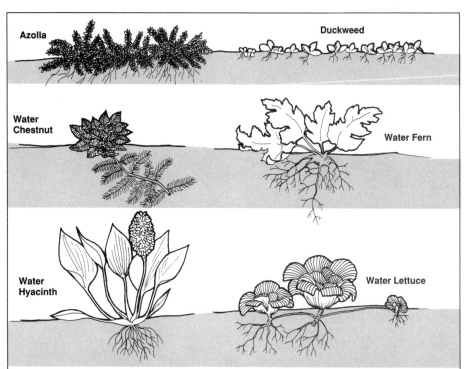

Floating Plants. Free-floating plants can be purchased in bunches and require no maintenance once you set them afloat. However, you may have to thin them out to keep them from taking over the pond.

drooping or tattered fins, dull or cloudy colors, or bumps and bruises on their bodies. If one or more of the fish in the tank looks sick, avoid the whole tank, because the other fish may also be infected.

Koi

Japanese koi (which means broaded carp) are a close relative of the goldfish, but they are easily distinguished from goldfish by the short whiskers around their mouths. Colors include silvers, metallic gold, bright oranges, whites, lemon yellows, and various tricolor combinations. As with goldfish, koi have been bred to produce many named varieties (Kohaku, Asagi, Shusui, Koromo, and so on). Under ideal conditions, these colorful fish will grow up to 4 feet long and live well over 100 years. However, their average life expectancy in a garden pond is about 15 to 20 years, and they will grow to only about 2 feet long.

Koi are easily trained to eat from your hand and do simple tricks, like jumping through hoops or sucking from a

baby bottle. They'll often follow their owners around the edge of the pond, waiting for a handout. Koi owners insist that each fish has its own distinctive personality.

Koi and goldfish live quite happily together in the same pond, but water requirements for koi are more exacting. Because of their large size, they require a pond depth of about 30 to 36 inches, although more shallow areas can be incorporated for better viewing of the fish. The banks should be steep, and at least 18 inches above water level, so the fish don't jump out of the pond. In colder climates, koi usually won't survive the winter unless they are taken indoors. Breeding koi is a specialized hobby beyond the scope of this book, but several good books have been written on the subject.

Mosquito Fish

A humble relative of the fancy guppies sold in pet shops, mosquito fish (Gambusia affinis) are native to natural ponds, lakes, and watercourses throughout the warmer areas of the country. They're often introduced into man-made ponds or lakes to control the larvae of mosquitos and other pesky insects. Resembling a small minnow, mosquito fish grow to about 1 inch long. These hardy little fish reproduce rapidly under a variety of water conditions, although their numbers are generally kept in check by the size of the pond and the available food supply.

Mosquito fish require no special care; they feed on small insects, insect larvae, and leftover bits of goldfish food. They're generally too small (and too quick) to be bothered by animal predators. Larger fish, such as koi and goldfish, may eat mosquito fish, but generally they prefer other food.

Mosquito fish are not nearly as interesting or attractive as goldfish or koi. But they can play an equally important role in maintaining biological balance in a water garden. At the same time, they will also significantly reduce the numbers of pesky mosquitos. In some areas, you can obtain these little fish free or at a minimal charge from a local mosquito abatement agency, a city parks department, or a county agricultural extension office. Or, you can get an aquarium net and bucket, and try your luck at a nearby lake, pond, or reservoir.

Game Fish

For various reasons, catfish, trout, crappie, bluegill, bass, and other gamefish usually don't do well in garden ponds. The main reason is that small, shallow bodies of water don't meet their temperature and oxygen requirements. Most gamefish have adapted to relatively consistent temperatures found in larger, deeper bodies of water. Gamefish are also aggressive by nature, and they will often pick on smaller fish or even eat them whole.

Amphibians

Frogs, newts, salamanders, and turtles are all likely candidates for the pond. Often, these creatures come to

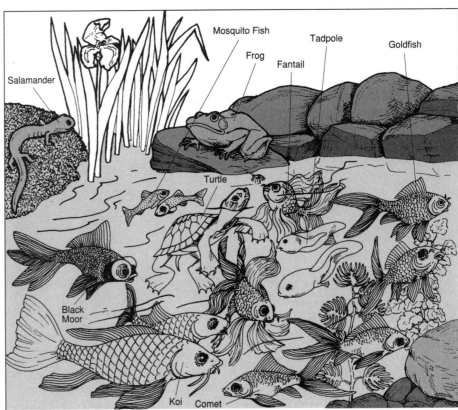

Fish and Other Water Creatures. Many types of aquatic life can be introduced to a garden pond. Some will visit on their own accord.

the pond uninvited, especially in rural areas. Besides being good pond scavengers, tadpoles and pollywogs are fun to watch as they grow legs and transform into frogs. Newts go through a similar aquatic pollywog stage, characterized by their feathery external gills. Frogs, turtles, salamanders, and newts are likely to visit the pond to lay their eggs, but they're equally apt to travel some distance from the pond to forage for food. And keep in mind that if you overstock the pond with tadpoles, you may end up with a backyard full of croaking frogs!

Other Water Creatures

As mentioned, water snails help keep the pond clean by consuming algae and fish waste. They also serve to maintain the ecological balance of the pond. They're best known as nature's "vacuum cleaners", removing algae from the stems and leaves of larger water plants. (They won't eat the plants themselves.) Numerous varieties exist, but the black Japanese snail (Viviparus malleatus) is the most

popular. Water snails can be purchased at any aquarium shop. Also, when you buy your water plants, you're more than likely to get a few of these tiny hitchhikers (or their eggs). But don't worry—they won't crawl out of the pond and eat your garden plants!

Freshwater clams and mussels serve much the same purpose as snails, although they're somewhat more reclusive. Clams bury themselves in underwater plant containers or in the muck at the bottom of the pond. Mussels attach themselves to submerged rocks and other underwater surfaces. Freshwater mussels are particularly useful for filtering out floating algae, to help keep the water clear. Bear in mind that snails, clams, and mussels won't remove all the algae from your pond, no matter how many you have. And they should not be considered substitutes for a good filtration system and other more effective forms of algae control mentioned in this chapter.

POND CARE & REPAIR

Once your pond is established, you'll need to clean and maintain it on a continuing basis. Many timesaving aids and devices are available to help. But caring for a pond isn't the drudgery you may think. It can actually be a pleasurable pastime, getting you in closer touch with the plants and animals that live there.

Pond Care

Maintaining a clean, healthy pond is like a cross between keeping up a garden and caring for an aquarium. Even during the summer months, when your pond requires the most attention, it shouldn't take you more than an hour or two every week to keep it in good shape.

Maintaining Water Quality

During the warm season, ponds lose water through evaporation, so you'll need to replace the water regularly. By doing so, you may introduce chemicals from the tap that can concentrate in the pond. These, combined with toxins produced by fish wastes and decaying plant matter, may eventually pollute the water and even disrupt the biological balance. This rarely happens in ponds with a good balance of plants and fish and adequate filtration systems. But it is possible, especially if you haven't been cleaning the filter regularly or the pond becomes overcrowded with fish and plants.

Ponds may also become polluted by runoff containing pesticides, herbicides, or other toxic chemicals.

For these reasons, periodically test the water (about once a month during the warm season), using a test kit as described on page 63. If the pond becomes polluted, correct the situation by partially draining it and adding fresh water. As a rule of thumb, you can replace up to 20 percent of the total water volume without affecting the biological balance of the pond. You should also test the water if your fish are showing signs of stress (gasping for air at the surface, swimming sideways or erratically, or acting lethargic). These conditions may also be symptoms of a biological disease, or simply a lack of oxygen in the water, which can happen during hot weather. If oxygen is the problem, partially drain the pond and refill it with fresh water. Run the pump continuously for a week or so; add more oxygenating plants, if necessary. If you suspect disease, though, consult your aquarium dealer for proper treatment.

Draining & Cleaning the Pond

If the water is severely polluted, choked with algae, or filled with sediment, you may have to completely drain the pond, clean it, and refill it with fresh water. Draining may also be necessary to find and repair a leak in the pond liner or shell. The best time to clean the pond is in late summer or early autumn. Plants are nearing the end of the growing season then, so you're less likely to stress them or to damage new shoots. Fish will also be less stressed at this time, and any fish that hatched in the spring should be big enough for you to net and remove from the pond. (If you clean the pond in the spring, you can disrupt spawning fish and amphibians, or damage the eggs.) Before you start, fill one or more holding tubs with some of the pond water. Drain the pond to within about 6 inches of the bottom; then carefully net out the fish and put them in the holding tank. (If you have a lot of fish, a kid's plastic wading pool or 50-gallon plastic trash can works well.) Add a few bunches of

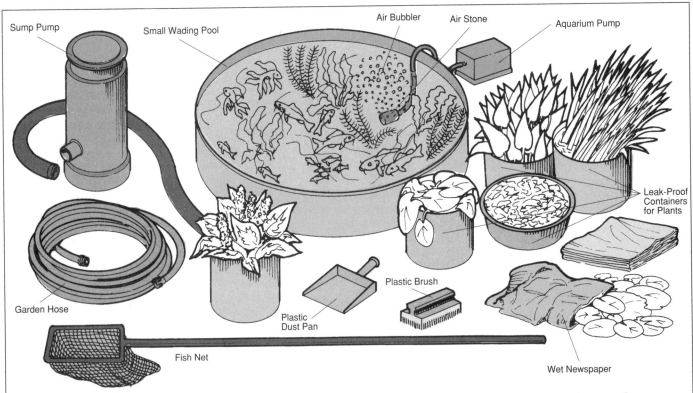

Draining and Cleaning the Pond. Shown is a basic collection of tools and materials needed to drain and clean a pond.

oxygenating plants to the tank, and place it in a shaded location. Allow about 1 gallon of water for each inch of fish. If the fish will be out of the pond for more than a few hours, place an aquarium air bubbler in the tank to provide additional oxygen.

Depending on the location of the pond, you can either siphon the water out with a garden hose that leads to a lower area in the yard, or you can pump the water out. Garden-hose adaptors are available for many pond pumps. If it's not possible to use the pond pump to remove the water (or it would simply take too long), you can rent a high-capacity sump pump at a tool rental shop. Run the pumped water into a nearby garden area; the nutrients in the water will benefit your plants. Don't allow the pump to run dry, though. Bail out any remaining water with a plastic bucket. Then remove the plants and place them in water-filled plastic buckets. If you have many large plants, like water lilies, wrap them in wet newspapers or burlap sacks; put them in a shady location; and spray them occasionally with a garden hose to keep them moist. When the pond is drained, sift through the silt and pick out as many snails as you can find. (You probably won't get them all.) Put these snails in the holding tank with the fish. Use a plastic dustpan to shovel out the silt on the pond bottom. Clean the sides and bottom with a stiff plastic brush or a strong jet from a garden hose. Do not use chemical cleaners—just water. As you work, be careful not to tear or puncture the liner or pond shell. Rinse and drain the pond several times to remove any remaining muck. Refill the pond with fresh water, and add a dechlorinating agent or water purifier, according to the manufacturer's instructions. Also pour a few buckets of the original pond water back into the pond to help re-establish the biological balance. Don't put the fish back into the pond until the water temperature returns to within 5 degrees of the temperature in the holding tank.

As with new ponds, you can expect increased algae growth until the ecological balance is reestablished.

Routine Maintenance

As in nature, garden ponds and their inhabitants go through seasonal cycles. With each season, you'll have a slightly different list of pond chores to perform.

Spring. In the spring, you may notice excessive algae blooms before lilies and other water plants have emerged to provide shade and consume nutrients. This problem will usually take care of itself once the aquatic plants have leafed out. Late spring is the time to introduce new aquatic plants, remove any dead foliage from existing ones, and clean out any debris in the pond that collected over the winter. After the last frost, you can divide, replant, and fertilize bog plants and water lilies. In cold climates, fish will still be lethargic and weak from winter hibernation, but they will begin to feed as the weather warms up. Now is the time to supplement their diet with easily digestible foods in small amounts (consult your aquarium dealer). Do not overfeed: The rule of thumb is to give the fish no more food than they can eat within 10 minutes. Fish are also particularly susceptible to diseases at this time, so keep a close eye on them. In mid- to late spring, many fish and amphibians will spawn and produce eggs. To assist the process, you can place spawning mats (available from mail-order water-garden suppliers) in the pond. If you haven't been running the pump over the winter, inspect the pump, filter, plumbing, and electrical connections for damage. Have the pump cleaned and serviced by a reputable dealer, if necessary.

Summer. Pond activity reaches its height during the summer months. Aquatic plants will be growing rapidly and sending forth their colorful blooms. Spend a few minutes each day snipping off faded blossoms and keeping plants trimmed. Insects will start to appear, so keep an eye on plants. Avoid the use of insecticides in or near the pond. Hand-pick caterpillars and other pests from plants, and toss them in the pond for your fish. Use a hose to spray lily aphids from the water lily leaves.

As the weather becomes hotter, water evaporation will increase, so you'll have to "top off" the pond

Routine Maintenance. Throughout the growing season, clip dead leaves and fading blossoms from aquatic plants to keep the pond looking neat and tidy.

Summer. Do not use insecticides in or around the pond. Hand-pick insects or wash them off the plant leaves with a garden hose.

every day or two in order to keep the water level up. It's best to add a little water each day, rather than a large amount once a week.

As water temperatures rise, fish become susceptible to various diseases caused by bacteria, fungi, and parasites. So, inspect the fish frequently for signs of illness, which could include blotchy or discolored skin, missing scales, or lethargic/erratic movement. Immediately remove sick fish from the pond, and treat them with the appropriate fish medicine. Refer to a fish book or consult a local aquarium dealer for advice on choosing the correct treatment. Because pond life of all types flourishes during the summer, you'll need to clean the pump strainer and filter more frequently. As the water heats up, oxygen levels will drop, so it's a good idea to run the pump continuously.

Autumn. This season brings falling leaves, which must be removed from the pond every day before they have a chance to decay and pollute the water. If the pond is located near or under a tree, stretch netting over the pond to catch the leaves. Any leaves that do sink to the bottom of the pond can be removed with a soft plastic rake, pool sweep, or spa vacuum (available at water-garden suppliers). Pool sweeps and vacuums are also good for removing excess silt from the pond bottom. Be careful not to disturb rooted plants in the pond.

Clean the pump filter frequently. Continue pruning yellowed foliage from water plants. Fish may become hungrier as they build up stores of fat to survive the winter.

Winter. When the water temperature drops below 45 degrees Fahrenheit, fish become inactive and stop eating. You don't need to feed them until the following spring, when they become active again. In warmer climates, fish may be fed all year around, or as long as they remain active. When ice forms on the pond, it can cut off oxygen to the fish, and trap toxic gasses beneath the surface. If the pond is frozen for more than a few days, the fish may suffocate. In mild climates, where ice is a temporary condition, you can place a pot of boiling water on the ice to melt a hole in it, as shown. In moderately cold climates, placing a circulating pump on the pond bottom (where the water is warmer) and directing the flow upward will prevent ice from forming in the middle of the pond. In extremely cold climates, use a floating pond de-icer to keep a hole open in the ice all winter. If you won't be running the pump during the winter, remove it from the pond and drain all pipes to keep them from cracking. To avoid damage to a biological filter, drain and rinse it. Allow it to dry out for the winter. When you put the filter back in service the following spring, it will take several weeks for the beneficial bacteria to reestablish themselves in the filter media. Move frost-tender plants indoors for the winter.

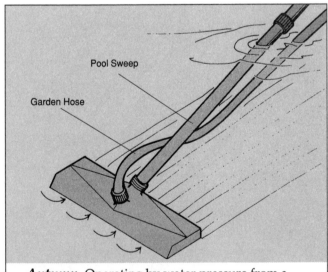

Autumn. Operating by water pressure from a garden hose, a pool sweep removes silt and sediment from the pond bottom.

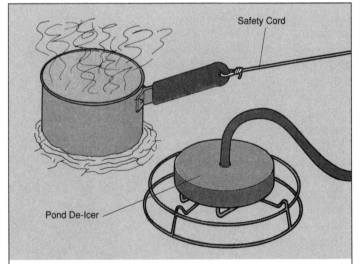

Winter. If pond ice is rare in your climate, use a pan of boiling water to melt a hole in the ice. In severe-winter climates, a floating pond de-icer keeps the hole open throughout winter.

Repairing a Pond Liner

Punctures and tears in flexible liners can be repaired with patching kits available from water-garden catalogs or the source where you bought the liner. The kits usually contain a small can of adhesive and a piece of liner for making patches. Tears in butyl rubber liners can also be repaired with a special laminate tape.

1 Completely drain the pond and locate the source of the leak. Make sure the tear or puncture is completely dry and clean. Before making the repair, find out what caused the tear or puncture (sharp rock, root, etc.) and remove it. Cushion the area behind the tear with damp sand or a piece of liner underlayment.

2 Cut a patch from the same material as the liner (butyl rubber or PVC plastic), about 2 inches wider and longer than the tear. Apply a thin, even coat of adhesive over the torn area, slightly larger than the patch.

3 Apply a coat of adhesive to the patch, making sure you cover the entire area. Allow the adhesive to become slightly tacky (about 2 to 3 minutes, or as recommended on the label directions).

4 Firmly press the patch in position, and smooth it to remove any wrinkles. Allow the adhesive to dry thoroughly before filling the pond with water.

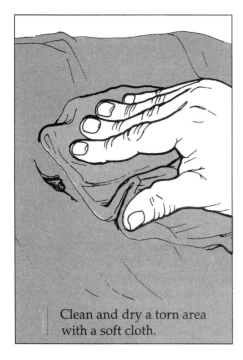

1 Clean and dry a torn area with a soft cloth.

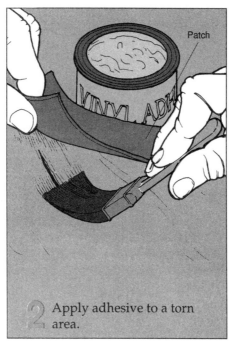
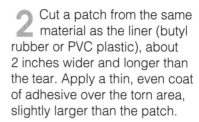

Patch

2 Apply adhesive to a torn area.

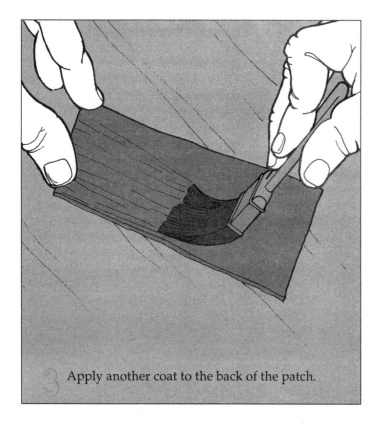

3 Apply another coat to the back of the patch.

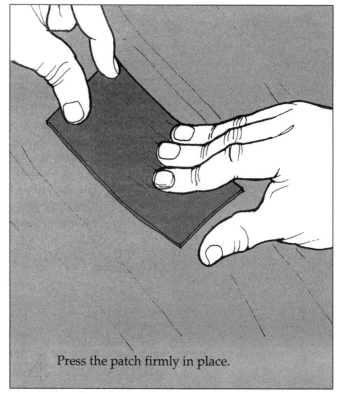

4 Press the patch firmly in place.

Hardy Water Lilies

Name	Description	Comments
Charlene Strawn	Clear, fragrant, medium-yellow blossoms with darker-yellow centers. Holds blossoms higher above water than most hardies. Plant has medium spread (6 to 12 square feet), is shade-tolerant (3 hours minimum sun per day).	Prolific bloomer with long blooming season. Easy to propagate, good for beginners.
Marliac Carnea (also called Marliacea Carnea in some catalogs)	Very pale pink, slightly fragrant flowers about 3 to 5 inches across. Small to medium spread (1 to 8 square feet) Slightly shade-tolerant (4 hours minimum sun per day).	Vigorous plant, prolific bloomer. One of first hardies to break dormancy in spring.
Pink Beauty (formerly Fabiola)	Clear, medium-pink blossoms that bloom in clusters of two or three at a time. Slight fragrance. Plant has small spread (1 to 6 square feet), requires full sun (6 hours minimum sun per day).	Prolific bloomer, with long blooming season. Compact plant size makes it excellent for smaller ponds.
Splendida	Strawberry-red flowers with slight fragrance; medium spread (6 to 12 square feet). Shade-tolerant (4 hours minimum sun per day).	Good, medium-sized plant for pond of any size.
Virginia	Large, nearly double, white flowers with yellow centers. No fragrance, long blooming season. Shade-tolerant (4 hours minimum sun per day).	Very showy flowers, reaching about 9 inches across. Although it tolerates partial sun, it performs best with full sun.

Tropical Water Lilies

Name	Description	Comments
Dauben (also called Daubeniana)	Light, lavender-blue to white, minature flowers (about 2 to 4 inches across). Highly fragrant blooms, small spread (1 to 3 square feet) when planted in containers. Tolerates some shade (4 hours minimum sun per day). Day bloomer.	Prolific bloomer; often has several flowers at once. Compact size makes it an excellent choice for tub gardens and small ponds.
Margaret Mary	Pale to medium blue, fragrant blooms, medium spread (6 to 12 square feet). Tolerates some shade (4 hours minimum sun per day). Day bloomer, slightly viviparous.	While medium in size, plant will adapt to a 3.5-quart container.
Panama Pacific	Description: Bluish blossoms that deepen to a rich purple, with bright yellow centers. Slightly shade-tolerant (4 to 5 hours minimum sun per day). Small to large spread, depending on container size. Day bloomer, quite vivaparous.	Good, medium-sized plant for pond of any size.
Red Flare	Spectacular dark-red petals with deep maroon stamens, and red-tinged foliage. Medium to large spread (6 to 12+ square feet). Requires full sun (6 hours minimum sun per day). Night bloomer.	Exceptionally striking red flowers. Good for medium- to large-sized ponds.
Texas Shell Pink	Very large, pale-pink blossoms, prolific bloomer. Medium to large spread (6 to 12 square feet). Slightly shade-tolerant (4 to 5 hours minimum sun per day). Night bloomer.	Good for medium- to large-sized pools. Giant, light-colored blossoms show up well at night in dark ponds.
Wood's White Knight	Large, pure-white flowers with yellow stamens; prolific bloomer. Fragrant blooms, medium to large spread (6 to 12+ square feet). Shade-tolerant (3 to 4 hours minimum sun per day). Night bloomer.	Good for medium- to large-size ponds. Very prolific bloomer, with clusters of three or more large flowers borne at one time.

Acrylonitrile butadiene styrene (ABS) A plastic formulation (typically black in color) used for some rigid pond shells, also for drainpipe in plumbing systems.

Aeration The infusion of oxygen into water by mixing it with air, usually by means of a fountain spray or underwater air bubbler (such as those used in aquariums).

Algaecide A chemical treatment that prevents or controls algae growth.

Backfill Earth, sand, or gravel used to fill the excavated space under a pond shell or liner.

Balanced water Water with the correct ratio of mineral content and pH level that prevents an alkaline or acidic buildup.

Catch basin In a man-made stream or watercourse, a small depression or basin beneath a waterfall designed to hold water when the pump is turned off.

Chicken wire Flexible wire mesh used to reinforce thin concrete structures; also referred to as poultry netting. Sold in hardware stores, lumberyards, and home centers.

Chloramines Complex compounds formed when chlorine (from tapwater) combines with nitrates present in pond water. Toxic to fish and plant life, chloramines are difficult to neutralize by chemical means— the pond water usually must be partially or fully replaced to reduce chloramine levels.

Conduit Metal or plastic pipe used to encase buried or exposed electrical cables and protect them from moisture or physical damage.

Coping Stones, bricks, or other individual masonry units used as a finished edging around the pond perimeter. Coping can be set loose or mortared in place.

Crown The growing tip of a root system, from which a plant sprouts; the point at which plant stems meet the roots.

Dry well A gravel-filled hole used to receive and drain water runoff; part of a drainage system to which water runoff is directed via a perforated drainpipe.

Ethylene propylene diene monomer (EPDM) A kind of synthetic rubber. Flexible sheets of EPDM are used for pond liners. EPDM has greater stretch and UV resistance than PVC.

Footing The widened, below-ground portion of a poured-concrete foundation or foundation wall.

Frost heave Shifting or upheaval of the ground due to alternate freezing and thawing of water in the soil.

Frost line The maximum depth to which soil freezes in winter; your local building department can provide information on the frost line depth in your area.

Game fish Large, usually carnivorous fish such as trout, bass, pike and catfish. Due to specific oxygen, space, and temperature requirements, game fish don't do well in small garden ponds.

Grade The ground level. "On grade" means at or on the natural grade level.

Ground-fault circuit interrupter (GFCI) A safety circuit breaker that compares the amount of current entering a receptacle with the amount leaving. If there is a discrepancy, the GFCI breaks the circuit in 1/40 of a second. The device is usually required by code in outdoor areas that are subject to dampness.

Head The vertical distance between a pump and water outlet, used to determine pump performance. Pumps are sized by how much water (in gallons per hour) they can deliver at different "head" heights above the water level of the pond.

Light well A lighting fixture recessed below ground level that directs light upward, typically used to highlight tall plantings or other features beside the pond.

Marginal plants Various plant species that grow in wet or boggy soil around the edges of a stream or pond; also called Bog Plants.

Mil One one-thousandth of an inch; the measurement used to gauge the thickness of PVC and rubber pond liners.

Nitrifiers Beneficial bacteria present in pond water that break down fish wastes and other organic matter, transforming toxic ammonia into harmless nitrates, which nourish plants.

Oxygenating grasses Various species of submerged plants used primarily to add oxygen to pond water.

pH A measure of acidity or alkalinity of soil or water. The pH scale ranges from 0 (acid) to 14 (alkaline). Midpoint 7 represents neutral (neither acid or alkaline). Healthy pond water ranges in pH from 6.5 to 8.5.

Photosynthesis The synthesis of carbohydrates by plants from carbon dioxide, water, and inorganic nutrients (nitrates and phosphates) using sunlight as an energy source with the aid of plant chlorophyll.

Pier A concrete or masonry block rising above ground level to support the structure above it.

Plastic cement A dry cement mixture that includes a powdered latex additive to reduce cracking and serves as a waterproofing agent.

Polyvinyl chloride (PVC) A type of plastic formulation. Thin, flexible sheets of PVC plastic are used for pond liners. Rigid PVC plastic pipe is used for water supply lines.

Reinforcement bar Often called Rebar. Steel rods used to reinforce thick concrete structures to prevent cracking.

Rhizome A spreading underground stem or runner, which forms the root stock for hardy water lilies and some other water plants.

Runoff Water traveling across the ground surface, caused by heavy rains or irrigation. If the surrounding ground is sloped toward a pond, surface runoff can wash dirt and garden chemicals into a pond.

Scavengers In garden ponds, creatures such as snails, mussels, clams, or tadpoles that feed on fish wastes, algae, and dead organic matter.

Sod Sections of turf or grass cut from a lawn (usually with a flat-blade shovel) that contain both the root system and topgrowth. Can be replanted if kept moist.

Swale A broad, shallow ditch or depression in the ground, either occurring naturally, or excavated for the purpose of directing water runoff.

Topography The relief features or surface configuration of an area; the contour of the land.

Tuber The enlarged fleshy portion of an underground stem or rhizome; a potato is one example. Tropical lilies are tuberous plants.

Ultraviolet light (UV) Invisible rays at the extreme violet end of the sun's light spectrum, which causes color fading and deterioration of certain materials, such as plastics. Most pond liners have chemical additives to inhibit the effects of UV rays.

Underlayment A thick fabric material placed under a flexible pond liner to protect it from sharp stones or other sharp objects in the pond excavation. Get underlayment materials from pond dealers.

Variance A formal waiver from a municipal building department or similar agency to allow an exception to local codes or ordinances on a nonconforming feature of a building project.

Weir A notched obstruction or spillway placed across a stream to create a waterfall.